AMERICAN SOCIETY: PROBLEMS OF STRUCTURE

SECOND EDITION

JONATHAN H. TURNER

University of California, Riverside

HARPER & ROW, PUBLISHERS
New York, Hagerstown, San Francisco, London

Credits

Below are listed the page numbers on which illustrations appear by special permission. We appreciate the right to reproduce the following illustrations:

1, Caraballo, Monkmeyer; 17, Wide World; 44, Wide World; 65, Orin, Woodfin Camp; 97, Beckwith Studios; 124, Joel Gordon; 150, Joel Gordon; 174, Conklin, Monkmeyer; 206, George Gardner; 232, Windsor, Woodfin Camp; and, 252, Wide World.

Sponsoring Editor: Dale Tharp
Project Editor: Karla B. Philip
Designer: T. R. Funderburk
Production Supervisor: Stefania J. Taflinska
Photo Researcher: Myra Schachne
Compositor: Monotype Composition Company, Inc.
Printer and Binder: The Maple Press Company
Art Studio: Danmark & Michaels, Inc.

AMERICAN SOCIETY: PROBLEMS OF STRUCTURE, Second Edition
Copyright © 1972, 1976 by Jonathan H. Turner

Library of Congress Cataloging in Publication Data
Turner, Jonathan H
    American society.

    Bibliography: p.
    Includes index.
    1. United States—Social conditions—1960–
2. United States—Civilization—1945–   I. Title.
HN65.T87   1976   309.1′73′092   76-2714
ISBN 0-06-046706-1

To my parents,
Hugh and Marie Turner

Contents

Contents in Detail

Preface

In the following pages, I have sought to improve upon the first edition of this book. I have rewritten and reorganized each chapter, while adding a new chapter on America's economic problems.

The intent of the book remains intact, however: to examine the social problems inhering in America's basic social structures. In reworking the book, I concluded that America reveals three primary forms of structural organization: institutional structures, distributive or stratificational structures, and community structures. Thus, I have organized specific chapters around these basic forms of social organization. Part One, the institutional section, contains chapters dealing with problems of the economy, government, law, and education. Part Two, the stratification section, analyzes problems arising from inequality, poverty, and racism. The final section, Part Three, focuses on community problems inhering in America's residential areas as well as in the ecological community.

Naturally, a structural approach to social problems requires that the *inter*relations among structures be examined. The problems of government, for example, are intimately related to economic, social class, and community patterns in America. Accordingly, I hope that students will begin to appreciate the root causes of social problems by visualizing the complexity of the structural relationships from which they arise.

As with the first edition, I have not included chapters on deviance. Instructors tend to have their own preferences for this wide-ranging topic. And since there are many good, short paperbacks on various forms of deviance, I hope that those instructors who do cover deviance in their courses will choose several of these short paperbacks as a supplement to the structural approach offered in this text. In this way, students can be exposed to a fuller range of problems confronting American society.

More tables and graphs are included in this edition in an effort to document important points. The extensive bibliography and bibliographic references provide resources for students to pursue further documentation.

As a final note, it should be emphasized that no book on as complex a topic as the structural sources of social problems can be all-encompassing. I have sought to offer only the beginnings of what is, in reality, a never-ending analysis. Instructors and students can hopefully supplement and expand on the analysis to be offered—thereby revealing to an even greater extent the fact that American social problems are built into basic structural arrangements.

Jonathan H. Turner

Chapter 1

INTRODUCTION: THE SOCIOLOGY OF SOCIAL PROBLEMS

DEFINING SOCIAL PROBLEMS

Sociology originally emerged as a self-conscious discipline because thinkers were concerned about the social conditions around them. For once people began to seek secular, as opposed to religious and spiritual, interpretations of the world, they began to ask: What is wrong with society? How can society be changed for the better? Sociologists still ask these questions since, like most members of society, they too are concerned about the conditions of society. Often the only difference between the professional sociologist and the "person on the street" is that sociologists seek to study objectively the facts behind problematic conditions.

To study objectively and scientifically a condition defined as a "problem" does not mean, however, that all people will agree on what conditions are problematic—one person's problem can be another's paradise. Even among sociologists there is disagreement over the problems of American society. And while social scientists may all agree to study problems objectively, they often choose different features of the society to study. For example, twenty-five years ago very few people, including social scientists, viewed the ecosystem and environment as problematic areas. Today the topic can hardly be ignored. And even when problems do not suddenly emerge from "nowhere," there are subtle shifts in what are defined as major problem areas. In the 1960s the "ghetto" and the associated racial turmoil was a major problem; now, this situation is viewed as less troublesome, despite the fact that ghetto conditions remain the same. Or, student activism was a major problem just a few years ago, but today student *in*activism over social and moral issues is viewed as a problem by some.

What is evident, then, is that defining social problems is a difficult task. Most might agree, in the abstract, that conditions which cause harm to people and society are problems, but disagreements over what is harmful would soon emerge. Is marijuana harmful? prostitution? gambling? homosexuality? divorce? capitalism? inequality? welfare? Answers would vary, and for a simple reason: It is sometimes difficult to know for sure if a practice or condition is harmful to either individuals or society. And sometimes we are put into the situation of determining if one "harm" is worse than another. For example, is a recession or its "cure" (high unemployment) more harmful? Or, is the loss of jobs more harmful than environmental controls that limit construction or production? The answer to these questions would vary, depending upon whom one asked.

As a result, there emerges a "problem" in studying social problems: What does one study? What criteria should students of society use in selecting problems for study? Below are some possible criteria:

1. conditions that violate a majority of the population's sense of right and wrong
2. conditions that a majority of social scientists agree are bad for individuals and society
3. conditions that politicians regard as bad for individuals and society
4. conditions that a highly vocal minority regard as bad
5. conditions that the "powerful" regard as bad
6. conditions that college students regard as bad
7. conditions that the media regard as bad
8. conditions that the author of a social problems text regards as bad, and so on, for any group, person, or segment of the society

If any one of the criteria listed above is chosen, many conditions that large numbers of people regard as bad would be ignored. For example, if only those problems defined as such by a majority of the population were analyzed, then many conditions defined as problematic by others, including most social scientists, would be ignored. If the majority ruled, for instance, inequality, sexual discrimination, poverty, racism, and environment would not—by recent opinion polls—be defined as *major* problems. The reverse would be true for many citizens if only the conditions selected by social scientists were regarded as problems.

For this reason, sociologists often introduce their texts with lengthy discussions on scientific criteria for isolating the problematic from the nonproblematic. Such discussions perpetuate an illusion: the belief that sociologists know what is good and bad in society. We do not. Science allows for the objective study of problems, but it cannot select the problems for study. This we must do as people and as citizens in American society. Thus, the social problems discussed in this book will be based on ill-defined criteria for selecting the problematic; but the scientific criteria for gathering evidence will guide the analysis of the topics selected.

As a general way of understanding why the problems analyzed in the following chapters were selected, a combination of the criteria listed previously were, at least implicitly, used: (1) The author thinks something is bad. (2) The author perceives that much of the general public believes some condition is problematic. (3) The author perceives, in his discussions with students over a number of years, that they see some condition as bad or problematic. (4) The author thinks that other social scientists—the instructors of courses on social problems—will agree that the conditions selected are problematic. This "definition" of social problems is not as scientific-looking as that found in other texts, but it is more honest, and most importantly, it recognizes that the selection of social problems for study is a subjective assessment. But once selected, subjectivity can hopefully be suspended. It is the desire of social scientists to suspend subjectivity when *analyzing* a social condition. Their objectivity separates them from the "person on the street" and enables them to reach insights and conclusions about the causes of events that others might not see.

CULTURE, SOCIETY, AND SOCIAL PROBLEMS

To classify a social condition as a problem is to say, in effect, that something is wrong with the structure of society. For any social condition to be sufficiently prominent to be labelled a problem, it must be rooted in the basic culture and structure of American society. For example, if pollution is defined as a problem, its causes are not the "evil profit motives" of industrial capitalists or "insensitive and job-hungry hard hats," but rather, the causes are in a *system* of beliefs and practices that (1) force industries to seek pollution-causing profits, (2) allow communities to dump sewage, regardless of environmental consequences, and (3) provide workers with few job alternatives outside environmentally harmful activities. Or, if poverty is viewed as a problem, its causes lie neither in the "laziness" of the poor nor in the malevolence of the rich, but in a system of beliefs and established practices that deny economic and educational opportunities to certain groups in the society.

Social problems are thus conditions whose causes—and of course, whose solutions—reside in cultural and social arrangements. In many ways these problem-producing arrangements may be defined as good or necessary. Social problems are, therefore, not always the result of structures that people would define as bad. For example, while many would view poverty as a severe problem of American society, they would not see the political and economic structure, as well as the cherished beliefs associated with these structures, as bad, even though the causes of poverty may lie within these structures and beliefs. Or, while most Americans viewed Watergate abuses, as well as spying on citizens by the FBI, IRS, Pentagon, and CIA, as bad, few are ready to reject the American political system, although it was the system, not its incumbents, that was the cause of these problematic events.

At this stage, of course, no evidence has been introduced to support the theme that social problems adhere in those cultural and structural arrangements that most Americans cherish. The body of the chapters that follow are dedicated to the task of demonstrating that problems reside in cultural and social arrangements. But the basic principle of the sociological approach to social problems must be stated early: *Social problems are caused by social and cultural arrangements in society.* But because people believe in the cultural values that legitimize the social structures that, in turn, shape their lives, they are often reluctant to see them changed. For this reason, a corollary to the above position can be offered: *Social problems are often difficult to eliminate because their solution would require a change—usually a great change— in the beliefs, values, and daily lives of the majority of citizens.* It is for this reason that sociological treatments of social problems appear both "radical" and "impractical." People often do not want to have their values, beliefs, and daily routines viewed as the causes of "evils" in the society, nor do they wish to change what, for the majority in America, has brought "the good life."

Few sociologists are political radicals; few are political conservatives; most lie somewhere between. Thus, a sociological analysis that appears radical does so not from political motivations, but from the simple truth that social problems—that is, social "evils"— reside in what for many people are "good" social arrangements. But if social problems are to be understood, it is necessary to suspend our commitments to existing cultural and social arrangements, lest we abandon the scientific goal of understanding the causes and conditions of the events defined, by various criteria and by different people, as problems.

To appreciate the sociological perspective, then, it is critical that our culture and social structures be examined. We must understand what they are, what they do, and how they operate. Only in this way can we begin to understand the social problems of American society.

CULTURE AND SOCIAL PROBLEMS

What is *culture?* For many, it represents the refined and cultivated aspects of social life—art, music, sculpture, the opera. But for social scientists, the concept of culture has a much more neutral meaning. Unfortunately, it has a different neutral meaning for different social scientists. To the anthropologist, for example, culture often refers to *everything* created by human beings—their freeways, their symphonies, their languages, their institutions, their religions, their bombs or spears, or "anything created by humans living in society." When anthropologists talk about an "American culture" or a "Samoan culture," they are referring to the totality of artifacts, beliefs, and institutions of a people. In contrast, sociologists define culture in much narrower terms. For many sociologists—although not all—culture refers to the "symbolic products of social life." What is a *symbolic product?* An answer requires some elaboration.

Humans are unique in their ability to create and use extensive systems of symbols. Chimpanzees and porpoises appear to be able to use some symbols, and perhaps they can even create a limited repertoire of symbols. But in comparison to humans, other life forms possess little culture—that is, few systems of symbols. A symbol denotes some feature of the world, and when combined into a system, symbols allow people to make very complex representations to each other about the world. Take language as an example. Words, sentences, paragraphs, and other features of our language system allow us to see and do things that would be impossible without language. We could not interact very effectively, we could not romanticize love; we could not build factories; we could not hate factories; we could not worship gods; nor could we proclaim our atheism. Thus, given the capacity for language, humans can construct and transmit a "new world"—a world not tied to the actual physical conditions of existence. Humans can now guide their conduct by other means than impulse, instinct, and environmental imperatives. They can shape their world with technologies (or knowledge about how to control the world) or with beliefs in the supernatural. For sociologists, then, culture refers to the symbol systems created and transmitted by humans.

Sociologists tend, however, to study only some portions of these symbol systems. Most particularly, sociologists study *idea systems* or those systems of symbols that guide and regulate concrete patterns of social interaction. In the chapters to follow, reference will be made to the values and beliefs of American culture. These are the most critical idea systems for understanding the root causes of social problems. Values and beliefs represent people's general conceptions of what should exist, what should be, and what is proper in the world around them. While sociologists often distinguish between values and beliefs, in the analyses throughout this text, we will use the concepts of values and beliefs interchangeably. What is important for our purposes is that, when dealing with people's conceptions of what is, what should be, and what is proper, values and beliefs reveal people's commitments to existing arrangements. And what people are committed to is difficult to change, even if it helps cause the problems that people define as bad.

Much of human conduct is guided by complexes of ideas—values and beliefs. Human society—its institutions, communities, and organizations—is circumscribed by these complexes of ideas. Humans are, in many ways, slaves to their own symbolic creations, for ideas not only say how we should behave in the world, but they legitimize and make the structures shaping our lives seem right and proper. And so, as we approach the analysis of social problems in America, it will be necessary in some chapters to be alerted to the influence of ideas in perpetuating these problems.

SOCIAL STRUCTURE AND SOCIAL PROBLEMS

What is *social structure?* Divorced from any substantive content, the concept of structure denotes the relationships among positions. The organizational chart of a business corporation is one way of visualizing structure. It outlines the positions—president, vice president, comptroller, payroll manager, and the like—as well as the relationship of authority among them. But as those studying business, or any type of organization, soon discover, this formal structure does not reveal the full extent of informal relations among the people who occupy these positions. Thus, a social structure is the totality of all relations—among all positions within a social context—whether formal or informal and whether involving authority, respect, love, or hate. Stated in the simplest terms possible, social structure is a map that relates positions to each other. But, of course, real social structures are continually changing, filled with processes occurring among interacting people. It is necessary, therefore, in studying society, to be attuned to both the dynamic and stabilizing processes as people create, maintain, and change the way they organize themselves.

The structuring of human affairs—in fact, the very existence of human interactions—is possible because we can create and use symbols. Symbols allow humans to communicate with each other and to regulate their affairs. Social structure is a "structure" because people elaborate ideas to govern their concrete relations, and then elaborate additional ideas to justify and legitimize their patterns of regulation. In this way people can "see" the world in much the same way, they can believe in the same goals, and they can view action from the same standards of approriateness and inappropriateness. The word *same* is, of course, an overstatement because *similar* is about as close as humans get to achieving consensus over ideas, and consensus is often fragile, easily degenerating into conflict and dissension.

One of the remarkable outcomes of humans' symbol-using capacity is the diversity of ideas and structures that they create. Perhaps even more remarkable, however, are the similarities in social structures that humans have created. In fact, all human societies reveal three basic types of social structures: (1) institutional systems, (2) community systems, and (3) distributive systems. The term *system* merely underscores the structure—or relatedness among parts—of these basic human forms of organization.

What are *institutional systems*? Social institutions, as such systems are often called by sociologists, are those structures in a society that resolve the most fundamental problems facing the organizing of humans into society: how to eat, how to govern, how to procreate, how to control tension, how to induce conformity, how to regularize sex, and how to coordinate activities. In most primitive societies, these protein problems are dealt with by the institution of kinship, or in modern terms, the family. Such family institutions are quite different from the ones with which we are most familiar, but it is not an oversimplification to view most activity as being family oriented. But in more developed societies, separate institutions evolve to cope with different types of problems. The institution of the economy evolves to deal with problems of securing resources from the environment and converting them into usable, life-maintaining commodities. Government becomes separated from kinship and deals with the problems of allocating power to organize and control society-wide action. Law emerges and comes to regulate and coordinate activities, while sanctioning certain forms of deviance. Education begins to assume many of the socialization functions formally performed by parents in the family. And thus, modern societies will reveal separate institutions (economy, government, education, law) for dealing with what appear to be universal dilemmas facing humans. It is in these "new" institutions that many of the problems facing American society reside.

Naturally, institutions are highly interrelated, enabling them to be called institutional "systems." For indeed, what happens in the economy affects government, and vice versa. Or, what the educational system does reverberates through society. Accordingly, what occurs in each institution has consequences for events in the others.

What are *communities?* Communities are geographical units that provide people with *places* to live and carry out their diverse activities. Just how these activities are carried out, however, is circumscribed by institutions. For example, how one works is determined by the economy; how one is governed, by the polity; how one is socialized, by family and education. The fact that institutions are involved in community processes raises an obvious question: Are communities a separate type of structure? Most certainly yes, because they determine *where* and *in what pattern* people will reside and act. But the influence of institutions on this geographical or spatial patterning underscores an important facet of human organization: Structures interpenetrate and influence each other. Just as the economy may affect the way people work and transport themselves, the patterns of the community—its zoning laws, its tax base, its size, its road system, and the composition of its citizens—will influence the types of economic organizations that can exist.

In fact, many social problems inhere in this fact of interpenetration. For example, the conflict between workers in search of jobs and environmentalists in pursuit of a clean ecosystem often represent two forces: the workers an economic force, the environmentalists a community force. One group wants economic expansion, the other greater community control over land use. Thus, in studying social problems, it is necessary to be attuned to problems *within* and *between* institutions and communities. For while institutions and communities are highly interdependent, if they were not separated in analysis, then much insight into the causes of, and solutions to, social problems would be lost.

What is a *distributive system,* the third basic type of social structure? All societies, except perhaps the most simple and primitive, distribute valued resources—money, power, and prestige, for example—unequally. Just how such distribution occurs is influenced by institutions and community patterns; for just as institutional and community structures interpenetrate, so do distributive systems, institutions, and communities. Government, for example, influences the distribution of power, and the economy the distribution of money. Communities, in determining where people live, can determine people's access to value resources, such as money-earning work opportunities, educational opportunities, or perhaps even political participation and the opportunities to acquire power.

The most salient feature of the distributive system in a society is its "social class" structure. Social classes are relatively homogeneous groupings of people in a society who possess a similar share of scarce resources. When we talk about the "working class," the "middle classes," the "rich," or the "poor," we are distinguishing large groupings of people in terms of their share of valued resources such as money, prestige, and power.

While the profile of distributive systems is often shaped by community and institutional forces, the reverse is also true. The structure of social classes and the kinds of resources that they possess influence basic institutions and the patterning of communities. Residential patterns are often a reflection of people's access to resources and their class position. Residential ghettos are, for instance, clear reflections of the distributive system in a society. Or, the nature of economic organizations is, to a very great extent, limited by the intellectual resources that the population has been able to purchase in the educational system.

Inhering in the distributive system in America are many social problems—poverty and racism being two of the most obvious. For indeed, much of the tension and conflict among members of society occurs over how resources are to be distributed. Ghetto riots, hardhat protests, wildcat strikes, and taxpayer revolts, are the result of an unequal distribution of scarce resources.

Thus, social problems ultimately inhere in the three basic structures of human societies: institutional, distributive, and community systems. Because of this, it is wise to pause briefly and indicate how these structures present problematic features.

PROBLEMS AND THE INSTITUTIONAL SYSTEM

As the institution responsible for securing resources, producing and distributing goods, as well as employing many Americans, the economy touches all other institutions and structures in the society. In America, many problems are evident in the economy, such as: How big should corporations be? How much political influence should they have? Should they seek to make the worker's life better, even if it means decreased profits? How are inflation and recession to be controlled? What should be the role of government in a capitalistic economic system? How are foreign cartels to be dealt with? Since the economy is so important in understanding all other social problems, these and other questions will be addressed in Chapter 2.

As the seat of power in society, government is always a center of controversy. For ultimately, government can regulate and control virtually all processes in a society. In America, there are many enduring controversies surrounding government: Who should control the controllers? Does the public have a voice? Are politicians responsive or are they corrupt? What should America's national priorities be? Who should set them? Who should have more power, congress or the president? These and other prominent questions will be addressed in Chapter 3.

Law is the institution concerned with regulating deviance and maintaining order. In so doing, it is, in America at least, supposed to render justice in accordance with cherished cultural ideals. In Chapter 4 our system of justice is examined, particularly as it relates to crime and criminals. Does the justice system prevent crime? Or, does it cause crime? Is it fair? Is it overburdened? These and other questions will need to be addressed when examining law in America.

The educational system in America has assumed much of the socialization process previously performed by the family. As an agent of socialization, elementary schools in America present a spectrum of dilemmas: Who should control the schools? Who should finance them? What is the most humane way to education? Whose values should dominate educational socialization? Schools also perform gate-keeping functions; they give credentials that facilitate access to desired jobs. Surrounding secondary and college education, then, are a host of issues which are the subject of constant controversy in America: Do the schools discriminate? If schools train for jobs, who should influence policies: government, industry, family, or community? As the centers of higher learning, what are the functions of the universities: to teach? to do research? Who should influence their policies: no one? the public? students? faculty? As the educational structure of American society has grown and assumed so many important functions that affect people's lives, it confronts many problems and dilemmas, as we will see in Chapter 5.

PROBLEMS AND THE DISTRIBUTIVE SYSTEM

There is a great inequality in the distribution of income and wealth in the American society. A relatively small portion of the population—as little as 1 percent—controls 30 percent of all wealth while 20 percent holds 76 percent of the wealth. The extent and consequences of such inequality will be thoroughly discussed in

Chapter 6 with an eye to such questions as: Is inequality a problem in itself? Does it contribute to other problems?

In Chapter 7 one facet of the distributive system is analyzed: the existence of a large poverty class in America. This poverty class (depending on whose statistical definition of poverty is used) totals between 35 and 50 million people and represents one of the more enduring problems confronting Americans. Important questions that this chapter will address include: Why does such a class exist in the most affluent land in the world? What perpetuates it? What problem does it cause for American society?

In Chapter 8 we will examine how inequality in America is compounded by another problem: racial and ethnic discrimination. Such discrimination has kept many minorities at the bottom of the social class system—a situation that has been a constant source of tension and conflict. How did this happen? Why does discrimination persist?

PROBLEMS AND THE COMMUNITY SYSTEM

America is an urban society—the entire population of 212 million is compressed into only 2 percent of the land area. America is also a metropolitan society with most of the population residing in areas with a large central city, surrounded by smaller suburban cities. How did this come to pass? Why does this urban profile cause problems of financing, decision-making, central-city decay, racial and ethnic tensions, and the other problems of the central city in metropolitan America? These issues will be discussed in Chapter 9.

America's cities, communities, and metropolitan areas reveal another problem: segregation. Within any community, blacks (and other "distinguishable" minorities) are segregated from whites. And within the entire metropolitan area, blacks tend to be confined to the decaying core of the large central city, surrounded by affluent, white suburbs. How did this come to be? What tension does it generate? How can the problem be solved, if at all? What does it foretell about the future of community life in America? Chapter 10 examines American community segregation.

A society is only a part of a much larger community: the ecological community. Humans are, in the end, only one species in a complex network of other species and life-sustaining substances of the physical environment. But humans are a very special population because their culture, institutions, and communities are structured in ways that could potentially destroy much of the ecosystem. Nowhere is this more of a problem than in America, the world's greatest polluter. How could this be so? And why are ecological problems so difficult to resolve? Population, culture, society, and the ecological community are the topics of Chapter 11, the closing chapter of this volume.

SOCIAL PROBLEMS: THEIR CULTURAL AND STRUCTURAL BASIS

This has been a long introduction and preview to the study of social problems, but in many ways much of the work involved in understanding American social problems has now been done. A general perspective for studying a very complex phenomenon has been offered. This perspective allows for the organization of the topics to be covered: Part One of the book will deal with the problems associated with the structure and, where appropriate, the culture of basic institutions. Part Two will focus on problems in the structure of the distributive system in America, and Part Three will analyze the structure of community problems. In addition to providing an organizational framework, our approach has provided key concepts—values, beliefs, and structural interdependence among the institutional, distributive, and community systems—for visualizing why a condition exists and persists in America.

It is to the application of this perspective to specific social problems that we now turn our attention. And as will become evident, America's social ills are indeed "problems of structure."

PART ONE
PROBLEMS OF BASIC INSTITUTIONS

Understanding American society would be impossible without delving into some of its basic social institutions—the economy, government, education, law. These institutions are central to any society because they resolve many of the exigencies of human survival such as how to secure resources, raise the young, organize activities, and maintain order. The institutional arrangements of *any* society, however, *systematically* generate strains, tensions, inequities, conflicts, dissensions, hatreds, violence, disease, hunger, and death. And because of their importance to social life, institutions can be a major fountainhead of social problems. Nowhere is this more evidence than in the United States. Much of what is problematic about American society can be traced to the internal structure of its basic institutions.

In Chapter 2 the structure of the American economy is examined and problems such as inflation, monopolization, price-fixing, recession, "stagflation," coordination and control, nationalization, consumer fraud, worker alienation, and pollution are analyzed as outgrowths of the structure and culture of the economy. This analysis of the economy opens the book because so much of what occurs in American society is influenced by economics. In later chapters attention will shift to other problems in non-economic contexts that are, in part, influenced by economic processes.

Government in America is analyzed in Chapter 3, with particular attention drawn to the problems of establishing priorities and making decisions. In a complex society the capacity of government to deal with all social problems can have profound consequences, as will become evident throughout the pages of this volume. In Chapter 4 the institution of law is analyzed, especially as it relates to problems of combating crime and administering justice. Education in America is examined in Chapter 5, with emphasis on the dilemmas of how to operate both lower- and higher-educational structures in a complex and pluralistic society.

These institutions are basic to the functioning of American society and their problems of structure are important topics in their own right. But, as will become increasingly clear in the chapters of Parts Two and Three, these institutions also determine the distribution of resources and the living patterns among Americans. It is for this reason, then, that the study of the problems of structure in America must begin with an institutional analysis, since such an analysis will provide a good foundation for examining other social problems.

Chapter 2

ECONOMIC PROBLEMS

Economic processes influence all facets of social life in America. Because the economy is one of the most basic institutions, an economic analysis is crucial to an understanding of all social problems in America. Not only does the profile of the economy affect virtually all social problems, many internal processes within the economy itself constitute distinct social problems; for example, rapid inflation, widespread unemployment, recession, the vulnerability of the economy to whims of foreign governments, the size of conglomerates and multinational corporations, the apparent increase in consumer fraud, the disproportionate influence of corporations on political processes, the perceived failure of federal regulatory agencies to work for the public, instances of price-fixing and monopolistic practices among large corporations, the waste and pollution created by many economic activities, the existence of a poverty class, and the frustration and alienation of many workers. The diversity and scope of this partial catalogue of economic problems precludes their detailed individual analysis, but fortunately, a structural approach allows insight into the underlying causes of specific economic problems. For indeed, all of these and other problems have arisen and continue to persist because of the cultural and structural dynamics of America's particular form of "liberal capitalism." By examining the structure of American capitalism, it will be possible to conceptually visualize, although only in a very general way, the apparent causes of current economic problems in America.

The word *capitalism* has now assumed an ideological status and it is no longer a simple matter to understand just what it denotes. While all would agree that capitalism is a particular form of economic organization, mutual agreement soon ends as conceptions of capitalist economies become obscured by arguments over whether they are good, bad, unavoidable, or a necessary evil. Probably the best way to understand the nature of capitalism in American society is to summarize the ideological tenets of "conservative" capitalism and "liberal" capitalism as well as the "collectivist critique" of all forms of capitalism. In this way the spectrum of advocacy, accommodation, and critique can be covered. To some extent, this spectrum represents a culture of capitalism since conservative, liberal, and collectivist beliefs are constantly invoked to justify, or criticize, various forms of economic activity.

THE CULTURE OF CAPITALISM

Both conservative and liberal capitalism hold a series of common beliefs:[1] (1) Capital—wealth and any asset that can be converted into money—should be concentrated in the hands of private individuals to invest as they see proper. The disagreement, however, between conservatives and liberals is not over private property (or private capital), but over how much capital should be held by government and whether government has any right to regulate capital accumulations among private citizens. (2) The accumulation of capital should be encouraged, since large sums of capital can be invested in economic enterprises, thereby encouraging increased productivity and the general welfare of all citizens. Liberals and conservatives disagree, however, over how far capital accumulation by one corporation or individual should be allowed to go. (3) The most efficient means for accumulating and using capital for the production of goods and services is the corporation that allows for the pooling of capital, the organization of labor, the development of technology, and the use of natural resources to produce and distribute goods and services. But, conservatives and liberals will disagree over the extent to which government should control and regulate corporate activities. (4) Corporations must be profit-making units if investors are to be encouraged to "risk" their money or capital in various economic enterprises. Conservatives and liberals will usually fail to agree on how much profits should be regulated. (5) The "market" is an efficient way to allocate the resources of a society, since the demand for goods and services will lead profit-making individuals and corporations to invest capital in activities that will meet the needs of citizens. Conservatives and liberals do not agree, however, on whether or not supply-and-demand in the market should be the only way to allocate resources. (6) A "free-market" where individuals and corpo-

[1] This section draws heavily from several useful references: Maurice Dobb (1946), Robin M. Williams (1970), and Neil J. Smelser (1963).

rations, all guided by a profit motive, can compete with each other is the best way to induce economic units to keep costs down, and hence, prices low. Conservatives and liberals will often disagree, however, over whether free competition will always occur, whether it will always lead to efficiency and low prices, and whether it is desirable in all sectors of the economy.

At the ideological level, then, capitalism can be defined as a "desirable" mode of economic organization that is presumed to provide an efficient way to organize capital, labor, technology, and resources so that low-cost goods and services can be produced to meet the needs and desires of the people as expressed in the free marketplace. Socialists, communists, and other collectivists criticize the ideology of capitalism because, as they would argue (Sherman, 1972): (1) Private ownership of capital creates privileged classes and vast inequality. (2) Corporations are wasteful and exploitive forms of organization because profits are not always used for production, but for opulent consumption. And in seeking profits, corporations are not inclined to pay labor more than minimally necessary, nor are they disposed to create meaningful and gratifying forms of work. (3) The market does not respond to the needs of those without money, only to those with enough capital to create market demand. (4) Because some corporations will be more successful than others in market competition, they can come to monopolize markets and thereby raise prices and exploit labor with immunity. (5) Even when government seeks to regulate corporate size, monopoly, and profits, their vast capital and wealth allow them to buy political power and hence influence government to regulate selectively and favorably. Collectivists argue that a radical change in economic and political organization is required to solve these problems inherent in capitalism. The specifics of various proposals vary enormously in different ideological circles, but the common features of proposed alternatives include: (1) severe restrictions on how much property or capital can be held by private citizens, (2) complete governmental control of basic economic units, (3) production of goods and services that meet collectively agreed upon priorities, (4) a more equitable allocation of goods and services to individuals and families in terms of their needs, and (5) the use of labor for work that is related to achieving the collective goals of the society.

As can be seen, capitalism and collectivism are radically opposed ideologies. Also very clear is the fact that American society is capitalistic and it is the collectivist ideology that is often used to indict governmental intervention in the economy. In Table 1 the basic tenets of these beliefs are summarized for convenient refer-

TABLE 1 CONFLICTING CULTURAL BELIEFS

Conservative Capitalist Beliefs	Liberal Capitalist Beliefs	The Collectivist Critique
All capital should be in the hands of private citizens.	Some capital should belong to government.	There should be severe limitations of private capital; virtually all capital should reside in the government.
A free market will automatically lead to the optimal allocation of resources in society.	Some control of supply-and-demand in the market is necessary to meet societal goals.	Markets should be totally controlled by government to correspond to the needs of people.
The laws of supply and demald should be free to operate in the market.	Free markets represent the best allocative mechanism in some sectors; regulation is necessary in other sectors.	A free market will respond to demands of the rich with buying power, not the needs of workers who have no money to translate their needs into market demand.
The profit motive is what brings capital to certain enterprises; as long as markets are free and allow for profit, then desired economic activities will be performed.	There is a tendency for corporations to begin to monopolize market, and hence, raise prices. Corporations will often fix prices and engage in other collusionary practices. Government must therefore prevent such domination in order to foster the competition that keeps costs and prices low.	Big corporations come to control the markets and governments that regulate them. Corporations must be abolished as productive units.
A free, competitive market guided by a profit motive keeps costs and prices down (since corporations must compete with each other).	Government must regulate profits in some key industries; it must also prevent practices that allow corporations to make excessive profits. However, by subsidizing profits in certain economic sectors, the government can encourage investment in that sector.	The profit motive leads corporations to find ways to keep costs low while keeping prices and profits high, thereby hurting consumers and workers.
Profits can be defended as rewards for those with capital taking risks in the market.	Because of the size of key corporations and the interlocking nature of economic activity, government must not allow vital industry to fail; profits must, at times, be maintained through subsidies.	Profits represent nonproductive labor, and allow capitalists to exploit workers and consumers. They should be eliminated for they promote vast inequality.

ence. In looking at these diverse ideologies, even a cursary understanding of the American economy will reveal the domination of the liberal position. This distinct ideology corresponds closest to the actual structural arrangements in the economy, and as such, legitimizes the operation of the economy in its present form (Williams, 1970:166). Yet, despite the effectiveness of this belief system in legitimizing current economic arrangements, there are certain inherent problems in the structure of the capitalist system that the collectivist critique highlights in extreme form. In many ways the structure of liberal capitalism in America has evolved primarily as a way to cope effectively, at least in the short run, with the problems that conservative capitalists refuse to acknowledge and that radicals proclaim are the impetus behind the ultimate downfall of capitalist forms of economic organization. Just whether these inherent problems can be resolved by liberal capitalism or whether the collectivist's ideology will have greater appeal as they become severe cannot be resolved in this volume. But the ideologies of liberal capitalism and collectivism will probably come into greater conflict if the economic problems built into the structure of capitalism intensify over the next decades.

STRUCTURAL DILEMMAS OF CAPITALISM[2]

MONOPOLY AND OLIGOPOLY. The basic assumption of the conservative capitalist belief system is that open competition among economic units in a free market is the best form of economic organization. However, as became evident during the last century, if left unregulated such a system soon becomes dominated by monopolistic practices that, in turn, cut down on competition and freedom. As some economic units are profitable in the market, they acquire the power to cut prices, absorb temporary losses, and thereby drive other, less solvent units out of the market. Or, by threatening to do so, they can begin to indirectly regulate the activities of other competitive units. And once economic organizations possess this kind of "overlord" power, they can not only dictate how competitors are to operate, but they can also control smaller units dependent upon powerful monopolies for their business. For example, at one time in America the Rockefeller family so dominated the oil industry that it could suppress or control all competitors, all smaller suppliers, and all buyers of oil. Once this kind of control of the market occurs, economic units are not free, competition is

[2] This analysis of problems draws heavily from Maurice Zeitlen (1970), Williams (1970), and Sherman (1972).

suspended, and goods are no longer allocated in accordance with the laws of supply and demand.

It is this inherent dilemma of capitalist forms of economic organization that has led to ever-increasing governmental regulation of economic organizations. Yet, increasing concentrations of capital and the growth of successful corporations are inevitable in capitalist systems, despite efforts to maintain competition (Sherman, 1968). Several forces work against governmental efforts to maintain the market mechanism for allocating resources: First, the profit motive mandates that economic units are to increase their profits by expanding and growing. Second, certain economic activities in modern societies—transportation, communications, utilities—can be more efficiently performed by large organizations controlling most of the market. Third, large and successful corporations that employ large numbers of workers can exert enormous political influence and thereby mitigate governmental efforts at regulation. And fourth, some forms of economic activity require substantial concentrations of capital, making it more profitable for corporations to be large and, hence, achieve the "economies of scale" that come with size and, coincidentally, market domination.

The result of these inherent forces in America is for large sectors of critical resource markets to be controlled by relatively few corporations that are subjected to some governmental regulation. As opposed to *monopoly*, where one corporation dominates the market, the situation of a few large corporations controlling the market is termed *oligopoly*. Competition is usually quite intense among smaller corporations in less central markets; but, with few exceptions, in markets where there is high consumer demand and where large quantities of scarce resources are utilized, the oligopolistic tendencies of liberal capitalism are most evident. In Table 2 an attempt is made to document the high degree of capital concentration in the American economy. Table 2 reports the percentage of manufacturing assets held by the 100 largest firms in America. As can be seen, these firms now control about one-half of the total economic assets—a rather high percentage when it is remembered that there are over 150,000 manufacturing firms in America. Supplementing the data in Table 2 is (as of yet unpublished) a report by Professor Willard Mueller of the University of Wisconsin which reveals that the 200 largest corporations (as opposed to the 100 largest reported in Table 2) now control two-thirds of all manufacturing assets. The significance of this figure lies in the oligopolistic trend it underscores: In 1941, the 1000 largest manufacturing corporations did not control this great a share of the manufacturing assets. Buttressing these data, and supplementing those in Table 2, is the report by William Shepard of the University of Michigan stating that industries in which as few as four corporations control 50 percent or more of the sales now account for 64 percent of all manufacturing sales—indicating again the increasing oligopolistic control of the American economy.

In Table 3 the percent of profits by corporations of varying degrees of capital (asset) formation offers another way to visualize the degree to which all economic activity is controlled by a few large corporations. And in Table 4, the percentage of total sales by the four largest firms in such key market areas as automobiles, aluminum, glass, tires, and steel are reported to provide but another indicator of large corporate domination of the American economy.

INTERCORPORATE CONTROL. As large *intra*national corporations come to dominate markets in mature capitalism, they develop complex patterns of *inter*corporate control of markets which further

TABLE 2 PERCENT OF MANUFACTURING ASSETS
         HELD BY THE 100 LARGEST FIRMS

Year	Percent held by 100 largest firms
1925	35.1
1931	42.3
1939	42.4
1948	40.1
1955	43.8
1960	46.0
1965	47.6
1971	48.9

SOURCES: *Studies by the Staff of the Cabinet Committee on Price Stability*, Washington, D.C., 1969, pp. 45, 92; *Statistical Abstract of the United States 1973*, p. 483.

TABLE 3 CONCENTRATION OF ASSETS AND PROFITS IN
         MANUFACTURING, FIRST QUARTER 1968

Corporations having assets of:	Number of companies	Percent of companies	Percent of manufacturing assets	Percent of manufacturing profits
$1 billion or more	78	0.04	43	49
$250 million to $1 billion	194	0.1	21	20
$10 million to $250 million	2,165	1.2	22	19
under $10 million	185,000*	98.7	14	12
Total	187,437	100.0	100	100

SOURCE: *Studies by the Staff of the Cabinet Committee on Price Stability*, Washington D.C., 1969, p. 92.
* Estimate

restricts competition, while subjecting smaller corporations to considerable regulation. There are several ways such as intercorporate control increases (Turner, 1972:46–47): (1) interlocking directorships, (2) conglomeration, (3) trade associations, and (4) price-leading.

1. An interlocking directorship exists if several corporations have common members on their boards of directors. While interlocking directorships among *competing* corporations are illegal under current antitrust legislation, the indirect connections among corporations are so extensive as to obscure whether companies are competitive or not. And even if interlocking directorships exist among noncompeting corporations, increased control over a wider spectrum of activities in the economy is still achieved.

2. Corporations can own other corporations; and while antitrust legislation prevents large corporations from buying out their smaller competitors, intercorporate stockholdings still put considerable control of diverse economic activities into the hands of huge conglomerate corporations. Such diversification of single corporations also allows them to resist supply-and-demand pressures in the market. It enables them to maintain higher prices in a slackening market because they have sources of revenue from other markets to "ride out" price fluctuations. Successful conglomerates can potentially remain unresponsive to the free market and thus achieve a competitive advantage over smaller and weaker corporations that must lower prices and profits in the face of slackening demand in the market.

3. Trade associations are established to disseminate information as well as to set standards and guidelines for economic activities in various markets—as in the case of banking, insuring, railroads,

TABLE 4 OLIGOPOLISTIC POWER IN SELECTED
INDUSTRIES, 1963

Industry	Percent of sales made by four largest firms
Automobiles	*99*
Aluminum	*96*
Flat glass	*94*
Steam engines and turbines	*93*
Light bulbs	*92*
Cigarettes	*80*
Copper	*78*
Metal cans	*74*
Soap and detergents	*72*
Tires and inner tubes	*70*
Blast furnaces and steel mills	*50*

SOURCE: U.S. Senate Judiciary Committee, Subcommittee on Antitrust and Monopoly, Washington, D.C., 1964.

and dairy products. While actual price-fixing is prohibited by law, the information of the market provided by the association, coupled with contacts and liaisons, allows individual corporations to co-ordinate their activities and often to reduce their competition.

4. In oligopolistic markets, where a few large corporations control the majority of sales in the market, the fixing of prices does not necessarily have to involve the actual collusion and conspiracy of corporate heads—a practice forbidden by law. Instead, in what one author called the "conspiracy of newspaper pronouncements," one of the dominant corporations announces its intent to raise prices or perhaps to lower them, or to engage in some other market activity. The other corporations then follow suit within several days. No behind the scenes fixing of prices has necessarily occurred, but the result is the same: prices are fixed, and oftentimes at levels that do not correspond to actual demand pressures in the market. For example, the steel companies are frequent users of the price-leading techniques: Typically United States Steel will announce a price increase and the other large steel companies will then follow suit and raise their prices to correspond to those of U. S. Steel. In this way prices can be regulated independently from the laws of supply and demand. For example, the economist Gardiner C. Means reports that between September of 1973 and September of 1974—a period of falling market demand (23% increase in unemployment; 25% increase in idle manufacturing capacity)—whole-sale prices increased less than 5 percent in "competition-dominated industries" such as farming, leather, lumber, and textiles; but in oligopolistic industries the rise was 27 percent, indicating that prices did not respond to changes in the market.

In sum, the tendency of capitalistic economies to become dominated by mammoth corporations is compounded by various forms of intercorporate control. This control is often difficult to uncover, but it appears that a considerable amount of coordination, as opposed to competition, occurs among corporations in America. Such coordination reduces the vicissitudes of competition and maintains profit levels, while typically keeping prices artificially high.

MULTINATIONALIZATION. Because capitalist corporations are regulated by profit considerations, they inevitably seek resources in their cheapest form. Coupled with the enormous capital of America's large corporations, this search for cheap resources—whether natural or human resources—has led to extensive international involvement of America's largest corporations. In fact, it is now clear that most large corporations are multinational with extensive holdings and projects in several countries. In the current energy crisis, attention has been drawn to the multinational profile of oil companies, but virtually all large corporations in all sectors of the American economy have considerable capital invested in other nations.

Multinationalization is perhaps an inevitable result of the logic of capitalist economic organization: First, as raw materials become scarce under the impact of massive domestic extraction, corporations inevitably seek new sources which can be extracted at lower costs. Second, in both extractive and manufacturing industries, labor in less modernized societies is considerably cheaper—allowing for lower labor costs and higher profit margins. Third, the very great manufacturing capacity of large corporations often allows for the production of goods in excess of domestic demand, with the result that corporations seek markets for their goods and services in other societies. And fourth, world markets still remain comparatively unregulated when compared to the domestic market, and thus, corporations will often seek a foreign market where a government cannot (or will not) regulate prices and profits, especially in those markets where the demand is high and supply is short.

As the data presented earlier document, the assets and manufacturing capacities of the American economy are not only controlled by a few hundred large corporations, but these same corporations also serve other nations and have extensive holdings in

SOCIOLOGICAL INSIGHTS

WHO OWNS THE LARGE CORPORATIONS?

Tables 1, 2, and 3 reveal the extent to which large corporations dominate the market. But who owns these large corporations? In other words, who owns the stock? And how concentrated is the stock in the hands of the rich? Can the "little guy" also share in ownership? Using data from Internal Revenue Service files, three researchers from the University of Pennsylvania have just completed a study of stock ownership of American corporations for the year 1971. Results: 1 percent of the nation's families—that is, those with incomes over $50,000 in 1971—own 51 percent of the stock and collect 47 percent of the dividends. The 53 percent of American families with incomes of less than $10,000 in 1971 owned less than 10 percent of the stock and collected about 11 percent of the dividends.—*Newsweek,* December 18, 1974 other societies. The result of this situation is to make government regulation of America's large corporations less effective since they can produce and distribute goods and services in the international market when government policies become too restrictive. Such a situation will, as is most dramatically evident for oil and other raw materials, make the American market increasingly influenced by supply-and-demand forces in the comparatively unregulated international market. And with modernization of the Third World, partly as a result of American capital investments, the world demand for all goods and services enjoyed by Americans will increase as other countries seek to raise their material standard of living. Such escalating world demand will increase prices in all markets and America's multinational corporations will, in accordance with profit considerations, seek to distribute goods and services to those areas of the world willing to pay the highest prices. Such strategies by American corporations will have profound consequences for the domestic economy.

UNIONIZATION. Workers in capitalistic economies become a type of "commodity" in a labor market. Whether such a dehumanizing situation is regarded as good, necessary, or evil is not at issue, but it is clear that labor costs are like other costs to a corporation seeking to make a profit—they will typically attempt to keep labor costs low in order to realize greater profits. During early capitalism, the labor market works in favor of the corporation since workers must often endure very low wages and poor working conditions or lose a source of income. Eventually, as workers become concentrated, as dissatisfaction increases, and as industries become large and in need of steady labor so as not to idle massive capital investments, labor succeeds in forming effective unions which become the bargaining agents of workers in the labor market.

The history of union organization in the United States is one of violence, but by the 1930s, unions overcame the resistance of large scale industry and began to bargain collectively with individual corporations and with groups of corporations comprising entire industries. As a result, union organization in America tends to be industry-wide as is the case with autos, steel, and mining; and if not industry-wide, smaller unions are organized into large umbrella unions such as the Teamsters or large confederations like the AFL-CIO. Such large-scale union organization is a direct response to the prominence of large corporations. And it is an inevitable force in capitalistic economies because: (1) workers need to protect themselves from abuses of corporate profit motives, (2) workers need to have some security from the recurring economic cycles typifying capitalistic markets, (3) the industry itself begins to seek stabilized relations with the large working labor pool that can easily disrupt and shut down the massive capital investments of large-scale industry, and (4) government itself has an interest in avoiding conflict between economic elites and the working masses of population. Under these pressures, then, unions have become an integral part of mature capitalistic economies.

Unions further restrict open competition, not just in the labor market, but also in other markets, because now another type of large-scale organization controls one of the key resources of any economy, labor. Such control has been undoubtedly necessary in terms of humanitarian values, but it creates one more rigidity in market: wages do not respond to supply-and-demand—that is, they rarely go down when the need for labor is less—resulting in a constant pressure for prices to increase as corporations seek to maintain and increase their profits in the face of rising labor costs. Further, the wage-price spiral of one sector extends to others, since labor in all sectors of the economy is organized to support the activities of labor in any other. There is no necessary good or bad in this situation—it is an inevitable dynamic of capitalism. As capital becomes concentrated, labor becomes organized, with the result that individual worker's lives become increasingly controlled, not just by the corporation but also by the union. And one outcome of these forces is for the laws of supply and demand in all markets to become increasingly suspended in favor of the organizational policies of corporations, unions, and government which are only partially affected by market forces.

BIG GOVERNMENT. Partly as a result of these pressures toward monopolization, intercorporate control, multinationalization, and unionization, government has been inexorably drawn into economic affairs in America. Such interference has clearly violated the conservative capitalist belief system, but so have all the forces that disrupt the operation of the laws of supply and demand. This involvement has been justified by the liberal capitalist ideology that recognizes those inherent processes of capitalism which, if left unchecked, would suspend completely the free and competitive market.

Much governmental intervention in the economy has occurred as the goals of government have grown. Whether military or social in nature, the federal government has sought to regulate market processes to meet national goals. In this effort, the pattern of government intervention in the economy has been greatly influenced by the power of large corporations, the formal and informal cartels of trade associations, the subtle power of intercorporate stock-holders, the international politics of resource distribution, and the power of organized labor. A pattern of involvement reflecting such multiple influences will, of necessity, be highly complex, but in general government has used a variety of mechanisms to achieve some degree of control over market processes: (1) cash subsidies to selected industries, (2) massive purchases of goods and services in the market, (3) regulation of money flows through the tax and Federal Reserve systems, (4) export-import policies affecting the export and import of goods to and from selected nations, (5) direct "control" through regulatory agencies and licensing policies, and (6) direct control of prices and wages in selected industries and, at times, in all or most industries. Just how these various types of regulation are used will be discussed in an analysis of specific economic problems, but for the present, it should be noted that government regulation has, in accordance with liberal capitalist beliefs, sought to maintain competitive markets when possible. But at the same time, the government has allowed and even encouraged those very processes that can cut down on the amount of competition in the market. Namely, the federal government has tolerated the growth of large corporations that seek to suspend competition; it has also encouraged large unions and noncompetitive relations between labor and management; and, it has regulated monetary, military, and export-import policies to protect big corporations and unions from foreign competition. Within these governmental efforts are many contradictions, perhaps underscoring the structural dilemma of mature capitalism.

It is in the context of these structural dilemmas, as compounded by various ideological beliefs, that current economic problems must be viewed. For indeed, in light of these basic dilemmas, many economic problems are inevitable, but equally important, solutions to one set of problems can often aggravate other economic problems. It is these facts that make the resolution of specific economic problems very difficult.

PRESENT ECONOMIC PROBLEMS IN AMERICA

INFLATION

For several years the American economy, as well as those in other capitalist societies, has seen steady increases in the prices of goods and services. As will become evident, inflationary periods or episodes are inherent to capitalistic forms of economic organization; but equally important, inflation may increasingly become a world problem that could prove difficult to resolve.

THE SHRINKING DOLLAR

The chart below reports the cost of key items over the last 30 years. Naturally, incomes for Americans have increased as prices have escalated—thus underscoring the inflationary trends in the American economy. The chart reflects the purchasing power of the dollar from October, 1944 to October, 1974.

Year	Round Steak (1 lb.)	Sugar (5 lb.)	Bread (loaf)	Coffee (1 lb.)	Eggs (1 doz.)	Milk (half gallon)	Lettuce (1 head)	Butter (1 lb.)	Stamp (first class)	Gasoline (1 gallon)
1944	.45	.34	.09	.30	.64	.29	.12	.50	.03	.21
1954	.92	.52	.17	1.10	.60	.45	.19	.72	.03	.29
1964	1.07	.59	.21	.82	.57	.48	.25	.76	.05	.30
1974	1.78	2.08	.36	1.31	.84	.78	.43	.95	.10	.53

Source: U.S. Bureau of Labor Statistics, Consumer Division, 1974.

While inflation is a complex process, the result of inflation—higher prices—is easily comprehended by the average American. What causes prices to periodically escalate? The answer to this often asked question resides in the structural dilemmas of liberal capitalism. One force causing higher prices is the size of economic units that no longer must be completely responsive to competition. For example, U. S. Steel, General Motors, and Exxon are capable of dominating their respective markets to the extent that it is not always necessary for them to lower prices in the face of slackening demand. In light of their partial immunity to effective competition, they are likely to *raise* prices to make up for decreasing sales and hence maintain their profits. Other "competitive" corporations must be careful of undercutting such corporate giants, for in an all-out price war, smaller competitors could not survive. Thus, there are pressures for smaller companies to follow the leads of the larger; and if larger companies raise prices, others will faithfully follow, raising prices across the entire market sector.

Once one sector of the economy raises prices, the price increases become higher costs for those companies using the goods and services in their manufacturing operations. For instance, should U. S. Steel raise prices, General Motors' costs increase and it too is likely to raise the price of its cars. Thus, price increases by resource and basic commodity industries reverberate throughout the economy, setting off waves of price increases by all the companies comprising the complex web of interconnections in a modern economy.

Another inflationary pressure comes from organized labor. Capitalistic economies are built around growth and expansion, creating a highly affluent standard of living for the majority of the population during mature capitalism. Labor thus becomes accustomed to a constantly escalating standard of living (which is possible by successful wage increases) and to buying the myriad of goods and services provided by mature capitalism. For this reason, unions constantly work for increased wages and other benefits which, from the corporation's viewpoint, represent higher costs. And unless savings can be made in other cost areas, or unless corporations are willing to decrease their profits, the prices of their products will increase. At times these cyclical processes escalate so rapidly as to create a wage-price spiral like that of the late 1960s and 1970s, with the result that in trying to keep up with higher prices, labor seeks higher wages, in turn assuring higher prices. Such wage-price cycles would be less likely (1) if Americans were not accustomed to ever-increasing levels of material well being, (2) if corporations were not oriented toward ever-increasing profits, and (3) if a few corporations could not so dominate markets. But as long as workers and corporations think in terms of short-range profits and wages, wage-price spirals are easily initiated in mature capitalist economies.

Such spirals are difficult to control by governmental regulation because government is not geared to establish and implement a national economic policy. First, the nature of political democracy in a society as diverse as that in America makes it difficult to agree on any unified national policy (see Chapter 3), especially in the economic sphere where there are so many inherent conflicts of interest. Secondly, even if agreement over a policy could be established by Congress and the president, implementation is difficult because of the nature of governmental intervention in the economy. Much of this intervention has been indirect, using the free market mechanism to stimulate or decrease demand. For example, rather than directly establish wages, prices, and supply levels of goods and services, government has sought to influence all of these through tax policies, Federal Reserve actions, import-export policies, and governmental purchases. Government in America is not set up to directly control supplies, prices, and wages since the government does not own the capital of the economy. To own the capital would, of course, transform the economy into a collectivist form—a solution to economic problems that would be resisted by most Americans.

When government does attempt to regulate prices and wages, then, it has little control over the supplies of goods since corporations will often cut back production rather than operate at a loss or marginal level of profit. In so doing, they exert vast political pressure on government to relax controls, and such pressure is particularly effective in America because the population is unaccustomed to shortages and is unwilling to tolerate a leveling off, or a decrease, in their usual standard of living. Thus, the dilemma of liberal capitalism is that in seeking to maintain the market mechanism, government decreases its capacity to regulate supplies when it does implement wage and price controls. And, corporations structured to make profits, workers used to higher wages, and citizens accustomed to increasing material well being exert enormous political pressure on government in an effort to realize their short-run interests—whether for profits or affluence. As a result, a democratic form of government will tend to shift economic policies as much in response to citizen demand as to economic realities.

A final inflationary force is the international involvement of the American economy. Basic resources are now in shorter supply because of growing international demand, coupled with less accessible supplies in the United States. Thus, Americans must now compete with other nations for many essential resources that were formerly purchased at low costs in Third World countries. As these countries have become aware of the growing dependence of the modern world upon their resources, they have begun to organize and exert monetary and political influence. The Arab oil cartel is but the first, and still the most conspicuous, example of a phenomenon which will become increasingly prevalent in the world market. Just as giant, monopolistic corporations can begin to dictate prices in a domestic market, so countries with large quantities of needed resources can begin to dictate prices in the international market. Such *monolistic* practices are inherently inflationary since Third World countries are likely to raise prices in order to increase their world power and to develop their own countries.

One of the curious factors in this situation is that giant American corporations are now becoming the "brokers" of the Third World. As nationalization of basic extractive facilities of American corporations is increasingly implemented by the host country, American corporations become the "middlemen" in the international market. As profit-making organizations, they naturally sell to the highest bidders, causing worldwide inflation in the international market. Such multinational corporations are not as easily regulated as national corporations by any domestic government, with the result that in America, multinational corporations chartered in the United States are increasingly becoming less responsive to domestic economic demand and political pressures. Such a situation will inevitably be inflationary, since America's multinational corporations will seek to increase profits through raising prices. And should price controls be implemented, these same corporations can keep resources out of the U.S. market while selling to other nations, thus creating shortages that would probably force political concessions under public pressure.

Inflation, then, is not easily controlled in America because of the structural dilemmas of capitalism. As long as the Third World countries sold their resources cheaply, as long as American corporations were small, as long as corporations were national in character, as long as labor was less accustomed to ever-increasing wages, and as long as Americans were used to shortages, government market policies could influence inflation. But now the very success of American corporations and labor unions, added to the new consciousness of the Third World, has made domestic inflation much more difficult to control, even when the government suspends the domestic market mechanism through wage and price controls.

ECONOMIC CYCLES AND STAGFLATION

Capitalist forms of economic organization are subject to what is now called the *business cycle* in which periods of economic prosperity—high profits, full employment, and higher wages—are followed by recessions, and on occasions depressions, declining profits, high unemployment, and lower wages. The American economy has been subject to many such vacillating cycles, but despite their inevitability and methodical frequency, economists still debate their causes.[3]

Since the 1930s, governmental policies have been directed at mitigating the consequences of the business cycle. Various programs have sought to assist unemployed workers, while government fiscal, taxing, import-export, and purchasing policies have been designed to keep demand for goods sufficiently high so as to prevent a severe cutback in capital investment. For example, by lowering taxes and altering Federal Reserve requirements, more money (hence higher demand) is pumped into the economy; or, by restricting imports and lowering export restrictions, demand for goods is increased; or, by increasing the federal budget (usually through deficit financing and tax increases), governmental purchases can create demand and encourage production in selected sectors of the economy.

Business cycles are sometimes compounded by an additional problem: inflation. At various times, and most recently in the 1970s, recession has been accompanied by inflation, making recent governmental policies of *pump-priming* the economy during recession much more difficult. For to increase aggregate demand is to put pressure on prices to rise. This situation has been called the dilemma of *stagflation*—an economy with decreasing productivity

---

[3] Two forces appear to set the business cycle in motion (Sherman, 1972: 82–90): (1) Wages as a proportion of aggregate or total income actually *decline* during periods of prosperity, eventually translating into decreasing demand relative to productivity. In absolute dollars, of course, wages increase dramatically, but relative to escalating profits, the buying power of wages as a proportion of all income (wages, profits, etc.) and production decreases. (2) During prosperity, the high demand for capital goods (machinery, factories, etc.) and basic resources (fuels and necessary minerals) increases their cost to manufacturers, with the result that profits per unit of production begin to decline. At some point, the slackening demand resulting from the aggregate decline in wages, plus lower per unit profits, discourages further investment in capital expansion, setting into motion decreased production, unemployment, and lower wages. But traditionally during recessions, wages, as a proportion of aggregate or total income, have *increased*, creating greater demand, which encourages the renewed investment that leads to fuller employment, higher wages, and even greater consumer demand. But eventually, all of these processes create an over-production relative to the demand from wage earners, and the cycle is set into motion once again.

and employment accompanied by rising prices. Ordinarily, decreasing productivity with the resulting high unemployment will reduce market demand (because people do not have income) and reduce prices (to induce people to buy), or at the very least, stabilize prices. But the inflationary pressures discussed previously have at times been sufficiently strong to prevent price stabilization in the face of slackening demand. And it appears that these inflationary pressures may become an enduring feature of mature capitalism in America. In this situation, government policies to reduce recession can aggravate inflation to such a point that the economy achieves only "paper" growth with inflated dollars. In fact, with severe inflation, paper growth in profits and wages can represent absolute declines in profits and consumer buying power. And when profits suffer from decreased consumer demand, corporations begin to hold back capital investments and/or to cut production, thereby furthering recession.

Such has been the dilemma facing government during the 1970s —how to deal with inflation *and* mitigate the apparently inevitable business cycle. As with any dilemma, solutions to one problem may create other problems, and it is perhaps wise to outline, in an order of increasing "radicalness," some of the dilemmas inhering in various solutions to stagnation:

PUMP-PRIMING. The traditional approach since the New Deal has been to stimulate the economy through policies increasing market demand. Tax cuts, lowering of prime interest rates through the Federal Reserve, deficit government spending, and lowering export quotas represent typical approaches. Such policies can work to reduce recession in the short run, but they aggravate inflation which, if allowed to continue, would throw the economy into an even deeper recession in the long run.

If stimulated economic growth can keep profits and wages ahead of inflation, then government pump-priming policies can prevent recession. However, while some industries (such as oil) have enjoyed record profits in the 1970s, others have been subjected to declining profits. Further, by the end of 1974 government statistics from the Labor department showed that the buying power of wages had declined to 1969 levels, indicating that rampant inflation was running well ahead of wage increases. Thus, extensive and broad based pump-priming presents the danger of aggravating inflation to a point where it could actually accelerate recession.

DIRECT CONTROLS. In times of war, and more recently in the 1970s, wage-price controls have been instituted to prevent inflation during times of economic growth and expansion. Wage-price controls usually create shortages, since industries are unable to make what they consider "adequate" profits and thus cut back on production. Government subsidies to such industries restore inflationary pressures that make tight administration of wage-price controls even more necessary. Such an enigmatic situation also pits two government bureaucracies against each other—one stimulating a flagging industry, the other keeping a lid on the amount of stimulation to be allowed.

Wage-price controls can create a recession by discouraging investment while encouraging production cutbacks, unemployment, and reduced consumer demand. They are also difficult to administer in a society which has typically used the market mechanism for setting wages and prices. And yet they are at time a necessary tool for fighting the inflation that can cause the same recessionary tendencies; and they can mitigate the effect of rampant inflation on workers' purchasing power. But without a long term program for directly controlling economic activity by government, wage-price controls can create extensive distortions in economic activity and generate severe shortages of basic goods and services. Long-range policies for directly controlling the economy will, of course, be resisted by corporations and individuals committed to free market processes; but without such policies, wage-price controls can probably be effective only as a stop-gap measure to mitigate the rate of inflation.

INCREASED COMPETITION AND TRUST-BUSTING. One possible long-term solution to the inflation side of stagflation is to decrease the size of corporations thereby increasing competition among them. Such a trust-busting program would go against basic tendencies for monopolization and oligopolization of capitalist economies; but if companies can be forced to compete, then prices can be kept down as long as costs for basic manufacturing resources (such as fuels and minerals) do not have to be secured on the international market. Increased competition among corporations would aggravate the business cycle but, with decreasing inflation, government pump-priming could be more effective. However, it is not clear if it is politically possible, or even desirable, to "bust" large multinationals. These multinationals control world markets for basic resources, and it is not yet apparent whether increased competition among them could significantly lower prices in the face of high world demand for raw materials and fuels.

NATIONALIZATION. The collectivist belief system advocates the ownership by the people of the means of production—that is, government ownership of basic extractive, manufacturing, servicing, and distributing companies. Through direct ownership, government need be less concerned with profit motives and can more directly control production, wages, and employment. In doing these, chronic inflation and recession can be better regulated. But such a program is ideologically abhorrent to most Americans; and it is not certain that state ownership increases the efficiency and quality of production. Nor is it immediately evident that such ownership would maintain the economy's capacity to compete extensively in world markets, especially if wages and prices were kept out of adjustment with world market conditions.

Many capitalist nations have partially nationalized industry—usually in transportation and communications—but such programs do not mitigate inflation or recession since they do not significantly affect the operation of basic extractive, manufacturing, servicing, and distributing industries.

Just how to cope with stagflation is thus a difficult problem, with no single solution having any unambiguous advantage over others. Combinations of solutions are perhaps necessary, but which ones? And answers to such a question are, in the end, simply conjecture. For if one thing is evident, it is that the business cycle and the inflation cycle are not among the easily resolved problems of economic structure.

WASTE AND POLLUTION

In an economic system guided by profit considerations, efforts are directed at keeping costs low in relation to prices, thereby increasing profits. Such considerations may at times allow organizations to achieve a considerable degree of efficiency in their internal operation, but they are likely to lead to wasteful and polluting manufacturing processes. Pollution control and abatement equipment is expensive, and it is unlikely that economic organizations will make purchases that drive up costs. Furthermore, it is often cheaper to extract resources and manufacture goods by letting much valuable material go to waste, only because to use all materials or to recycle other resources is more costly than wasteful extraction and manufacturing. Only when it becomes less expensive to conserve and recycle can there be any strong imperative to use the least wasteful forms of manufacturing. And only when pollution becomes costly in terms of profit considerations are organizations likely to be concerned with ecological questions.

This situation is equally prevalent in societies guided by collectivist beliefs since rapidly increased productivity—and hence increasingly wasteful and polluting manufacturing—is usually the primary collective goal. Industrialization creates waste and pollution problems, but capitalist economic organizations present a different set of obstacles to their resolution than communist economies: Without direct government controls over economic processes, how is the government to induce or coerce corporations to employ less wasteful and less polluting forms of extraction and manufacturing? Problems of overcoming corporate and union political influence, of effective monitoring of pollutants and wastes, and of assessing taxes or fines make it extremely difficult for government in an economy dominated by large, private corporations and large unions to impose rules and regulations that might cut into profits, lower productivity, or cost workers jobs. (See Chapter 11 for a fuller discussion of pollution problems and solutions.)

CONSUMER DECEPTION AND MANIPULATION

In recent years a considerable amount of consumer deception has been exposed. A high degree of consumer manipulation, deception, and outright fraud is probably inevitable in an economic system structured for profit in a quasi-competitive market. Competitive markets encourage extensive advertising to induce consumers to purchase goods and services, and the drive for profits can sometimes lead corporations to deceive consumers about the nature of various products. Advertising is also necessary to encourage the growth so essential to maintain capitalistic economic systems. Thus, corporations seek to expand the demand for goods by creating "needs" in consumers for more goods. Instilling new needs for the "latest" model and a plethora of "new and improved" goods constitutes a form of corporate manipulation which, at times, extends into deception about the true nature of a product.

As the economy becomes dominated by large corporations, advertising assumes a new function: to convince the public that giant corporations are in the public's best interest. For example, oil company advertising has often assumed a "public information" format, seeking to convince consumers that oil cartel control of the world market is necessary and desirable to meet America's energy needs. As competition among giant corporations decreases, advertising becomes much more deliberately manipulative and seeks to persuade the public that the current state of economic affairs is desirable. Moreover, advertising costs enormous sums of money without adding to consumer knowledge and product superiority. The result of this situation is that consumers pay more for goods whose prices are inflated by advertising costs.

Regulating small and large companies in a quasi-competitive market has proven difficult. Many of the regulatory problems are endemic to capitalist forms of economic organization: First, the large number of manufacturing corporations producing millions of goods makes it extremely difficult to monitor advertising integrity, product safety, and various fraudulent activities. Second, there is a tendency for regulatory agencies to become co-opted by the larger organizations they are set up to regulate because day to day contact is not with consumers but with corporate officials. Third, the political power of corporations has often worked to weaken regulatory laws and make government agencies impotent, and hence, easily co-opted. As a result of at least these forces, then, a considerable amount of abuse, deception, and manipulation of the consumer occurs; and without consistently effective regulation by such agencies as the Food and Drug Administration, Civil Aeronautics Board, Interstate Commerce Commission, Public Utilities Commissions, Department of Agriculture, Department of Interior, Department of Justice, and the many other agencies with regulatory responsibilities, it is all but impossible to prevent every instance of consumer abuse.

The failure of government to effectively protect its clients, the public, has forced nongovernmental organizations like the Consumers Unions and the Ralph Nader organization to investigate and bring suits against both corporations and government for initiating and tolerating consumer abuse. This conflict between nongovernmental organizations and corporations is probably inevitable in mature capitalist systems where large corporations, unions, and government agencies can, at times, work against as much as for consumers' interests.

WORKER FRUSTRATION AND ALIENATION

Early capitalism tends to be highly exploitive of unorganized labor since individual workers are not in a position to bargain with corporate management over salary and working conditions. But as labor becomes organized in the mature stages of capitalism, it acquires considerable bargaining power, especially in industries with heavy capital investments where a shutdown becomes enormously costly. Under these conditions, organized labor is able to improve wages, working conditions, and fringe benefits.

Large and effective labor unions are a response to corporations that, as they become larger, are vulnerable to strikes and shutdowns. In organizing, however, industrial workers place themselves between two bureaucracies: the corporation and the union. Work within the corporation tends to be monotonous, highly regulated, uncreative, and, therefore, ungratifying, while union membership imposes restrictions on occupational mobility, job classification, and take-home pay. As industrial workers have become somewhat affluent and secure in their work, it appears that they also become more attuned to their dependent situation. Such awareness has created the "blue-collar blues" in which the lack of individual freedom and the incessant monotony of work in large industries has stimulated a search for more meaning and satisfaction in work.

This problem is endemic to corporate desires for profits using the most efficient and least expensive production process in which machine and human labor are made highly standardized. However, the "blue-collar blues" have become costly, resulting in poor job performance, high absenteeism, and high worker turnover. Alternative work settings have been sought by industry, but it is not yet clear whether profit-oriented corporations can implement work settings with less supervision and monotony on a wide scale. As a result, blue-collar dissatisfaction and corporate-union efforts to create more meaningful work is likely to be one of the basic problems of mature capitalism in America.

Much of the work force, however, does not belong to a union. As will be emphasized in the chapters on inequality and poverty, many workers are subject to hardships generated by the business cycle and the low wages stemming from intense competition in the unskilled labor market. Such workers experience enormous dissatisfaction and frustration with an economic system incapable of providing them with meaningful and well-paying work. The race riots of the 1960s were, in large part, an expression of such frustration to participate in the mainstream of the economy. Whites also experience these same impediments, and during times of deep recession, this marginal labor force can pose a threat to civil order.

Without union organization, these marginal workers must rely on government to protect and assist them; yet, only during a deep recession or outright depression has government been willing to provide an extensive system of public service jobs. But even these jobs have been defined as temporary measures to "take up the slack" in the employment picture of the economy. The unskilled, non-union worker must endure constant employment uncertainty in a cyclical economy that is only partially regulated by government, thus heightening frustration and, at times, rage against not only the economic institutions but the entire society.

COORDINATION, CONTROL, AND NATIONAL PRIORITIES

Like most mature capitalist systems, the American economy is a "mixed" economy with the free market mechanism operating in some sectors and government regulation in other sectors. Any large economy, whether patterned after capitalist or collectivist ideals, presents problems of coordination and control in meeting politically established goals. In capitalist systems, growth and profits are the primary goals of economic units, while high wages, security, and meaningful employment are the major goals of workers. To some extent, these goals correspond with national priorities, but in some instances, they do not. Goals such as racial equality, ecological preservation, international humanitarianism, national self-sufficiency in energy, consumer protection, community planning, and many other national goals come into conflict with the priorities of corporations and unionized workers.

Coupled with the economic and political problems associated with the business cycle and inflation/stagflation, government inevitably intervenes in the market mechanisms and seeks to allocate human and material resources to meet *political* goals. In so doing, government usually attempts to utilize the market mechanism as much as is possible, resulting in a system of market incentives and subsidies for economic organizations conducting certain types of economic activity. Tax credits for manufacturers, cash subsidies to farmers and airlines, price supports for dairy products, depletion allowances for extraction corporations, accelerated depreciation for real estate activity, and a host of incentives and subsidies usually operate to leave some semblance of the market mechanism. Control and regulation is, therefore, indirect, and it is not always possible to precisely coordinate economic activity in pursuit of political goals.

With government increasingly concerned with the well being of citizens, it is inevitable that economic and political goals will come into conflict. Capitalist systems are simply unprepared to coordinate economic activity, not only because of the indirect nature of regulation through the market, but also because large corporations, large unions, large conglomerates, and foreign governments are able to exert an independent base of power in a political democracy. This power is disproportionate, but as long as government is designed to be receptive to influence by private citizens' interests, then it is inevitable that well-financed and organized interests will exert more influence on political decisions than individual citizens.

This conflict between citizens and economic organizations in establishing national priorities and allocating societal resources is inherent in capitalist systems that rely on a quasi-market mechanism. As a result, coordination and control of economic activity in pursuit of political goals will in all probability pose a constant problem of structure in American society.

THE FUTURE OF THE AMERICAN ECONOMY: LIBERAL CAPITALISM VERSUS COLLECTIVISM?

One of the persistent themes in the collectivist critique of liberal capitalism is that, to paraphrase Marx's well-known statement, it will "sow the seeds of its own destruction." For according to this critique, the dilemmas of capitalism outlined in this chapter create such regular disruption through recession, inflation, fraud, and political disorganization that frustrated and alienated workers become disposed to initiate a revolution that restructures the economy in terms of collectivist beliefs. Such a scenario has never occurred in a mature capitalist society, so it is not entirely clear whether the problems inhering in capitalism do create sufficient discontent to encourage political revolt. And significantly, there are few signs that liberal capitalism is incapable of preventing such a revolt.

The collectivist critique does, however, highlight (albeit in somewhat extreme and polemical form) some of the problems of structure in the American economy. As the analysis of inequality, poverty, and racism in later chapters will reveal, economic arrangements in America support vast inequality, extensive poverty, as well as racial, ethnic, and sexual discrimination. Moreover, general unemployment at a 5 percent level, jumping to 9 percent and perhaps even higher during deep recessions, appears endemic to American capitalism. Monopoly, high prices, and exploitive profits are also common in the American capitalist system, as are considerable waste and pollution. But on the more positive side, American capitalism is capable of enormous productivity which translates into a notably high standard of living for the majority of its citizens.

Collectivist economic systems avoid, to a greater extent than American capitalism, extreme inequality, racial, ethnic, and sexual discrimination, chronic unemployment, exploitive prices, and inflation. Such systems, however, exhibit considerably less political freedom, while erecting large, inefficient, and at times, repressive bureaucracies. Collectivist systems, too, have their own problems of structure, and it is not immediately clear whether their problems are any less severe than those of American capitalism.

Thus, all forms of economic organization in modern and modernizing societies reveal rather fundamental problems that create inequalities, abuses, conflicts, and tensions. The structural source of these problems will differ somewhat depending upon the nature of economic organization, but in American society, they inhere in the cultural conflicts and structural dilemmas of liberal capitalism.

Chapter 3

PROBLEMS OF GOVERNMENT

Social problems in America are intimately connected to political processes. Many have their roots in these processes, and all problems can be resolved only with the political will to confront and eliminate their causes. When government does not adequately address social problems, it can be said to have its own problems of structure. For even in the post-Watergate era, the problems of governance are not caused by corrupt and evil politicians; rather, corrupt politicians are allowed to flourish only in a system that tolerates and rewards political abuses. It is not the individuals that must be examined; they enact roles from a script written by the structure of government.

While the individual incumbents in Congress, the judiciary, and the presidency obviously "make some difference" in what social problems are considered sufficiently grave to address, and in what solutions are considered appropriate, there are problems in the structure within which these individuals operate. It is these problems of structure that will be analyzed in this chapter, for in the long run, social problems in America will not be abolished by any politician until some of the structural dilemmas in government itself are overcome.

This chapter will focus on two such structural problems: (1) The difficulty of effective society-wide planning by government; and (2) the problems of reordering national priorities to address such problems as racism, pollution, inequality, and segregation. In turn, these two basic problems are a reflection of the pattern and distribution of power in America. To unravel these patterns and the basic problems inhering in them, we must first analyze the structure of federalism in America, and then the structure of the executive, legislative, and judicial branches of the federal government.

PROBLEMS OF FEDERALISM: CENTRALIZATION
VERSUS DECENTRALIZATION

Government in America reveals an inherent dilemma: It is a decentralized, federalist system with 50 individual states and thousands of local communities supposedly determining much of their
own destiny. Such a decentralized system represents the original
conception of the federal government as one that will perform best
when its duties are restricted to "housekeeping" chores: defense
and security, coinage of money, and regulation of trade. Comple-
menting this conception of the federal government was a laissez
faire ideology stressing that the free enterprise system of competitive markets and privately owned corporations is necessary for
prosperity and progress. In contradiction to federalism and laissez
faire is the second feature of American government, a trend toward
centralization. Increasingly, decision-making power is passing from
states and local communities to the federal government, and,
within the federal government, into the hands of the president and
away from Congress and the judiciary. And while Watergate and
similar illegalities by the agencies of government, such as the CIA,
IRS, Pentagon, and FBI, can be viewed as a commentary on the
morality of the participants, these actions can more accurately
be seen as one result of the growing concentration of power in the
federal government, and in particular, in the executive branch.
Such concentrations of power could potentially make reordering
priorities and national planning somewhat easier, but they also
open the way for the abuse of power—thus underscoring the
dilemmas facing America's federalist system.

In all federalist systems, the problems of planning and arranging
national priorities are a reflection of the contradictions in federalism and laissez faire on the one hand, and a large, centralized
government on the other. A decentralized federalist system is
attuned to local rather than national interests, with the result that
efforts by Congress to create national programs are likely to encounter resistance by coalitions of local interests. Furthermore,
when national programs are enacted, the federalist structure of
government and the remnants of laissez faire can potentially
neutralize them. In an attempt to work through local governments
and to utilize the private sector of the economy, many federal
programs are rendered less effective because of waste, inefficiency,
graft, and corruption at the *local* level. Thus, national planning,
coordination, and control are inherently difficult in a political system that values competition and decentralization.

The trend toward centralization in American government would seemingly eliminate the problem of national planning, but the *pattern* of centralization has aggravated the problem of national priorities. Ignoring for the moment the merits of the fact, centralization of government in America has involved the creation of a large and powerful "military establishment" that consumes close to one-half of all tax dollars, thereby making massive government expenditures on social and domestic programs more difficult. Whereas the original Social Security Act, housing legislation, welfare laws, and many other *domestic* federal programs were initiated with the dramatic centralization of government during the 1930s, the post-Korean War period has seen domestic programs take up a smaller proportion of the federal budget than before World War II. Meanwhile the military has maintained its grasp on the tax dollar at a level not much less than that during the Korean mobilization (Lieberson, 1971).

In essence, the political process in America exhibits some of the less desirable features of both federalist and centralized governments. Federalism, backed by laissez faire and a suspicion of big government, has made national planning difficult. Centralization has evolved along the path toward a military, as opposed to a social service, profile. In turn, these problems of America's federalist structure are, to a very great extent, a result of changes in the balance of power *within* the structure of the federal government.

PROBLEMS IN MAINTAINING THE BALANCE OF POWER

THE EXECUTIVE BRANCH OF GOVERNMENT

THE GROWING POWER OF THE PRESIDENT. The U.S. Constitution originally defined the powers of the presidency rather ambiguously. But over time, in response to a long series of national crises ranging from war to economic depression, this ambiguity has become translated into far-reaching power: to appoint and remove administrators from office, to direct administrative agencies, to initiate most legislation for Congress, to direct and control the military, to make war without congressional authorization, to regulate the budget by selectively administering funds granted by Congress, and to appoint and direct cabinet officers and the administrative bureaucracy under them.

This centralization of power has occurred in the face of a strong laissez faire ideology and a cotitutionally established federalist system. To have overcome these traditions means that powerful forces had been operating to create a centralized political system.

One of these has been the sheer growth in the size of the nation—from a small, agrarian population to an industrial urban populace of over 200 million. Large urban and industrial societies probably cannot be governed by local government because the proliferation of nationwide problems makes decentralization most difficult. A second force leading to government intervention has been the potential destruction of a capitalist economy through monopolization by a few corporations. And the "boom and bust" cycles of the economy, culminating in the Great Depression, have necessitated further control and regulation of the economy. Still more pressure for centralization has come from the redefinition of citizenship and

---

SOCIOLOGICAL INSIGHTS

DID THE SYSTEM WORK?

In many ways, the abuses of Watergate and the presidential cover-up activities were the result of the growing perception by the Nixon administration of their power. Many commentators have noted that the "system worked," for indeed, the abuses were uncovered, a president was forced to resign under threat of impeachment, and key figures in the Nixon administration were prosecuted.

But other commentators have noted that the system did not work. They ask a simple question: What if there had been no White House tapes? Would Watergate cover-up activities have been exposed? Would the President have been forced to resign in order to avoid impeachment in the House and prosecution in the Senate? And would key Nixon administration figures have been successfully prosecuted? Would, in fact, the public know much about the abuses of power by the executive branch of government? It may be that the system worked rather badly since the impeachment process was never completed and would never have been initiated without the tapes.

No president is likely to tape himself again, and thus, it can be asked: Can abuses of power be uncovered again? And can the impeachment processes ever be an effective check on presidential power? Or, is there something about the structure of government in America that bestows enormous power on the president? Or, is it possible for Congress to regain much of its lost power?

These are the questions that a structural analysis can help answer.

civil rights for formerly disfranchised groups who have demanded federal intervention in the social and economic spheres.

But perhaps the most persistent pressure for centralization has come from war. For example, from 1776 until 1900 American army units participated in an estimated 9000 battles and skirmishes, while naval units engaged in 1100 missions involving violent conflict. These figures average out to 90 violent conflicts per year for the first 125 years of American government (Wright, 1942; Dentler, 1967:57). When twentieth-century conflicts are added to this inventory, the military involvement of American government becomes clear. For example, aside from the first and second world wars, the United States in recent decades has engaged in numerous limited wars: Korea (1950–1953), Indochina (1951–1953), Guatemala (1954), the Congo (1960), Cuba (1961), Laos (1961), Vietnam (1962), the Dominican Republic (1965), Cambodia (1970), and Laos (1971).

Whether a full-scale or limited involvement, war activities encourage centralization of government since people and resources need to be mobilized on a national scale. War activities create both social (protests, hardships, veterans' benefits, etc.) and economic (inflation, for example) problems, thus furthering the need for centralized power. And once a large military establishment is created, economic, social, monetary, and political policies become interwoven with this establishment. Such interconnectedness with the centralized military establishment not only furthers the power of the president (as commander in chief) and the Pentagon, it makes redirection of national priorities toward domestic issues by the executive branch of government more difficult. The problems of government structure, then, are intimately tied to the rise of the military establishment in America.

THE MILITARY AND GOVERNMENT. The military establishment emerged during World War II and its aftermath. The rapid conversion of the depressed American economy to wartime production in the early 1940s created, for the first time in ten years, full employment and prosperity. This transformation established an unfortunate association between military production and economic prosperity: One inevitably followed the other in the minds of most Americans and economic advisors to the president. The Korean War added the specter of a world communist conspiracy, with the result that Americans were most willing to accept, out of fear, the rhetoric and reality of the cold war. The significance of the Korean War and fear of world communism in creating a military establishment is best reflected in the growing budget of the Pentagon. In 1945, the last year of full wartime production, the budget was $80.5 billion. By 1950 the military budget dropped to $13.3 billion; but by 1960 it had climbed to $45 billion (Melman, 1970: 210).[1]

In the 1950s the Penatgon was granted expanded power to purchase what it wanted in order to promote national security. During World War II the government procurement rule requiring that all purchases be made through written competitive bid was suspended. After the war, the Armed Services Procurement Act was passed, reestablishing the general procurement rule, but with 17 major exceptions. By 1970 nearly 90 percent of the procurement contracts of the Pentagon and 98 percent of the National Aeronautics and Space Administration (NASA) were concluded under these exceptions. President Harry S Truman clearly recognized the dangers of such exceptions when he wrote to the heads of the armed services:

> This bill grants unprecedented freedom from specific procurement restrictions during peacetime. . . . There is a danger that the natural desire for flexibility and speed in proceurement will lead to excessive placement of contracts by negotiation and undue reliance upon large concerns . . . (Kauffman, 1969).

Truman's fear of an alliance between the military and America's large corporations became more of a reality by the late 1950s, causing President Dwight D. Eisenhower to label the alliance "the military-industrial complex"—a powerful coalition of military, business, and congressional leaders.

Yet, it was probably not until the 1960s that a true military establishment emerged. President John F. Kennedy made a campaign on military issues such as the missile gap between the United

---

[1] Lieberson (1971) has argued that the military budget as a proportion of the total federal budget has always been high during wartime and has always dropped during peacetime. More significantly, he argues that the post-Korea military budget, as a proportion of the total federal budget, has been no greater than it was in the 1840s, another period of relative peace. This comparison has little meaning. The United States in the 1840s had only a small federal budget, which dealt primarily with housekeeping chores. There were few large federal domestic programs. Under these conditions the federal budget should reflect a large proportion of expenditures for military spending. The important point is that military expenditures remain a large proportion—about half—of the federal budget in an era in which the budget must finance a myriad of domestic programs. During the depression—another era of intense domestic imperatives—the military budget was less than 10 percent of the total budget. Since that time the military has been able to increase its budgetary power five times over, even in the face of domestic needs rivaling those of the depression.

States and Russia, and thereby activated both real and imagined feeding of fears of imminent danger from communism. Once in office Kennedy increased the power of the military by declaring that the United States must be prepared to fight "aggression" in Asia, Europe, and the Western hemisphere. More importantly, Kennedy designated Robert McNamara, a businessman and a top manager of Ford Motor Co., to reorganize the Pentagon in order to increase its efficiency and to reinforce civilian control.

As secretary of defense, McNamara used tested management techniques to convert the Defense Department into an organization with a multidivision corporate structure. McNamara was given expanded powers, and he, along with top military and congressional leaders, constituted a "management team." The Pentagon was converted from a loose military complex of informal allegiances and alliances among military, business, and congressional leaders into a highly centralized military establishment with the elites of the Pentagon possessing increased control of defense contractors. As one polemicist has remarked, many defense contractors became divisions of a militarized "state management" (Melman, 1970). A giant and highly centralized governmental corporation that now controls around 80 billion tax dollars per year and around 30 percent of the gross national product was thus created under the Kennedy administration. The distinction among economic, political, and military elites is now less sharp, for they are all converging into one centralized establishment with an affinity of interests in a powerful military profile in America.

Much of the power of the Pentagon is, of course, necessary in the face of the political and military realities of the modern world. And given the complexity of the technology and machinery used in modern warfare, it is also inevitable that alliances among the Pentagon, business, and higher educational organizations would emerge. Once such alliances emerge, however, those organizations— such as corporations and research oriented universities, and all who own and work for these organizations—have a financial interest in perpetuating the alliance. As will become evident, efforts of the Pentagon, labor unions, manufacturing representatives, and even educators now generate political pressure supporting continuation of the military establishment. In this way a subtle and yet profound cooptation by the Pentagon of organizations in many institutional spheres has occurred. Much of this cooptation is probably necessary, but once some degree of power exists, it is perhaps inevitable that the Pentagon would seek more influence. For example, a list of Pentagon contractors and contractors for the allied Atomic Energy Commission and NASA reads like a "who's who" of large American corporations. Since these corporations control smaller companies, the amount of direct and indirect control of the economy by the military establishment can be far-reaching. Some major corporations, such as General Motors, Ford, and Standard Oil of New Jersey, have only a relatively small proportion of their production geared toward the military. Many corporations, however, such as General Dynamics, Lockheed, Boeing, North American Rockwell, Ling-Temco-Vought, may soon become completely dependent upon the military (Weidenbaum, 1963:113–117; Lapp, 1968:184–190). Although these companies are not owned by the military establishment, they are under its influence because a clear majority of their total sales are to the government. Other major corporations, including General Electric, General Tire, Sperry-Rand, Westinghouse, RCA, Bendix, IBM, Kaiser Industries, General Telephone, Litton Industries, and Pan American, sell a large proportion—but not a majority—of their products to the military. In many cases, if these corporations were to lose their defense contracts, they would suffer financially—thus giving the Pentagon tremendous influence.[2] If the trends of the last 20 years continue into the next decades, the Pentagon could have direct and indirect control of a major part of the economy, with the result that it will be increasingly difficult to convert economic enterprise toward non-military goals.

What is particularly problematic about military influence over the economy is the waste created by military production. First of all, military products have no real economic utility. They cannot be used in the economy and hence increase its productive capacity; rather, they are either stockpiled, scrapped, or redesigned. Second, government-subsidized corporations, especially those in aerospace and defense weaponry, have in many instances become inefficient and top-heavy with management personnel. Since many defense-oriented corporations become less dependent upon the open competitive market, they do not need to be as efficient as those competing in the private market where laws of supply and demand are more likely to operate. Should they run over their cost estimates, as they usually do, the Pentagon bails them out—although recent policy statements indicate that the Pentagon's willingness to do so may be declining. Finally, defense spending is inflationary and hurts those who must live on stable and limited incomes. Inflation also disrupts civilian capital available to the economy because it decreases the value of money while increasing the risk of invest-

---

[2] This is not to argue that economic prosperity depends on military spending. On the contrary, most experts argue that a cut in the defense budget would *increase* economic prosperity. See, for example, Koat, 1967:805–819.

ment. The result is to reduce private investment in new machinery, which is becoming increasingly noncompetitive in the world market.

One of the most damaging features of an economy oriented to military production is the waste of research manpower that could be used for other purposes. Approximately 63 percent of research and development (R & D) personnel work for the military, with only around 259,000 R & D workers currently available to non-military production (Melman, 1970:187). Compared to the 466,000 R & D personnel in Western Europe, most of whom work on civilian projects, the nonmilitary sector in the United States suffers from an acute technical manpower shortage. Deprived of civilian research, major problems like pollution, urban decay, inadequate transportation, and the declining technical dominance of the American economy are aggravated.

Even in higher education, where values of academic freedom and pursuit of pure knowledge dominate, the Pentagon, NASA, or the Atomic Energy Commission (AEC) have become prominent.[3] Among the approximately 300,000 scientists in the United States, about 35 percent work in universities. Of this group, the work of around 43 percent is supported in part, or wholly, by the federal government. Of the 1.5 billion in federal dollars fed into the university research machine, close to 40 percent comes from the Pentagon and allied agencies, such as the AEC and NASA. This research runs the gamut from pure science to development of weapons and social control techniques. In addition to these direct inputs into university research by the military establishment, many defense contractors in private industry subcontract much of their R & D work to major universities, thus increasing the dollar flow into universities from the Pentagon.

The political power of the Pentagon is revealed by two interrelated facts: (1) It is the largest and most influential agency in the executive branch of government. (2) It commands nearly one-half of all tax revenues allocated by the legislative branch of government. The large size of the Pentagon's administrative empire is a reflection of its dominant financial position, while in turn, the Pentagon's wealth reveals its capacity to influence political decision-making. Until this cycle is altered, the Pentagon will continue to expand its size, influence, and command over the nation's resources. And even in the face of considerable congressional and

[3] There have been numerous studies on universities and the impact of the federal dollar, for example, Kidd, 1959; Orlans, 1962; Hirsch, 1968:51–78. For a more polemic analysis concerning the effects of government (especially the Pentagon) on universities, see Ridgeway, 1968; Melman, 1970:97–106; Maccoby, 1974.

public criticism of the Pentagon, this cycle is not easily broken because of the diverse sources of political power possessed by the Pentagon.

With respect to influencing Congress, the Pentagon has accumulated enormous influence. Because some of America's large corporations are under the managerial control of the Pentagon, they are willing lobbyists in Washington. These corporations have much to lose should the defense budget be cut, and accordingly maintain very active lobbies in Washington. Since, as noted earlier, they do not always have to venture into a competitive marketplace and advertise like most nondefense-oriented corporations, these contractors can divert their advertising budget into lobbying activities. Corporate leaders in the defense industry now have an ally in their lobbying efforts to keep the Pentagon well heeled: organized labor. As the American economy is increasingly geared toward defense production, the labor force, particularly organized unions, has begun to lobby in favor of Pentagon policies in order to protect their jobs. Another related source of political control by the Pentagon comes from the saturation of certain geographical areas with defense-oriented industries. Once an area is dominated by defense industries, it becomes economically dependent on the Pentagon. Under these conditions, the dependent constituency is likely to elect congressmen and senators who look favorably upon defense industries. For example, the transformation of Texas into the second largest military-industrial area in the country (after California) increases the likelihood that senators and congressmen sympathetic to the Pentagon will be elected. Similarly, it is unlikely that antimilitary candidates would be elected in rural Georgia and in southeast South Carolina—the local economies are dependent on the military.

Another source of Pentagon power comes from its own lobbying activities. The Pentagon has a large public relations division that attempts to mobilize public support for Pentagon policies while exerting direct pressure on the Congress. The formal budget for such lobbying activities was reduced to 30 million by the Congress in 1971, but, informally, the monies allocated to the selling of the Pentagon approach $200 million per year. Under this kind of well-financed pressure, congressional decisions will often reflect the priorities of the Pentagon rather than those of domestically oriented agencies.

The Pentagon poses a dilemma for American society. On the one hand, an active military is a long-standing tradition, one that reflects the willingness of citizens to assist other troubled nations. Extensive military expenditures are, to some extent, necessary in

SOCIOLOGICAL INSIGHTS

A CULTURE OF DEFENSE?

Enduring and pervasive social structural arrangements are usually justified and legitimized by beliefs. Many authors have criticized the "military ideology" justifying the military establishment (Yarmolinsky, 1971; Melman, 1970; Kauffman, 1969). Below, a list of ideological tenets favoring the increased expenditure of money for the Pentagon is listed, with each one followed by the typical critique. The list was developed by Seymour Melman (1970:103–183) and the reader is invited to assess critically both the ideological assertions and the critique:

1. *Additional offensive weaponry increases America's deterrence capacity against nuclear attack.*
   The critique: The United States is no safer today than it was 15 years ago from nuclear attack, despite a threefold increase in defense spending. Since each nuclear power has an overkill capacity, it makes little difference if people can theoretically be killed 20, 30, or 100 times over—they still die only once.
2. *The United States would be overrun without continued military buildup.*
   The critique: Overrun by whom? And how? Where? With an overkill capacity of 20 or 30, it borders on paranoia to think that China, Russia, or anyone else would try to attack the United States. Increasing the overkill capacity to 50 will not make America safer.
3. *The United States must be competent to deal with all military contingencies.*
   The critique: With nuclear overkill capacity, the United States is competent to react anywhere in the world. But no nation can be competent to police the world; the costs are too great, as has been discovered in Vietnam, and as China and Russia would similarly discover.
4. *Defensive systems can be developed to ensure an ongoing society after nuclear attack.*
   The critique: With nations possessing an overkill of at least 20, no such defensive system is possible—including expensive antiballistic missiles.
5. *Nuclear war cannot yield victory, but small, conventional wars must be fought and won to preserve our deterrence capacity.*
   The critique: As Indochina convincingly demonstrates, small,

conventional wars cannot always be won—short of using nuclear weapons, in which case the tenet becomes invalidated.

6. *Military organizations and defense industries advance technology in other important spheres.*

The critique: Military technology does not spill over in great quantities to the civilian sphere, since much of it is for weapons and/or is kept secret. It is not clear how military technology will build better transportation systems, house the nation, rehabilitate the cities, or check pollution.

7. *Defense spending is necessary for continued economic prosperity.*

The critique: Defense spending promotes a product that is useless in the domestic economy; defense spending has created inflation; defense spending overseas has depleted America's gold reserves and has caused instability of the dollar on the world market; defense spending has deprived civilian industries—from steel to metal working—of capital desperately needed to modernize their obsolete production facilities; and defense spending has tied up most of the research and development manpower for projects that have no direct benefit to industry or the public. It is, therefore, ludicrous to think that defense spending stimulates the economy.

8. *The Pentagon uses the latest systems analysis technology to assure economic efficiency and effectiveness.*

The critique: The Pentagon uses systems technology to increase its managerial control, not to prevent waste and inefficiency. The fact that when defense contractors such as Lockheed and General Dynamics have entered the civilian market they have virtually gone bankrupt is sufficient to reveal the effectiveness of the Pentagon's latest system analysis.

9. *Some waste and failure is inevitable given the complexity of the technology being developed by the Pentagon.*

The critique: It has been estimated that components for military hardware have a failure rate of 40 percent. The technology is not that advanced; rather, high failure rates due to inefficiency are justified by proclaiming the complexity of the technology involved.

10. *Defense industries can always be readily converted to civilian work when needed.*

The critique: In 1963 Senator George McGovern attempted to establish a National Economic Conversion Commission. The Pentagon lobbied for its defeat, revealing its "concern" for the conversion of defense industries to civilian use. Furthermore, even given the will to convert, it is one of the delusions of the Pentagon and the public that defense industries can be reconverted rapidly to new, socially beneficial tasks, such as antipollution and transportation research and production.

11. *The United States is sufficiently affluent and does not have to choose between guns and butter: it can afford both.*
   The critique: The United States will have to choose between guns and butter. It is impossible to rebuild cities, eliminate hunger and poverty, fight pollution, reconstitute the courts, and quell the racial fires when one-half of the tax dollar goes to the Pentagon.

12. *Whatever may be said about the military, its activities are ultimately controlled by Congress and the president.*
   The critique: The military controls itself. Executive orders are constantly ignored and congressional mandates are easily violated, as was evidenced by incursions of military personnel into restricted areas of Indochina. The only real power over the Pentagon is the capacity to pull its purse strings; so far, neither Congress nor the president has been willing to do this to any significant degree.

the present world political environment. On the other hand, however, the power of the Pentagon has become so great as to make difficult any drastic reordering of national priorities. Further, considerable power to control many segments of the society has become concentrated in the hands of the military establishment elite. And when this power is coupled with the power of the presidency, such a high degree of power is accumulated as to make Watergate, CIA domestic spying, and Pentagon surveillance of citizens more likely. This is the basic dilemma of structure in the executive branch of government in America.

THE LEGISLATIVE BRANCH OF GOVERNMENT

THE DECLINE OF CONGRESSIONAL POWER. In the system of checks and balances, Congress is to mitigate the powers of the president. Under the provisions in the Constitution, Congress was empowerd to initiate most legislation, to establish national priorities, to set up and regulate executive agencies, and to determine the structure of federal courts. Since Congress was set up as a representative body, the will of the populace was to guide the form and direction of the federal government. In reality, however, Congress has abdicated much of its power to the executive branch. Now the president and executive agencies, such as the Department of Defense, establish national priorities and initiate the most important legislation.

Yet, Congress has retained some power in that it can still fail to pass programs initiated by the president, refuse to confirm his appointments, block attempts at reorganization of departments, and most importantly, withdraw funding of most government programs or agencies, and of course, impeach and convict the president. But even in the post-Watergate era, when Congress was to regain much of its lost power, it has remained more of a *reactive* than active force in determining the direction of the nation. The Senate and House are more likely, though not always, to check rather than initiate national policies and priorities. Furthermore, despite changes in campaign-spending laws, congressional action (or reaction) tends to reflect the power of well-financed and well-organized interests rather than the will of the poorly organized general public. As such, Congress has often been a conservative force preserving the status quo.

PROBLEMS OF DECISION-MAKING IN CONGRESS. The fact that Congress is an elected body would seemingly assure representative democracy in America. Two features of representation, however, have tended to skew congressional decision-making in a less representative direction. First of all, to be elected in a media-dominated society costs money. Candidates for either the House or Senate inevitably become indebted to those well-financed interests that provide major financial backing. The effect of the new campaign-spending laws on this problem has yet to be determined, but since the federal law provides for limitations only on the presidential race, not on Senate and House races, it can be assumed that little change from past practices is likely. Some state laws, as well as an increasingly suspicious public, may have some impact in reducing the influence on monied interests, but it is presently difficult to determine if any significant changes in the financing of Senate and House campaigns have occurred. Second, the House of Representatives has a definite rural bias. Despite Supreme Court decisions requiring that representation in the House reflect the distribution of the population, reappointment has not eliminated overrepresentation of congressmen from rural areas. The fact that these congressmen are frequently the chairs of important committees makes the rural bias in Congress even more pronounced. In a society that is highly urbanized, the overrepresentation of rural populations can at times pose a roadblock to needed urban-oriented

Problems of Government 59

legislation. For example, the respective power, influence, and current level of funding in the Department of Agriculture and the Department of Housing and Urban Development is a testimony to the antiurban profile of the House, since the Agriculture Department's budget is many times that of HUD.

Within Congress, legislation on a national level (except on defense and safe issues such as social security) at times is rendered less effective by local interests. To get to the floor of either the House or Senate, legislation must pass through the appropriate committee. Committees have virtually complete control over the fate of legislation in that they can pigeonhole, rewrite, stall, or kill any bill. Committee chairs, usually selected on the basis of

SOCIOLOGICAL INSIGHTS

SIGNS OF CONGRESSIONAL REFORM?

In January of 1975 a reform movement swept the House of Representatives—perhaps signaling the beginnings of change in congressional decision-making. Three of the oldest and most powerful committee chairs met their downfall: The Democratic caucus in the House voted to unseat the chairs of the Armed Services Committee, the Agriculture Committee, and the Banking and Currency Committee. Coupled with the forced resignation of the chair of the House Ways and Means Committee, the seniority system that has for years prevented the enactment of comprehensive and change-oriented legislation began to break down. The downfall of these committee chairs may indeed be followed by further changes, and at the very least, other chairs will be less arbitrary and dictatorial in their actions.

The replacements on the Agriculture, Banking, and Ways and Means committees are more urban- and change-oriented than their predecessors and, thus, they more accurately reflect the needs and priorities of the nation. The new chair of the Armed Services Committee, which rules over the Pentagon budget, differs little from his predecessors, although there is some indication that he is more sympathetic to domestic programs.

Thus, the rigid seniority system is no longer intact. These recent changes perhaps signal the beginnings of congressional reform that can make Congress a more active, as opposed to reactive, force in American government.

seniority, have enormous power to prevent legislation from getting through their committees. They can delay committee hearings and prevent legislation from coming to a vote. Because seniority rather than competence is the most frequent basis for selecting committee chairs, senators and representatives from states and districts where the constituency and interests are stable, and hence conservative, will be most likely to chair important committees. Since rural areas tend to be the most stable, committee chairs in the House will tend to evidence a rural bias. In the Senate, committee chairs will most likely come from small states with comparatively homogeneous constituencies and stable interest groupings, as is evidenced by the large number of Senate committee chairs from the South. In a nation that is highly urbanized, constantly changing, and rife with diversity, the overrepresentation of chairs of crucial committees by representatives from rural, conservative, homogeneous, and stable areas renders decision-making on the critical issues of the time more difficult.

When a piece of legislation does get to the House or Senate floor, it faces another challenge—particularly if the legislation involves national planning for change—for now it must confront a

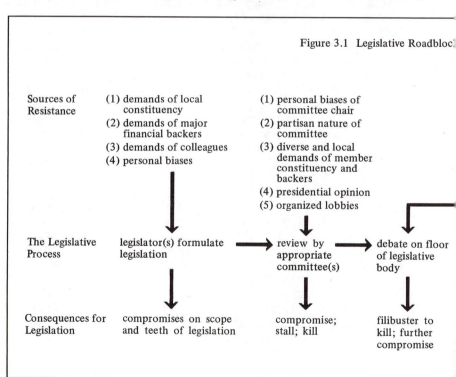

Figure 3.1 Legislative Roadblock

Sources of Resistance	(1) demands of local constituency (2) demands of major financial backers (3) demands of colleagues (4) personal biases	(1) personal biases of committee chair (2) partisan nature of committee (3) diverse and local demands of member constituency and backers (4) presidential opinion (5) organized lobbies	
The Legislative Process	legislator(s) formulate legislation	review by appropriate committee(s)	debate on floor of legislative body
Consequences for Legislation	compromises on scope and teeth of legislation	compromise; stall; kill	filibuster to kill; further compromise

multitude of local and national interest, groupings that have helped finance campaigns. Legislation that proposes change on a national level will usually go against a coalition of some of these interest groups which, because of their contributions, have influence with the senators and representatives.

INTEREST GROUPS AND LOBBYING. In any large and complex society there will be many diverse groups pursuing different goals. Many of these groups are highly organized to exert political influence and, hence, can be labeled *interests*. These interests often maintain elaborate offices in Washington, staffed with paid professionals. Frequently, former employees of legislators are kept on a staff to provide a particular interest with the necessary informal contacts to exert influence.

Traditionally, the most intense lobbying activities have come from organizations in the private sector. However, over the last 20 years, executive departments, most notably the Pentagon, have become conspicuous lobbies on Capitol Hill. For example, the yearly lobbying expenditures of the Pentagon in Washington alone probably approach many millions of tax dollars. The fact that executive

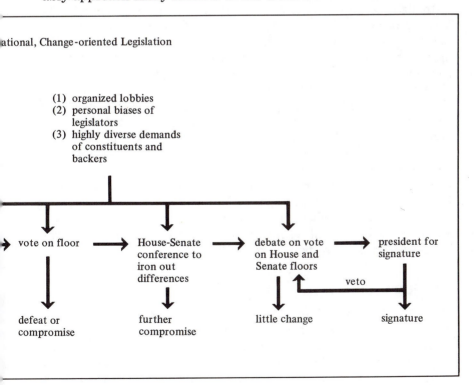

branches of government have become some of the most well-financed lobbies, exerting the most influence, is perhaps another indicator of the centralization of power into the executive branch. Yet, departments such as the Housing and Urban Development, Health, Education, and Welfare, and Interior are among the *least* well-financed of the executive lobbies, with the result that lobbying activities that advocate domestic priorities are less effective than those stressing military-related goals.

In the abstract the principle of effective lobbying sounds democratic because it enables diverse segments of society to have the ears of legislators. However, access to legislators can at times depend on wealth and degree of organization. This indicates that well-financed and well-organized groups are likely to have more influence on the legislative processes than the poorly organized public. As long as this situation persists, national planning will be more difficult, since change-oriented, national legislation will often run up against the resistance of some de facto coalition of interests that may have little in common except their opposition, perhaps even for different reasons, to a comprehensive piece of legislation.

In light of this situation, the only recourse for the public has been to become organized. For the poor, the black, the victims of industrial pollution, and even for middle America, organization may increasingly become a last recourse, and the beginnings of a movement toward such organization are currently evident. For example, the National Welfare Rights Organization, the Consumer's Union, Common Cause, and the Sierra Club all reflect a newfound awareness of the only alternative available to a public that is becoming increasingly aware of, and dissatisfied with, the disproportionate influence of interests. Just how effective these new public lobbies can be in the face of the well-entrenched Pentagon, Department of Agriculture, big business and industry, and affluent labor is unknown at present. But until these newly emerging people's lobbies display more organization, broad-based support, and increased financial resources, national planning and reordering of priorities will be, at best, very gradual.

THE JUDICIARY

Probably one of the most effective forces for social change in America is the federal court system, culminating in the Supreme Court. The list of reforms by the Court—from school desegregation and protection of civil liberties in criminal cases to draft reform and reapportionment—is impressive, coming close to equaling those of either Congress or the presidency. In passing on the constitutionality of various laws and practices, the Supreme Court has been able to legislate new, reform-oriented laws. Contrary to the Court's detractors, this legislative function of the Court is not an abuse of its power, but rather, an obligation imposed by the Constitution.

For disfranchised, poorly financed and organized segments of the population, the sympathy of the Supreme Court has represented one of the few legitimate channels for addressing grievances. With comparatively few resources and only a small organization, groups can initiate test cases to challenge unfair laws and practices. In many ways, the court system has represented a counterforce for the public and small interests against the well-financed and organized interests exerting disproportionate influence on Congress. Further, the Court has forced consideration of issues such as civil rights, which Congress might prove incapable of resolving in a clear and forthright manner.

Naturally, there are limitations on the Supreme Court's capacity to initiate change and reform in American society. First, the Court rules on the constitutionality of practices, but it cannot administer in detail the required action. The courts are not regulatory agencies, and in fact, they must often await a law suit to determine if rulings are being carried out properly. Thus, the courts can set general policies, but they cannot dictate just how these policies are to be implemented. The result of this fact has, at times, been inefficient, reluctant, and even subversive administration of court rulings. Probably the best example of the problems of governmental administration of unpopular court decisions is in the area of school integration. Some 20 years after *Brown* v. *Board of Education* integration is still resisted, often with considerable violence by the public. And as long as public resistance is high, representative bodies at all levels of government will be reluctant to enact clear administrative guidelines and to enforce those established by lower federal courts.

Secondly, the Court rules on *specific* issues brought before it; it cannot always establish comprehensive policies that take related issues into consideration. Such comprehensive policies should ideally come with legislative action by Congress, but as emphasized previously, the structure of government presents a number of roadblocks for change-oriented, national, and comprehensive legislation that might reorder national priorities.

And third, the composition of the Supreme Court determines, to a great extent, just how change-oriented decisions will be. The Supreme Court is inevitably a political body that can evidence a liberal, moderate, or conservative profile. Over the last 20 years the Court has evidenced a liberal profile, but in recent years, its composition appears to have shifted toward a more moderate profile. While specific decisions can still be labelled "liberal" or "conservative," the cumulative impact of many decisions appears to have shifted judicial policies toward a more moderate and less change-oriented profile.

These limitations suggest that the court system is inherently less capable of generating national planning or reordering national priorities than either the executive or legislative branches of government. It is only in the face of the growing power of the Pentagon and the president—coupled with the structural impediments to congressional consensus and concerted action—that a reliance on the courts seemed necessary to change national policies. But the appropriate limitations on the power of the courts simply dramatize the current problems of structure in American government. Many social problems—urban decay, transportation, pollution, discrimination, poverty, inequity, and inequality—will remain prominent in American society because of the dilemmas of decision-making in government.

Chapter 4

PROBLEMS OF LAW: CRIME AND CRIMINAL JUSTICE

From one perspective law is merely a part of the political system in a society. For indeed, the laws themselves are enacted by political bodies, such as city councils, state legislatures, and the Congress. And the key legal decision makers—judges, district attorneys, police chiefs, and the like—are either elected through the political process or appointed by political leaders. But in another sense, law is a separate institution. Once enacted, laws have an autonomy to control and regulate societal processes, including political actions. And once appointed or elected, incumbents in the legal structures of American society are supposed to remain *a*political, although such is not always the case. Perhaps most important, the political and legal systems have different consequences for the society: Government sets goals and allocates resources for their attainment; law maintains order, control, and some degree of integration in a society.

Thus, while many consider law to be simply a part of the government, it can be visualized as a separate institution with its own unique structure and implications for society. In this chapter attention will be drawn to the criminal justice system since it is in the areas of crime, criminals, and the administration of justice that the most acute problems of structure reside.

CRIME IN AMERICA: AN OVERVIEW

THE REALITY OF CRIME

Crime is an act that violates criminal laws.[1] Since most people violate the law, everyone has probably been a criminal at one time

[1] Admittedly, this definition ignores much of the debate over definitions of crime from the legalistic one offered here to broader conceptualizations. However, present purposes do not require that the text become involved in this debate, and therefore, the simplest of definitions is offered here.

or another. For example, a survey of 1700 persons in the New York area revealed that, in response to a list of 49 criminal offenses, over 90 percent of the anonymous respondents admitted they had committed one or more offenses for which they could have received a jail or prison sentence.[2] The majority of these "criminals" were never detected in their crime, nor were many of their crimes reflected in official statistics. These findings reveal that criminal behavior and its consequences for society cannot be understood without focusing attention on the nature of laws that would formally define 90 percent of the population criminal, and on the structure of enforcement and administration of those laws that make only a few people actual criminals.

THE CRIME STATISTICS

The 1967 President's Commission on Law Enforcement (hereafter referred to as the President's Commission) noted that "there has always been too much crime. Virtually every generation since the founding of the Nation has felt itself threatened by the spectre of rising crime and violence." Indeed, current *official* statistics document a rapidly rising crime rate. The most comprehensive statistical summary of crime in America comes from the yearly publication of the *Uniform Crime Reports* (UCR) by the FBI. Using three types of property crimes (burglary, larceny over $50, and motor vehicle theft) and four types of crimes against persons (willful homicide, forcible rape, aggravated assault, and robbery), an index is constructed to reveal the amount of and trends in serious crimes. The data for this index represent "crimes known to the police" and are gathered from local and state police officials throughout the country. Although it is usually cautious about claiming this index reveals *all* crime, the yearly report, as interpreted by the media and the public, is at times accepted uncritically and without necessary qualifications as a rough revelation of crime in America. The report portrays the following picture of crime over the last 20 years:

1. Each year the number of crimes against persons, especially aggravated assault, robbery, and forcible rape, show a sharp increase. Willful homicide appears to remain fairly constant, showing only small increases in recent years.
2. The number of crimes against property show an even more dramatic increase each year.

[2] This study is summarized in the President's Commission on Law Enforcement and Administration of Justice, *The Challenge of Crime in a Free Society*, 1967. (Hereafter referred to as the President's Commission.)

3. While the volume of crime is greatest in large cities, property and personal crimes are up everywhere, in the biggest and smallest cities, in the suburbs, and in rural areas.
4. Even when increases in the size of the population are taken into account (i.e., there are more people than ever), the *rate* of crime per 100,000 people shows a large increase.

What do these figures actually reveal about crime in America? Unfortunately it is difficult to know exactly what they tell because a number of problems are involved in their collection.

First, the study cited earlier reveals quite clearly that most crimes are not reported, indicating that crime is considerably more widespread than revealed by official crime statistics. A number of data sources underscore this fact. For example, the National Opinion Research Center (NORC) of the University of Chicago surveyed 10,000 households and asked if the person questioned had been a victim of a crime and, if so, if the crime had been reported to the police. Upon comparison, it became apparent that the survey crime rates, except for willful homicide and motor vehicle theft, were higher than the UCR crime rates. Overall, the amount of personal-injury crime was nearly twice as high by the NORC survey as that reported by the UCR index, while property crimes were well over twice as high by NORC as by UCR tabulations (Biderman, 1967). More detailed surveys by the Bureau of Social Science Research in high- and medium-crime rate areas in Washington, D.C., Chicago, and Boston portray a similar pattern (President's Commission, *The Challenge of Crime*, 1967:20–23). A more recent study by the Law Enforcement Assistance Administration in 1973 reveals that from a survey of a sample of 125,000 citizens and 15,000 businesses, several conclusions can be reached about crime in the general population: Of the 16.6 million major crimes in the first six months of 1973, only about 5.3 million persons reported them to the police. Moreover, only 3.9 million of this total were relayed to the FBI from local police departments. Thus, it is clear that official crime statistics underreport the amount of crime in America.

A second problem with the official FBI crime statistics is that they do not incorporate crimes committed by organized syndicates (gambling, narcotics, prostitution), police crime, or professional and *white-collar crime* (income tax evasion, antitrust violations, restraint of trade, and misrepresentation in advertising). Just how extensive such forms of crime are cannot be known precisely, but they are certainly more widespread than the "conventional" crimes reported in the UCR index. These forms of crime are committed by the wealthy and by the highly organized and would raise the UCR index by several fold is incorporated into official statistics.

This underreporting of crime in official statistics poses a number of interpretive problems. With such a vast pool of unreported crime, any change in police reporting practices or any improvement in policing techniques will cause a sharp increase in the amount of crime reported or known to the police. Although it is impossible to determine for sure, it is likely that at least some of the dramatic increase in crime over the last decades reflect not so much actual increases, but rather changes in police practices that have led the police to dip into the heretofore unreported pool of crime. For example, the President's Commission undertook an extensive examination of police reporting practices and found that, from 1959 to 1965, a change in the criminal reporting procedures by police was followed by jumps in the crime rate. These represent "paper" increases that are impossible to distinguish from real increases in crime. Another factor causing a seeming acceleration in crime rate is police professionalism, which, as is discussed later, has resulted

SOCIOLOGICAL INSIGHTS

CRIME STATISTICS AND PUBLIC REACTION

Is real crime increasing in America? Or are rising rates a statistical artifact? The statistics are such that it is impossible to know, but it is likely that, while crime has probably increased, some of the increase as reflected in the *Uniform Crime Reports* index is a "paper" increase. This fact indicates that some anti-crime legislation and public concern is in response to a crime wave that may not exist except in official statistics and in people's minds. Ironically, legislative and public concern over crime can have the consequence of statistically raising crime rates, since political and public pressure usually results in greater police efficiency in the name of "law and order," which in turn forces police to dip deeper into previously unreported crimes and thereby raise the crime rate. Such an increase in the crime rate (not necessarily crime) generates more public and political concern, and hence, even more pressure for "law and order." Thus, to some unknown extent, public reaction and concern about rising crime may be a self-fulfilling prophecy: the more pressure for law and order, the more diligent the police, and the more they dig into previously unreported crimes—thereby increasing the rate that generated public reaction in the first place.

in greater police efficiency through the use of new technologies and patroling practices. Furthermore, the increasing use of computers, clerical personnel, and statisticians has resulted in more accurate and complete police records, which, when reported to the FBI, raise the national crime rate.

RISING CRIME: ITS INEVITABILITY IN AMERICA

What causes increased crime? This question is impossible to answer because many of the answers lay buried in the psychological processes of individuals. Moreover, as the above discussion illustrates, it is very difficult to compute accurate statistics, thereby making imputed increases in the crime rate, and inferences about a rise in criminally disposed individuals, ambiguous. Furthermore, Americans should expect increased crime for several reasons: (1) There are more laws to break than previously, (2) the demographic trend toward a younger and urban population assures increased crime, and (3) Americans own more material goods than ever and, thus, there is more to steal.

1. LAW-MAKING AND CRIME. If crime is defined as a violation of criminal laws, then it can be expected that the greater the number of laws, the more crime. Over the last 50 years the United States has undergone profound changes associated with industrialization and urbanization. Accompanying these changes, new laws have proliferated at an incredibly rapid rate so that today there are more ways to violate the law than there were 70 years ago (Allen, 1964). Crimes such as disturbing the peace, traffic law violation, automobile theft, cheating on tax assessments, income tax evasion, violation of interstate commerce regulations, and the carrying of a gun without a permit result from law enactment in this century. Thus, an increase in crime is an inevitable by-product of a modernizing society and its ever-expanding body of law. Ironically, as the public and legislators become concerned over rising crime, they may hastily enact new laws to deal with crime and, by this very process, force crime rates to rise—perhaps setting off a new cycle of public concern, legislative law enactment, and increased crime rates. Just to what extent current increases in crime *rates* are the product of such a process is impossible to assess. Probably only a small impact on crime rates, in the short run, is registered by an expanded body of criminal law but, over several decades, the influence on crime rates may be more profound.

2. DEMOGRAPHIC FACTORS AND CRIME. Without delving into the "criminal personality" and without assuming a shift toward a more

crime-oriented "cultural ethos," increases in crime can be seen as inevitable in light of basic demographic trends in the United States (President's Commission, 1967). One of these trends is the urbanization of the population. Crime has always been more predominant in urban than rural areas; thus, as the American population has become urbanized, crime has increased. Furthermore, the racial and ethnic pattern of urbanization has forced minority groups into the decaying and impoverished city cores; it seems inevitable that the crime rate of these slum dwellers, who must remain deprived in the midst of affluence, would be higher than that of their rural ancestors, who did not have to endure such relative deprivation.

Another major demographic trend has revolved around changes in the age composition of the population. Because of the post-World War II baby boom, the younger age groups have increased dramatically as a proportion of the population. Since it is in this age group that crime rates have always been highest, it can be expected that as it increases in size, the national crime rate will rise. For example, using UCR index crimes, over 40 percent of those arrested for forcible rape and robbery and nearly 30 percent of those arrested for willful homicides and aggravated assault are in the 18- to 29-year-old group. For property crimes such as burglary, larceny, and auto theft, over 50 percent of all arrests are among those under 18 years old. While high arrest statistics for the young may be the result of their criminal inexperience and inability to avoid the police, it is more likely that they just commit more crimes than other age groups, especially those crimes on the UCR index. It is impossible to judge whether crime within younger age groups is rising, but as the young increase as a proportion of the population the national crime rate will no doubt increase. Even without a rise in criminality among youths, the fact that a million additional youths are added to the late-teens and early-20s age groups each year makes increases of crime inevitable.

3. AMERICAN AFFLUENCE AND CRIME. Crimes against property have shown the most dramatic increase (by official statistics). More property is being stolen today than ever before. However, this does not necessarily mean that a larger proportion of the population is prone to theft, robbery, or larceny; rather, these data could reveal that there is more to steal in an affluent society and that property is less well protected than formerly (President's Commission, 1967). For example, car theft has become widespread because there are more cars to steal; and since they are insured, owners tend to be more careless. To take another example, the rise in thefts of over $50 may reflect the impact of inflation as

much as an increase in serious crime. Thirty years ago $50 represented much more than it does today, with the result that stealing $50 today is really petty larceny, except for the fact that it is recorded as a serious crime and included in the UCR index. If $100 were used as the dividing line between petty and grand larceny, the grand larceny rate would drop and the petty larceny rate would represent about what a dividing line of $50 did in 1940.

Aside from generating more to steal and inflating the value of what is stolen, affluence creates frustrations among those who do not participate in that affluence. As long as the whole society was relatively poor, the poor could be content, knowing that most people were not much better off. But with the growth of affluence, those without much property have an escalated sense of deprivation. Looting during the ethnic and racial riots of the 1960s is perhaps the most dramatic example of how such deprivation causes crime, but the less visible day-to-day thefts and robberies among the poor also reflect the desire to share in American affluence.

After all these qualifications are tacked onto official crime statistics, the question still remains: Is crime increasing dramatically? Some of the increase in crime rates is probably a statistical artifact, while another portion of the increase appears inevitable as more criminal laws are enacted, as the population becomes urbanized and younger, and as affluence increases the deprivations of the poor while providing more property to steal. Above and beyond these forces, it is impossible to know if individual Americans are more criminally inclined than 10, 20, or 50 years ago. There is simply no way to know.

THE COSTS OF CRIME

Curiously, the public appears most concerned about one of the *least* costly forms of crime, in terms of dollars lost to individuals and society: crime in the streets—assault and robbery. If crime is a social problem because it costs a lot of money and disrupts society, crime in the streets is of less significance when compared to drunken drivers, organized syndicates, fraud, embezzlement, unreported commercial thefts by employees, and willful homicides (70 percent of whose victims are known to their killers).

Crime is expensive in two senses: (1) It involves the loss of property and money, as well as income through death of or injury to the victim. (2) It costs the government tax revenues since lost money and income cannot be taxed. More significantly, organized crime dealing in illicit cash flows, narcotics, loan sharking, gambling, and prostitution deprives the government of enormous tax revenues that could be used to help resolve other social problems. From only a cost perspective, the crimes that occupy the public's attention—assault and robbery—are less problematic. In fact, UCR index crimes are not nearly as significant as many crimes not included in this index. To quote from the President's Commission (1967:32):

1. Organized crime takes about twice as much from gambling and other illegal goods and services as criminals derive *from all other sources of criminal activity combined.*
2. Unreported commercial theft losses, including shoplifting and employee theft, are more than double those of all reported and commercial thefts.
3. Of reported crimes, willful homicide, though comparatively low in volume, yields the most costly estimates (income loss from death) among those listed on the UCR crime index.
4. A list of the seven crimes with the greatest economic impact includes only two, willful homicide and larceny of $50 and over (reported and unreported), of the offenses included in the crime index.

Organized crime syndicates derive enormous profits from gambling activities, narcotics rackets, high-interest cash loans, prostitution, and alcohol. Operating much like business corporations, criminal syndicates have been able to avoid prosecution.[3] One of the principal reasons for the success of organized syndicates is that they provide services demanded by the public—gambling, drugs, quick cash loans, and prostitution. Furthermore, since the clients of crime syndicates commit criminal acts simply by being clients, they are not likely to register complaints, as would victims of more conventional crimes. Thus, the real "victim" of organized crime is not the user of illicit services, but the federal government, which is deprived of tax revenues. Recently, crime syndicates have taken their untaxed profits and moved into many legitimate enterprises, including bars, taverns, securities, restaurants, and vending machines. These businesses tend to be heavy cash-flow enterprises in which "skimming off" tax-free cash for sheer profit or investment in other legitimate and illegitimate enterprises is relatively easy. Aside from depriving the federal government of needed tax revenues, such infiltration can undermine basic economic traditions

[3] For a detailed analysis of organized crime, see: Cressey, 1969; *Report of the Special Committee to Investigate Organized Crime in Interstate Commerce;* and the President's Commission, *Task Force Report: Organized Crime,* 1967. Also, see Chapter 10 for a more detailed discussion of organized crime in America.

and institutions by creating a thin line between what is legal and illegal in the society (Cressey, 1969).

Probably the second most costly form of crime is what has been labeled *occupational crime* (Quinney, 1964; Clinard and Quinney, 1967:130–132). A partial list of occupational crimes would include tax evasion, embezzlement, restraint of trade, employee theft, misrepresentation in advertising, black marketeering, misappropriation of public funds, fee splitting, price fixing, infringements on patents and copyrights, unfair labor practices, falsification of records, padding of expense accounts, and corruption in the handling of trusts, receiverships and bankruptcies. Originally such crimes were labeled white-collar crimes because of the high proportion of middle-class professionals and corporate executives involved (Sutherland, 1940; 1967). However, somewhat later it was recognized that "farmers, repairmen, and others in essentially non-white-collar occupations could, through such illegalities as watering milk for public consumption, making unnecessary 'repairs' on television sets, and so forth, be classified as white-collar violators" (Newman, 1958:737).

Occupational crimes can be separated into three categories: (1) those involving individual against individual, such as lawyer fraud and doctors' fee splitting; (2) those involving employees against corporations, such as embezzlers; and (3) those involving the decisions of top management of major corporations, such as is the case with price-fixing, willful pollution, and misrepresentation in advertising (Clinard and Quinney, 1967:132). All of these forms of occupational crime are costly to individuals, the public, and government. Losses each year in the form of unreported commercial losses (e.g., employee theft) alone cost considerably more each year than the combined losses due to willful homicide, assault, arson, and looting. Such losses raise consumer prices, limit the availability of capital funds for the economy, and deprive government of tax revenue. To illustrate further, the costs of false advertising and misrepresentation are enormously high in that people end up buying what are sometimes unnecessary goods whose prices are inflated due to advertising costs—costs which in turn are deductible under tax laws and therefore deprive the government of further revenue. Or, the willful violation of antipollution laws by corporations is horribly expensive in terms of health costs and expenses for resource restoration. Thus, occupational crime is costly because its deprives the government of revenue, raises prices for the consumer, deletes the amount of capital available to the economy, and is often injurious to people's health.

It is somewhat surprising that occupational criminals usually escape punishment, and when they are caught, penalties are comparatively light. There are several reasons for these differences between treatment of conventional and occupational criminals. First, occupational criminals are often of high prestige (doctors, lawyers, businessmen) and powerful (e.g., corporation presidents), with the result that police authorities are reluctant to pursue violations, especially when they must fight well-paid lawyers in expensive court trials. Second, occupational crimes are hidden in that the victim is the public, or an entire corporation, who remains ignorant of the crime or too apathetic to do much about it. Third, violations by occupational criminals, especially corporation executives, are usually handled as infractions of civil and administrative rather than criminal laws. For example, in a classic study, Sutherland (1967:22–26) found that 70 large corporations in nearly 980 violations of the law—restraint of trade, misrepresentation, unfair labor practices, and so forth—were forced to undergo criminal proceedings in only 16 percent of the cases; the remaining 84 percent were handled by civil courts and administrative agencies. Similarly, violations of pollution control regulations by large corporations are rarely prosecuted criminally, although their acts can at times threaten people's lives and are often enormously costly to the public.

The public concern for crime is thus curiously selective because it concentrates on visible crimes committed more frequently by lower-class individuals. These differences in concern stem from the comparative invisibility of occupational and organized crime (and hence public ignorance about it) and from the power of these criminals to influence law enactment and enforcement, as well as judicial processes. While data are scarce on the subject, the greatest increase in crime in America is probably among organized and occupational crime rather than conventional crime.[4] Currently the public has yet to define these hidden crimes as a serious social problem. Although concern over organized crime is growing, it has yet to reach the magnitude of the virtual panic exhibited by the general public over crime in the streets.

THE CRIMINAL LAW: THE PROBLEM OF OVERCRIMINALIZATION

What is and what is not crime is ultimately a matter of legal definition. It is thus impossible to separate crime from the legal statutes defining behavior as criminal. This conclusion may at first appear banal but, in reality, the nature of criminal laws pro-

---

[4] Naturally, this statement in no way mitigates the problematic nature of conventional crimes. Being raped, mugged, and robbed is still not much fun.

foundly affects the amount of crime in American society and the way in which it is dealt with by the police and courts.

CRIMES WITHOUT VICTIMS

Criminal law is supposed to prohibit harms against private property, other persons, and the state. However, in the American legal system a large body of criminal laws has accumulated prohibiting acts that do not directly harm other people, the state, or property. For example, many laws prohibit certain kinds of sexual acts, ranging from "abnormal" sexual intercourse to public solicitation by prostitutes and homosexuals. Another large body of criminal law deals with gambling and the use of narcotics. These crimes do not have victims in the conventional sense, and the existence of these laws is the result of pressure by various segments of the population.[5]

In a free society, with its enormous diversity in tastes and lifestyles, there is always a conflict among the values of different segments of the society. For even in the face of legal codes reflecting the "morality" of only some, people still gamble, use drugs, and enjoy all forms of sex. Most persons run little risk of police sanctions because many no-victim laws—especially with respect to sexual acts—are not enforced. As Thurman Arnold caustically observed, they "are unenforced because we want to continue our conduct, and unrepealed because we want to preserve our morals" (Kadish, 1967:161–162). However, many others of these laws are enforced, even though no harm to property, other persons, or the state has occurred. The persistence of such laws has created a number of serious problems.[6]

1. Laws denoting crimes without victims, such as those concerning certain forms of sex, drug use, public drunkenness, gambling, and vagrancy are so encompassing and broad that they make potential criminals of everyone. In effect, they hold criminal sanctions over people's head for behaviors that do no harm except to the precepts of some segments of the population. In doing so, such

---

[5] Obviously some criminal acts, such as heavy narcotics use, can indirectly have victims; those users with expensive habits must commit conventional crimes, usually robbery, to secure the funds necessary to support their habit. However, were drug use not illegal, drugs would not be so expensive and users would not have to rob to secure necessary funds. It is likely that those who insist that drug use be a crime are also appalled at the result of their moral crusading: increases in other crimes by those with expensive habits. Unfortunately, they rarely see the connection and the solution it suggests: legalize drugs use and make drugs cheap, while providing the facilities to help people get off the habit.

[6] See Kadish, 1967; President's Commission, *Task Force Report: The Courts,* 1967:97–107; Quinney, 1970:86–97; La Fave, 1964:63–84.

laws potentially limit people's right to self-determination and self-expression.

2. Since many people in modern societies appear to enjoy getting drunk, using drugs, having sex, seeking out prostitutes, and gambling, these laws go against widespread behavior patterns. It is always dangerous to have vast bodies of laws on the books that people insist on violating. It is possible that as people violate the law, they lose respect for not only its codes and statutes, but also for those who enforce it.

3. Prohibitions against prostitution, drugs, and gambling have created a vast illegal marketplace for organized crime. Since people demand these services, they tend to be provided by illegal syndicates that derive enormous untaxed profits. In turn, these profits are used to subsidize harmful crimes, such as loan sharking, extortion, and bribery. Additionally, these profits are used to infiltrate and invest in legitimate businesses and enterprises, making the distinction between law and lawlessness difficult to maintain. From one perspective, no-victim crimes *create* organized crime. It is no coincidence that organized crime in America emerged during Prohibition, when such a large market for liquor existed that criminals needed to become organized in order to deliver the goods demanded by the public and avoid prosecution by the police. A similar situation currently exists with respect to drugs and gambling; as long as legal prohibitions against these widespread acts remain, organized crime will persist.

4. Perhaps one of the most serious problems created by no-victim laws is the waste of manpower and other resources involved in enforcing and adjudicating them. In any large urban area, public drunkenness and disorderly conduct constitute close to one-half of all arrests and thereby clog up the courts (President's Commission, *The Courts*, 1967:20). Detective man-hours spent on drug use come close to one-third of the total in large urban areas; court costs for just marijuana offenses run into the millions of dollars each year—nearly $80 million in California alone in 1970 (Skolnick and Currie, 1970). This diversion of police man-hours and resources, to say nothing of court time, deters the police from catching, and the courts from adjudicating, criminals who commit crimes with victims. It has been estimated that well over 50 percent of total police work and court time is spent on catching and prosecuting people who have not hurt anyone else, taken property, or damaged the state.

5. The persistence of a large body of laws pertaining to crimes without victims creates a situation in which not all of the laws can be enforced; there are simply too many of them and they already

consume most police resources. When not all laws can be enforced, *police discretion* in law enforcement is inevitable. The existence of unenforceable and outdated laws can, at times, grant the police license to selectively enforce the law—a situation that goes against all basic American tenets concerning due process of law. The greatest danger of granting discretion to the police in one area, such as crimes without victims, is that discretion and selective enforcement may be extended into all areas of criminal law. Furthermore, to encourage discretion in police enforcement sets a dangerous precedent in that it gives the police the power to remain autonomous from, and at times even in violation of, their legislative mandate. When the police increase their autonomy from the law and those bodies that enact the law, a society can become subject to the will of agencies and their administrators rather than the rule of law. Finally, outdated and unenforced laws can, on occasion, allow the police to use such laws to prosecute persons on grounds unrelated to the crime against which the laws were purportedly addressed. For example, vagrancy laws have traditionally been used to arrest "suspects" from lower economic groups who cannot be arrested or detained on other criminal charges. Thus, no-victim laws not only give the police the power to selectively enforce the law, but they also enable the police to change the intent of law and use it for their purposes rather than those dictated by the law.

CRIMINAL LAW AS A SOCIAL AND CIVIL SERVICE

Another form of overcriminalization through law is the extension of criminal sanctions into areas that might be more efficiently handled by social service agencies (Kadish, 1967). For example, laws against public drunkenness cause a staggering number of drunks to be fed daily into the enforcement and judicial machinery. In fact, more arrests are made for public drunkenness than any other offense. While a drunk behind the wheel of a car does pose a harm, the use of police sanctions against alcoholics, skid-row residents, and other persons with drinking problems is probably a less than efficient use of limited police resources since to attempt to solve problems of poverty and personal failure with criminal rather than social and psychiatric procedures is not possible. In reality, the existence of such public drinking laws forces the police to provide a social service for the community; and when police are called upon to provide social services as well as law enforcement, neither duty is performed well (Allen, 1964; President's Commission, *The Courts*, 1967:106).

In addition to using the law to provide social services, criminal law is often extended into areas more properly handled by civil codes and statutes. For example, criminal laws and enforcement agencies are often used to secure payments for debts. Frequently, bad checks do not involve either fraud or criminal intent on the part of the debtor, yet in many states criminal laws and the threat of sanctions are used to resolve what are really civil matters. The existence of such criminal laws forces the police to investigate and then to threaten debtors with criminal sanctions, hence tying up manpower and resources. In such cases, the law and police are being used as a collection agency—a function unrelated to serious crime.

Sometimes criminal law is used simultaneously to settle a civil matter and provide a social service. For example, laws, police, and the courts are frequently invoked in family nonsupport cases to force the father to pay for the support of his wife and family (President's Commission, *The Courts*, 1967:101). In these instances, criminal law is being used as a legal aid society for indigent families—a function performed much better by social agencies in a civil court.

In sum, the extension of criminal law into the area of crimes without victims and into the social service and civil sphere has created a "problem of overcriminalization" (Kadish, 1967). Overcriminalization has, in turn, generated many problems for the police and courts in America.

THE POLICE: DILEMMAS OF LAW ENFORCEMENT[7]

In principle, laws define crimes. The police are to enforce *all* laws and thereby deter crime. During enforcement, the police are supposedly guided by the rule of law (procedural law) that guarantees the civil liberties of suspects and makes the police accountable for their actions. Ideally, just as substantive codes and statutes define criminal behavior for the public, procedural laws define what is criminal for the police. While this principle is simply stated in the abstract, it can at time be violated in practice. The potential dangers of this situation in a free society—police abuse of citizens' rights, police discrimination, police brutality with impunity, police as makers of law through selective enforcement, and police as a political force with sufficient power to overrule the law—need not be dwelled upon.

The discrepancy between the operation of police in theory and

[7] For basic references on the police in America, see: Bordua, 1967; Skolnick, 1966; Niederhoffer, 1968; Wilson, 1968; Banton, 1964; Smith, 1960; Chevigny, 1969; President's Commission, *Task Force Report: The Police*, 1967.

in practice is perhaps inevitable in light of current conditions. First, the broad scope of criminal law makes the enforcement of all the laws impossible, but does not reveal to the police which ones to enforce (La Fave, 1964). Lacking a clear mandate from legislatures, the police must use their own discretion in deciding what is and what is not the law. Second, even though Americans value law and order, resources made available to the police are typically inadequate. Without resources, and burdened with a vast amount of no-victim and unenforceable laws, the police have inevitably begun to establish their own policies and priorities of law enforcement. As they do so, they can begin to divorce themselves from their legislative mandate, public scrutiny, and the constraints of procedural law.

While these two conditions help account for police deviations from procedural law, several additional forces also contribute to this situation: (1) police and community relations, (2) the internal structure of the police, (3) police ideology, (4) police professionalism, and (5) police political power.

POLICE AND COMMUNITY RELATIONS

According to most opinion polls, the American public holds the police in low esteem (Savitz, 1967). Yet, great expectations and demands are placed upon the police within any community. One of these expectations forces the police to engage in a wide range of peace-keeping activities, some of which have little to do with law enforcement. For example, one study found that nearly one-half the requests for assistance received in a police station were for help in health care (such as providing an ambulance service), in handling problems with children and incapacitated persons (a welfare service), and in supervising recreational activities. While such tasks need to be performed, they can divert police attention away from the enforcement of serious crimes and make the policeman, as the authors of this study proclaimed, "philosopher, guide, and friend" (Cumming et al., 1965). One danger in forcing the police to become involved in peace-keeping instead of law enforcement is that these duties extend beyond the bounds of substantive and procedural criminal law (Wilson, J., 1968:16–56). As police assume the ambiguous role of peace-keeper, they are granted enormous discretion in defining what is necessary to preserve the peace (not to uphold the law). Some suspects, usually from the lower classes, can be arrested to preserve the peace; others, usually middle class, can be let free; and still others can be illegally detained (Esselystn, 1953; Bittner, 1967). Thus, besides diverting resources away from law enforcement, the peace-keeping role can

SOCIOLOGICAL INSIGHTS

YOUTH AND THE POLICE

A number of studies have sought to determine what characteristics of suspects and situations affect the way police will act in the field. Below is a partial catalogue of relevant findings for police and youth encounters (Schrag and Kuehn, 1976):

1. Deference to police by juveniles is as likely to lead to arrest as an antagonistic attitude, with a civil attitude least likely to result in arrest.
2. Race and ethnicity influenced arrests of juveniles with, for example, black arrest rates nearly twice as high as for whites.
3. Children from broken homes are more likely to be arrested than those from intact homes committing the same offense.
4. The more a community defines as severe a crime—and this varies enormously from community to community—the greater the chance of arrest of a juvenile.
5. Females are less likely to be arrested for some crimes than males.
6. Court referrals of juveniles vary by community, with upper-, lower-, and middle-class communities having much different referral patterns.

easily be used to justify discriminatory and selective law enforcement—which violates the basic tenets of the rule of law.[8]

The police in any community are also subject to pressures from the public and local political leaders who demand that the "streets be kept clear of crime." In any community the police are highly responsive to this form of pressure, with the result that they can at times violate procedural law and arrest, under various cover charges, deviant and outcast groups such as homosexuals, prostitutes, drug users, and skid-row drunks, in order to show their efficiency and capacity to keep the streets clear—even though to do so diverts resources away from action on serious crimes. This need for the police within any community to constantly demonstrate efficiency is one of the most persistent conditions promoting

[8] One solution to this problem might be to have a large social service staff attached to the police force. This *unarmed* force could perform most of the social services, from ambulance driver to traffic cop, required by a community. In this way peace-keeping, public service, and law enforcement roles would not be confused.

procedural shortcuts in the name of maintaining an arrest record that will satisfy the public and various pressure groups in a community.

INTERNAL STRUCTURE OF THE POLICE

Partly in response to pressures to demonstrate efficiency and partly as a result of the volume of activity, the bureaucratization of police forces is inevitable. Police bureaucracies are basically command hierarchies arranged into major units such as traffic patrols, street patrols, investigative units, undercover units, and quasi-military units for riot control (Quinney, 1970:101–136). Extensive bureaucratization of the police has at least two consequences for the rule of law. First, bureaucracies tend to develop their own internal rules and procedures in order to generate greater efficiency. However, since these rules are established to increase efficiency, they can sometimes violate the principles of due process of law. In fact, as Skolnick (1969) has noted, the efficient administration of criminal law *will always be hampered* by the adoption of procedures designed to protect individual liberties. The second consequence is that bureaucratization also allows the police to "hide" their illegal acts. Bureaucracies are always difficult for outsiders, such as civilian review boards, to penetrate or investigate. In addition to the many formal rules of any bureaucracy, a large number of informal rules among law enforcement officials have emerged, emphasizing police secrecy and keeping matters "within the department." This bureaucratic autonomy from public scrutiny can allow the police to remain aloof, if they choose, from both the substance and procedure of criminal law.

POLICE IDEOLOGY

It has been known for some time that, in any large police department, there exists an ideology that, stated in somewhat extreme form, commands the police to (1) maintain secrecy about practices from the hostile public, (2) get respect from the public, even if it must be coerced, (3) by any means, legitimate or illegitimate, complete an important arrest (Westley, 1953; Quinney, 1969). Putting the tenets of police ideology this bluntly is perhaps an overstatement; and yet, behind much police activity—especially for the poor—these values are prominent. Some might view this ideology as an outgrowth of the authoritarian personality of each policeman. However, several studies reveal that the "raw recruit" to the police force is about the same in terms of beliefs and attitudes as his counterpart in the general population (McNamara, 1967; Niederhoffer, 1968). Furthermore, in their training at the police academy, a civil libertarian viewpoint stressing procedural law and the rights of the accused is a prominent part of the curriculum. These facts indicate that there is something about the bureaucratic structure of the police force and the nature of police work that soon sours young recruits into veterans who can, at times, harbor a somewhat antidemocratic ideology.

Three facets of police work appear to be responsible for the existence of such an ideology. First, the dangers of police work make the police suspicious of the public, especially in lower-class neighborhoods. Such suspicion isolates policemen from those they serve, while driving them together as a body of close-knit comrades engaged in mutual protection. Second, policemen will at times have to assert their authority to perform law enforcement duties against a hostile public that holds them in low esteem (Savitz, 1967). Maintaining this authority frequently becomes the policeman's on-the-beat credo, for, as recruits are told again and again by department veterans, "you gotta be tough." The combination of suspicion of the public and the desire to be tough can become volatile when applied to many segments of the population, such as low-income racial and ethnic minorities. Because these are prime areas of crime, police are already suspicious of these residents so when they attempt to assert their authority they are resisted, often violently, by minority group members who see this "get tough" approach as one more abuse not to be endured. The third facet of police work sustaining the police ideology is the internal bureaucratic structure of the force. The bureaucracy must continually demonstrate its efficiency in the eyes of the public and politicians. One indicator of efficiency is the number of criminal cases "cleared" by an arrest. Since the department as a whole, and each individual patrolman, is gauged by his arrest efficiency, policemen are often anxious to make arrests, even if it may mean violating some aspect of procedural law. Another police practice stemming from the need to have high arrest statistics is the arrest quota system, whereby police units are required to show a certain number of arrests. One way to fill quotas is to arrest suspects without much evidence, or to clear the streets by arresting vagrants, drunks, and prostitutes. Police vehemently deny the existence of such quotas, but there is too much evidence suggesting their use in some police departments to accept these denials without skepticism. Such concern for arrest is perhaps inevitable in light of the bureaucratic imperative to demonstrate efficiency. It is difficult to document statistically the efficiency of the police in preserving civil liberties and thus, by default, the yardstick of efficiency becomes the arrest record.[9]

POLICE PROFESSIONALISM

The drive toward police professionalism represents an attempt to overcome the widespread corruption and inefficiency that existed at one time in many police departments in America. Civil service examinations became a basis for promotion; education of the police in academies became required; and the use of new technologies, from computerized auditing to newer and better police cars, became emphasized (Skolnick, 1966:238–240). While these changes have certainly cut down on the amount of corruption among the police, they have caused police professionalism to be based on technological efficiency more than the preservation of procedural law and basic civil liberties. In some police departments professionalism has become defined as using technical gadgetry—telephone wiretaps, police helicopters, computerized files, unlawful buggings, and so on—in fighting crime (Quinney, 1970; Skolnick, 1966). Politicians at all levels of government have supported the direction of such police professionalism by allocating, with little hesitation, funds to buy technical equipment to be used for riot control and surveillance of citizen activities.

While new technologies can make the police more efficient and competent in fighting crime, a potential danger resides in this definition of police professionalism: Police use of technological devices in the name of law and order can create a climate in which technology, rather than procedural law, dictates the way law enforcement will occur. The use of newer, more technical equipment should be supplemented by a new professionalism based on the ideals of a democratic order (Skolnick, 1966:238–239).[10] Yet, under grants from the Law Enforcement Assistance Administration, most federal funds made available to police departments are for technical equipment rather than for research on how to train the police to

[9] One solution to this problem is to have differential weights attached to different kinds of arrests for both the individual policeman and the force as a whole. A cleared arrest for a homicide, for example, should be given greater weight—in terms of prestige, efficiency ratings, promotional considerations, and so on—than for a marijuana case. What is necessary is that the police stop being rewarded for enforcing the law with respect to the least harmful crimes. In fact, the budget of the police force might even be linked to an efficiency rating computed by a weighted system in which clearing the streets would have little reward value.

[10] Again, this is not to deny that technical gadgets are necessary enforcement tools in a modern society. What is dangerous is the trend toward visualizing these tools as the *single most important facet* of law enforcement.

adhere strictly to the rule of law, even in the face of the many dangers associated with their work.

POLICE POLITICAL POWER

The police are, to a very great extent, caught in the middle of public demands for law and order, political pressures, the perception of rising crime, and the Supreme Court decisions stressing civil liberties. Under these kinds of cross-pressures, the police have sometimes retreated behind the walls of their bureaucratic technocracy and are likely to perceive of themselves, in the words of Robert Kliesmet of the Milwaukee Professional Policeman's Protective Association, as "the new niggers of the world." Undeniably the police are subject to a wide variety of pressures; but it is often the police themselves who have exerted pressures on politicians and created the sense of crisis over rising crime. Even though the police can be a defensive organization, they are not passive and have become a powerful political lobby. While such lobbying activities are perhaps necessary for any organization charged with performing a difficult task on limited resources, the current direction of police pressure appears to be lobbying for even more discretionary power. Such lobbying is against the tenets of procedural law that emphasize the "rights of the accused" over and against the needs of the state for order.

THE COURTS: THE DILEMMAS OF ADMINISTERING JUSTICE

THE IDEAL OF JUSTICE

EQUALITY UNDER THE LAW. The image of justice weighing all people impartially on her scales is a dominant ideal in the American legal system. Citizens are to be subjected to an impartial application of substantive and procedural law by unbiased judges.

THE PRESUMPTION OF INNOCENCE. In American courts, suspects are presumed innocent until proven guilty. On the basis of this assumption, suspects are entitled to a speedy arraignment where charges are to be read, a reasonable bail set, and where protection from police harassment and punishment is to be assured.

THE RIGHT TO A JURY TRIAL. It is basic to the concept of American justice that the accused have a right to a trial overseen by their peers. Embodied in this concept is the adversary principle, whereby the accused have a right to a counsel who must be allowed to confront the state and cross-examine those who support the state's accusations. From this confrontation between the defendants and their accusers, the truth is persumed to emerge.

THE REALITY OF JUSTICE

Few will maintain that American courts do a good job in maintaining the ideals of justice. As will be documented, the courts often violate these ideals: Judges are, at times, biased; laws are unequally applied; procedural rules can give way to bureaucratic expediency; suspects are sometimes presumed guilty; arraignment can become slow; bail can be excessive; and few ever have a trial by their peers, much less a full day in court.

Just about everybody recognizes that courts need to be overhauled. Most Americans, however, would seemingly reform the courts in a direction that would move them away from the ideals of justice. For example, when asked in a Gallup poll "What ails American justice?" 78 percent of the sample asserted that "convicted criminals get off too easily" (*Newsweek*, 1971). While 68 percent recognized that "it takes too long before accused people are brought to trial," the public appears more concerned with *convicting criminals quickly* than with maintaining the ideal of justice. However, to the extent that the ideals of American justice are worth maintaining, the problem with the courts is not their conviction rate—which is really quite high—but in *how* they convict suspects. When the problem is phrased in this way, the question of how and where, in the criminal court process, the ideals of American justice can be suspended becomes prominent.

ARREST AND DETENTION. Within a "short time" after being arrested a suspect *must* be brought before a lower court, such as that presided over by a magistrate or justice of the peace, for a preliminary examination. If the offense is minor, the magistrate often has the power to determine the guilt or innocence of the suspect. However, if the case involves a felony, the function of the magistrate is quite different: to determine if sufficient evidence exists to hold the suspect over for trial, and if there is, to set the bail.

Even at this early stage, violations of the ideals of American justice occur. First of all, suspects are frequently detained for much longer than a "short time." One study in Chicago revealed that 50 percent of a sample of prisoners brought before a felony court were held without being booked (formally charged with a crime) for 17 hours. By the time the magistrate's hearing rolled around, some suspects had been detained in jail for more than several days without bail—a practice that amounts to illegal detention and goes against the ideal of "innocent until proven guilty" (Savitz, 1967:81).

The whole process of setting bail in the magistrate's court can be highly unjust (Goldfarb, 1965; Quinney, 1970; Skolnick, 1966). The Eighth Amendment of the Constitution provides that bail shall not be "excessive"; but what constitutes a "reasonable" bail is left to the discretion of poorly trained magistrates who sometimes set bail in accordance with their own personal, political, and moral biases. Furthermore, the practice of bail discriminates against the poor, who do not have either the collateral to put up their own bail or the money to pay the fee of a bail bondsman. If persons cannot meet the bail set by the magistrate, they must remain in jail until their trial. In this way bail discriminates against the poor and forces them to remain in jail with others who have been convicted of crimes. It becomes difficult to "presume people innocent" when they must go to jail with those who have been proven guilty. In most cases, rather than endure months in crowded jails awaiting trial, suspects plead guilty to a lesser charge and thereby get their case immediately adjudicated by a judge without benefit of a trial. Thus, bail can be used, in violation of the Eighth Amendment, as a means of detaining suspects and as a way of coercing defendants to plead guilty. The use of bail in this way against the poor violates almost all the basic tenets of American ideals of justice: equality before the law, the presumption of innocence, and a trial by one's peers. Another injustice occurring in a magistrate's court stems from the fact that magistrates sometimes do not have any formal legal training. They are usually elected and have fixed political ties and social attitudes. As a result, the lower courts in many cities are less than partial, with little decorum and attention to procedural law. Under such conditions, the pretext of impartial justice is difficult to maintain.

ARRAIGNMENT AND PLEA. At a pretrial arraignment, the defendant and prosecutor face each other in a court of record. The formal charges are read by the prosecutor, and the defendant is asked to enter a plea of guilty or not guilty. However, it is behind the scenes, outside the courtroom that the real drama of arraignment and plea usually takes place. The pretrial appearance in court is typically just a formality that finalizes a bargain between prosecutor and defendant concerning what the charges and plea will be. By all estimates from 80 to 90 percent of criminal cases are resolved before arraignment, with the prosecutor negotiating with the defendant's lawyer in an effort to secure a guilty plea in exchange for a reduced charge and/or sentence.

There are three parties in plea negotiations: the prosecutor (district attorney), the defendant's lawyer, and the judge.[11] The most important of these parties is the district attorney, who is empowered by law to negotiate a plea, drop a case, or push for a maximum sentence. The district attorney has considerable discretion in dealing with a case. Prosecutors operate under two heavy constraints that limit their powers, however. They are, first of all, elected officials who are sometimes using the prosecutor's office as a stepping-stone to higher political office. As a result, prosecutors are under public, political, and media pressure to appear efficient and effective. They must "win the big ones" to appear effective and dispose of the multitude of minor cases to appear efficient. These factors indicate that the charges in the indictment brought against the accused and the willingness of the district attorney to negotiate pleas are often a reflection of political considerations— a fact that seems to run against the tenet of equal and impartial justice.

A second constraint on prosecutors comes from the large administrative bureaucracy in which they work. Bureaucracies need to appear efficient; but the judicial bureaucracy is faced with an overwhelming overload of cases that would impede efficiency if each case were adjudicated by an actual trial. Under these conditions, the only way to maintain the appearance of efficiency is to process rapidly, without trial, as many cases as possible. For this reason the prosecutor must seek to negotiate a plea of guilty in exchange for a lesser charge and sentence—thereby keeping the case from going to trial and jamming the already crowded courts.

To negotiate pleas successfully, prosecutors use a number of strategies, most of which violate the ideal tenets of American justice. In serious felonies, prosecutors usually "recommend" bail pending trial: by recommending high bail (forcing incarceration of the defendant until trial), prosecutors can put pressure on the defendants to plead guilty to a lesser charge. Prosecutors also have influence in selecting the judge; by threatening to select one who is "tough" on the alleged crime of the defendant, they can coerce negotiation. Prosecutors also decide how the indictment, or list of specific charges, at the pretrial hearing will read. Frequently, they use the practice of *multiple indictment*, or several different

[11] For a detailed inside description of this process in a large metropolitan court, see Blumberg, 1970 and Newman, 1956. For a secondary treatment of this process, see President's Commission, *Task Force Report: The Courts,* 1967 and Quinney, 1970:140–155.

charges for one criminal act, to their advantage in forcing a plea of guilty. For example, a typical indictment for possession of an eighth of an ounce of heroin could read as follows (Blumberg, 1970:56–57): Count 1—Felonious possession of a narcotic; Count 2—Felonious possession with intent to sell; and Count 3—Unlawfully possessing a narcotic. A charge for armed robbery might read: Count 1—Robbery, first degree; Count 2—Assault, second degree; Count 3—Assault, third degree; Count 4—Grand larceny, first degree; Count 5—Carrying a dangerous weapon; and Count 6—Petty larceny. By threatening to "throw the book" at defendants through multiple indictments, prosecutors pressure the accused to seek a compromise by pleading guilty to only one of the charges, preferably the least damaging. Finally, prosecutors can threaten to delay bringing the case to court; when coupled with a high bail that forces the accused to remain in jail, they can again coerce defendants to plead guilty. As is clear, all of these practices are not in response to the imperatives of justice but are a reflection of the political and bureaucratic pressures on prosecutors. The result is that equality before the law, the presumption of innocence, and right to trial can be suspended in the name of expediency.

Supposedly, in terms of the ideology of justice, defense lawyers are to have an adversary relationship with prosecutors. However, in practice the defense lawyer readily enters into negotiations with the prosecutor. If the defense attorneys bargained only for their clients, it might be possible to maintain some resemblance of the adversary principle of justice. But as A. S. Blumberg (1970:95–115) describes, defense lawyers are often "double agents" who represent not just their clients, but also themselves and, surprisingly, the need of the court system to adjudicate without trial. The ties of defense lawyers with prosecutors and with the court bureaucracy are often much stronger and binding than are those with clients. A defense lawyer who has been an assistant district attorney at one time may personally know the district attorney; but even when this is not the case, defense lawyers and district attorneys establish personal relationships that must endure beyond the transitory needs of one client or case. Perhaps more importantly, prosecutors must rely on defense lawyers to negotiate in order to keep cases from going to trial, while conversely, most defense lawyers must rely on the court to secure their fee. Collecting fees in criminal cases is always problematic, with the result that some lawyers collect in advance for each stage of a trial. The amount of the fee can, on occasion, determine the vigor with which they defend their clients.

Much of this vigor is evidenced outside the courtroom, where the defense lawyer pushes extra hard for a negotiated plea and reduced sentence. The defense lawyer is likely to draw upon the obligations for past favors owed by the prosecutor to secure a favorable charge and sentence. Since these negotiations are hidden, the defense lawyer must justify high fees with some form of performance within the courtroom. In this performance, defense lawyers are sometimes aided by the judge and the district attorney, who tolerate excesses and rhetoric. The defense lawyer acquires a vested interest, much like the prosecutor, in a system of negotiated rather than adversary justice; to have a real adversary trial would cost the defense lawyer enormously in time, energy, and fees. Thus, much like the overcrowded courts, the busy defense lawyer comes to rely on "bargain-counter justice" outside the courtroom. To the extent that lawyers rely on this system, loyalties to clients must be balanced with those to the organization and persons with whom they must maintain an adversary relationship.

This system works well for the affluent, who can afford good lawyers who will bargain effectively. But for the poor, who must rely on a court-appointed lawyer or the public defender, "plea copping" works more to the benefit of the prosecutor and court than to the defendant. Court-appointed lawyers are often the failures of the legal profession. They have little skill or "pull" with the prosecutor, and they are most interested in quickly securing their small fee. The result is a negotiated or "copped" plea that does little for the accused, but much for the court in terms of saving time and money.

More competent is the public defender, who is supported by the county or charitable organizations. But much like the courts, the public defender is burdened by an excess of cases, making it necessary to negotiate pleas with the prosecutor in order to keep up with an awesome caseload. Hence, when public defenders cannot defend clients except through negotiation, they lose the very weapon that could make them effective in those negotiations: the threat of taking the case to trial and tying up court time and personnel. Therefore, the public defender has less leverage against the district attorney than lawyers for the affluent, resulting in a situation in which the poor are more likely to be found guilty. Because poor defendants are denied a real trial and presumed guilty (for they must eventually plead guilty in a negotiated system), it is clear that they do not have equality before the law.

The final parties to the negotiated plea are the judges. It is in their courtroom that the pretrial hearing and arraignment occurs. And it is the judge who will ask defendants how they will plead. If defendants plead not guilty, the judge will add the case to an already heavy load and set a trial date. But if the accused pleads guilty, the case can be disposed of quickly. Judges clearly have a vested interest in adjudicating a case without trial because, like the prosecutor, they are part of a bureaucratic system demanding the efficient processing of an enormous caseload. The popular image of the aloof, brooding, reflective, and dispassionate judge is not entirely accurate at the lower court level, where most criminal cases are tried. In reality a working judge "must be politician, administrator, bureaucrat, and lawyer in order to cope with a crushing calendar of cases" (Blumberg, 1970:122–123). As such, the judge actively, although discretely, is forced to enter into plea negotiations by agreeing to abide by the decisions of the prosecutor concerning the charge and sentence. In fact, under some circumstances, actual meetings may be held behind closed doors in the judge's chambers as the final deal is hammered out. Judges must participate in the negotiated plea, for they must not accumulate too great a backlog of cases. Once the agreement has been struck between the prosecutor and defense lawyer, the judge allows the defendant to plead guilty at the pretrial hearing (Blumberg, 1970:65).

The majority of the cases brought before a judge are resolved in this manner (Newman, 1966:304). This pattern reveals that the judges will have difficulty in remaining impartial, for they inevitably have a vested interest in plea negotiations. The fact that judges enter into the negotiations makes it hard to visualize them as the neutral arbitrator of justice. And the fact that they are likely to encourage plea negotiations reveals a presumption of guilt and an unwillingness to grant every person a trial by their peers. It is likely, of course, that many clearly guilty persons are able to use the court system to avoid the full impact of the law. But it is difficult to separate those guilty who fair well in the system from those innocent who must plead guilty. And it is in this sense that the actual operation of the courts can, in many instances, suspend the ideal of justice.

In addition to violating the precepts of justice, the dangers of the current pretrial arraignment and plea process are perhaps obvious: The problem of processing volumes of cases now influences, disproportionately, how justice in America is administered. The whole process of adjudication occurs, at times, in secrecy, outside the court; thus it does not have to be guided by procedural rules and law. Coupled with the fact that the police are able to hide their enforcement practices (as discussed previously), similar practices of adjudication in the courts reveal a somewhat closed and hidden legal process in America.

SENTENCING. After a trial in which the defendant is found guilty, or after a pretrial plea of guilty, the judge is to pronounce sentence.[12] Judges must do so within the limits of the law, but even so, they have wide discretionary powers in imposing the sentence. Many legal innovations, such as the indeterminate sentence and probation, have greatly increased judges' discretion in sentencing, as has the general movement toward individualizing the treatment of criminals (Quinney, 1970:166). Discretion allows for bias on the part of judges. Contrary to their image as impartial figures coldly and rationally applying the law, judges are human and have many of the same biases as anyone else. Nowhere is this more evident than in their sentencing practices.

While personal bias ultimately determines, within the broad limits of the law, the defendant's sentence, judges can usually legitimize pronouncements in cases that have gone through a trial, or that were set in a pretrial agreement, by invoking a presentence report compiled by the probation department. (Such reports are not always compiled; only some states mandate them.) Frequently, the probation report is the sole basis upon which judges make sentencing decisions. This *presentence probation report* is compiled by a social worker, who collects data on the defendant from social agencies, relatives, friends, schools, police, employers, psychiatric testimony, and any other available source. Often, they are based on uncorroborated, hearsay data that would not be admissible during the trial. And yet, it is just this evidence that a judge can use to justify a decision made on the basis of personal biases. If judges use the presentence report as the sole basis of their decisions, they are granting enormous power to an overworked probation officer who has only the slightest familiarity with the defendant and the case. Thus hearsay evidence is used in a court of law to determine the fate of a defendant. What makes this practice questionable is that defendants do not have the right to cross-examine or confront their accuser—the probation officer or the judge.

The U.S. Supreme Court has upheld the use of these presentence

---

[12] The trial phase in the administration of justice has not been discussed because most cases are adjudicated without trial. Had the trial process been discussed, these facts could be established on the basis of current data: (1) Juries are biased (Robinson, 1950; Strodtbeck, 1957; Bevan et al., 1958; Simon, 1967; H. A. Bullock, 1961; Carter and Wilkins, 1967). (2) Witnesses are likely to be unreliable in their testimony (Gerver, 1957; Morris, 1957). (3) Psychiatrists are likely to abuse their medical prerogatives in their evaluations of the defendant (Halleck, 1966; Szasz, 1965; Blumberg, 1969). These facts make it less likely that even a jury trial assures the impartial rendering of justice.

ALTERNATIVES AVAILABLE TO JUDGES MAKE SENTENCING CHAOTIC

By JAMES A. KIDNEY

Washington (UPI)—In the same courthouse, two men convicted of identical crimes stand before separate judges for sentencing. Both defendants are young, lower-income family men without previous criminal records.

Both black-robed judges are middle-aged men who left prosperous law practices for the bench, thanks to good political connections and impeccable backgrounds.

As judges, both believe they are fair-minded.

Under state law, the crimes for which the two defendants were convicted carry any sentence up to 20 years in prison. There is no other standard.

The first defendant is sentence to 12 years in prison.

The second is admonished by his judge and gets three years, suspended.

This scene is commonplace in courtrooms across the land, and it troubles the consciences of many jurists and lawyers. Thousands of men and women languish in prison frustrated and angry, knowing that others who committed the same crimes were inexplicably set free.

During trial, defendants enjoy what the Supreme Court calls a "panoply of rights," but once a conviction is handed up, the sentencing process is chaotic.

With almost no standards for judge's guidance, the severity of a jail term frequently depends on the mood, prejudices, and political pressures of the time. The judge's alternatives are many, including probation, a minimum sentence, or special rehabilitation program, and are often arbitrary.

Sentencing laws also differ drastically from state to state. A crime might carry a maximum four-year prison term in one state, and a 10-year sentence in a neighboring state.

"The almost wholly unchecked and sweeping powers we give to judges in the fashioning of sentences are terrifying and intolerable for a society that professes devotion to the rule of law," says U.S. District Court Judge Marvin E. Frankel.

The staff of the American Bar Association's commission on correctional facilities and services, which has studied the problem, says reform is not enough that the system must be entirely rebuilt.

A recent federal study of judges in the 2nd Circuit Court of

Appeals in New York acknowledged that sentencing varied widely among jurists, but offered no immediate solutions.

Reformers find themselves in a quandary because no authority has ever decided what sentencing is supposed to accomplish. Should the sentence reflect the desire to punish? Is rehabilitation the goal? Or are harsh jail terms meant as a deterrent to crime?

Another problem is indeterminate sentencing, best known in California, where open-ended terms are handed down on the theory that a felon should be released only when he is reformed. A universally used variation involves the legislature setting only a maximum term, with judges allowed the discretion to apply any lesser sentence.

Indeterminate sentences sounded like fair play and drew wide praise at first, but now are sharply criticized because of the questionable underlying assumption that prisons rehabilitate.

"Jails ruin young men," says. Dr. Karl Menninger, Kansas psychiatrist and penologist. "Can't the public grasp this indisputable fact?"

"How can a decent prison attempting a rehabilitation program do anything for a boy who comes to it from a jail where he has been raped, battered, vomited and urinated upon, mauled and corrupted by some of the old-timers in the bullpen?"

Among prisoners, sentences with no fixed release date feed hopelessness and despair. Overworked parole boards tend to give cursory attention to each applicant. If a parole request is denied, the inmate often doesn't know why—or what standards he must meet to win his freedom.

Anthony Partridge of the staff of the Federal Judicial Center says it is impossible to write a sentencing standard that guarantees reform.

"We may not agree on whether a crime deserves 3 years or 20 years, but we surely can agree that the sentence should not depend on which judge a person gets," he said.

There are many reform proposals. All have demonstrable flaws and few have been put into use. They include:

• Setting a single sentence for each crime, so judges will have no discretion. Critics say this would leave no room to consider mitigating circumstances.

• Sentencing councils in which judges confer with their colleagues in the hope of narrowing the extremes of harshness or leniency. The 2nd Circuit study found the councils did not work as well as expected, and increased court workloads.

• More thorough presentencing reports to give judges greater background information before sentencing. The ABA staff, however, said concise reports would get more attention because most judges base their sentencing on only a few factors.

• Allowing appellate review of criminal sentences in ordinary cases, just as courts allow review of civil damages on appeal. Opponents fear overburdening the courts, but reformers say the loss of individual freedom is no less important than loss of money.

• Establishing computerized data banks for every legal jurisdiction so one judge can see quickly how other judges have treated defendants in similar circumstances.

Partridge said one difficulty with computer banks is deciding how far to go in classifying defendants, such as an auto thief who is an eighth-grade dropout with a record of drug addiction. Overclassification would make the system unwieldy.

Whatever the cure, the experts agree the problem goes to the heart of the criminal justice system.

An ABA staff study concluded that because legislatures have failed to decide society's purpose in sentencing, the judges' arbitrary discretion reigns and "equity and justice remain unapplied concepts."

Source: From the *Press-Enterprise*, Riverside, Cal., December 8, 1974.

reports on the assumption that the probation department functions autonomously from the court and can thereby mediate between the court and defendant (Blumberg, 1970:146). But in reality, the probation department is an adjunct to the court. The budget and the recruitment and supervision of personnel, policies, and administrative directives all flow from the court. As a part of the court bureaucracy, the probation department becomes involved in the processing of large numbers of cases. The ideology, and the desires of most officers, of the probation department stresses concern for the problems and needs of the defendant, but their burdensome administrative mandate forces the quick and efficient categorization of defendants into what can be inaccurate and stereotyped psychiatric categories. To incarcerate a defendant on the basis of such categories, or to use them to justify the biases of the judge, violates basic tenets in the American ideal of justice.

JUSTICE IN AMERICA: AN OVERVIEW

The ideology surrounding American justice could never be perfectly realized. It is probably impossible to have perfect equality before the law, total presumption of innocence, and every case adjudicated by trial. By definition, ideologies describe unattainable states, and American conceptions of justice are no exception. It appears, however, that the gap between ideology and practice, between what is and what should be, has not closed or even remained the same. It may have widened in recent years. The need to process large quantities of cases on limited funds has frequently worked against the realization of justice. And the hope for the future does not look bright; the pressures are toward more rapid production, not more justice.

In a society valuing justice, it is unfortunate that *investments* in justice are less than necessary to realize this value. Justice takes more time, costs more money, and perhaps enables some criminals to "beat the rap." While more money, judges, lawyers, and court personnel will be necessary to assure justice, the logjam in the courts will require that most laws pertaining to crimes without victims be written off the books. The bureaucratized court system, with its emphasis on efficiency, may have a tendency to take on only those cases that are *easily* processed. This can mean that the limited resources of the courts will be spent on prosecuting addicts, alcoholics, gamblers, sexual deviants, and vagrants, for these "criminals" are readily available and likely to cop a plea. The result for the court is a high production rate and statistical evidence of efficiency. To remove these crimes from legal codes and statutes will cut down on the statistical evidence of efficiency and also the jam in the courts. It may be inevitable in a highly industrialized, assembly-line society that justice must be measured by a production quota. If this is so, it will be difficult to realize the ideal of justice in America.

Coupled with the dilemmas facing the police and the pressures on the prosecutor to seek "copped pleas," realization of the ideal of justice becomes even more problematic. While America's laws, police, and courts are, by comparison with other societies', certainly among the best, many problems and dilemmas remain to be resolved. For indeed, Americans have always extolled that all citizens are "equal before the law," but the fact that such is not the case reveals the extent to which crime and justice will remain one of America's most enduring problems of structure.

Chapter 5

DILEMMAS OF
EDUCATION

In many respects the American educational system has been successful. Virtually every child in America receives a high school education, with close to one-half of these going on to some form of college. It is perhaps only in the context of such success that two dilemmas become markedly evident in American lower education: (1) Despite the fact that American schools have "acculturated" several generations of immigrants, while providing opportunities for millions, the schools still appear to exacerbate general problems of social class, ethnic, and racial discrimination. (2) And despite the success of schools in reaching nearly all Americans, the dilemma of *how* best to educate is still present. These problems are, of course, highly relative, since they can be raised only for a system that has been, in so many ways, highly successful. Questions about the subtle forms of discrimination in schools can become salient only where all people go to school, for in many societies, the discrimination is more open, obvious, and blatant. And questions of how best to educate can seem trivial in societies where many receive little formal schooling. Success in providing universal education, then, highlights the remaining dilemmas confronting the lower educational system in America.

The turmoil of the late 1960s and early 1970s placed into bold relief some of the dilemmas facing higher education. Again, many of these problems seem significant only because so many receive college instruction but, nevertheless, the "functions" of colleges and universities have been increasingly called into question: Who should higher education educate—the masses or the few? How should students be educated? What is the research function of universities to be? How independent of government, military, economic, and domestic interests should the universities be? While these questions are asked with less intensity and violence in the mid 1970s, no clear answers have been given, revealing the extent to which they pose an enduring set of dilemmas for higher education in America.

LOWER EDUCATION IN AMERICA

QUESTIONS OF HOW TO EDUCATE

Since much of the questioning of the educational process in primary and secondary schools represents a reaction to the present system, several features of this system should be highlighted:

First, American lower education is "massified," providing education for all school-age children. The very size and scope of this task inevitably leads to bureaucratization of public school structures, often resulting in the emergence of a "bureaucratic ethic" revolving around the processing of students and the maintenance of control and efficiency. Such an ethic, as it is translated into a myriad of concrete educational practices, can at times create problems concerning how to impart flexibility, humaneness, and innovativeness to students within a structure emphasizing control, order, and efficiency.

Second, compared to other modern societies, American education is highly decentralized; it is financed and administered primarily at the state and local levels. The United States is without any clear national educational policy, system of financing, or administration. Although supplemented by federal funds flowing from an often bewildering array of agencies, lower public education is financed principally by state and local taxes and administered primarily by local school officials. Such financial and administrative decentralization results in enormous discrepancies in the quality of education in different school districts, cities, states, and regions. Furthermore, dependency on local property taxes, as well as local administrative control, subjects American schools to social and political pressures within the local community, creating problems concerning how the schools should be run and by whom. Moreover, the financing of schools through local property taxes aggravates the inequity of the tax system, since these taxes are less progressive than income taxes; that is, the poor and middle-income groups must pay a greater portion of their incomes in property taxes than the highly affluent and rich.

Third, it has been noted by many that American public schools are dominated by middle-class values emphasizing competition and achievement. While such an emphasis can encourage high levels of performance for some, it can become highly discriminatory against those students who are not middle class and/or who do not learn well under conditions of competition and constant evaluation for achievement. To the extent that educational attainment determines one's social status as an adult, this situation increases the likelihood that those from the middle classes will have a competitive advantage in school, and later on the job market, over those from different class and cultural backgrounds—thereby perpetuating inequality.

It is these three basic features of the primary and secondary school system in America that present two specific dilemmas on how to educate: (1) control versus freedom of students in the schools, and (2) decentralized versus centralized administration.

CONTROL VERSUS FREEDOM OF STUDENTS. Americans value "conformity" to authority and accepted practices as well as "individual" creativity and innovativeness (Williams, 1970:433–499). This conflict of values is reflected in educational ideology and practice since the schools are charged with imparting both the capacity to conform and innovate. Values of conformity, however, are more likely to dominate schools in America. One reason for this domination may reside in the fact that American schools were often expanded in the late 1800s to assimilate masses of diverse immigrants into "the American way of life." Another reason lies in the nature of the job market for which schools prepare students—a market dominated by routine, standard, and bureaucratic jobs requiring considerable control of worker activity. Even aside from these two forces, the very fact that American society seeks to educate all its young requires a mass educational program that, in turn, creates extensive school bureaucracies; and bureaucratization generates its own imperatives for conformity, control, and regularity.

Thus, the goals of mass assimilation and vocational preparation have become bureaucratically institutionalized. Given a commitment to mass education and the resulting crush of students, bureaucratization is inevitable; and given an emphasis on vocationalism, this bureaucracy, as it emerges in thousands of local communities, would be expected to be concerned with efficiency in imparting basic skills directly relevant to a job or college. And because educational bureaucracies are presently dependent on the goodwill of the local community for financing, they are particularly anxious to demonstrate their efficiency to the watching public. This efficiency is often demonstrated by maintaining an orderly, serene, and controlled school environment.

Jonathan Kozol (1967) found an unusual degree of emphasis

on cultural uniformity and order stated explicitly in the teacher's manual at a Boston public school:

> Character traits to be developed: Obedience to Duty [and] Constituted Authority . . . Self-Control . . . Responsibility . . . Gratitude . . . Kindness . . . Good Workmanship and Perseverance . . . Loyalty . . . Teamwork. . . .

On the one hand, students are to be controlled to maintain the appearance of efficiency in the school bureaucracy while, on the other hand, they are to manifest those work habits necessary to fit into the urban-industrial workplace. Such an emphasis has been observed to operate in many subtle ways (Silberman, 1970:113–157; Friedenberg, 1968:155–158). For example, in most American schools there is an overconcern with the clock, time, and schedule. School can at times become a place where the clock and the schedule, rather than the needs and desires of students or teachers, determine what should occur. Such scheduling can be exacerbated by the lesson plans used by most schools to implement a standardized curriculum. Further, administrative rules can emphasize silence, with a sign of "good teaching" and "efficiency" being a quiet and orderly classroom. Compounding the concern for silence is the restriction of free movement within the school. By governing movement, much like that on an assemblyline, the appearance of efficiency and order is again maintained. The grading system in most American schools, with its emphasis on competitive evaluation, further orders and constrains school activity. The use of standardized IQ and achievement tests, the daily evaluations of teachers, and the term grading system have allowed some schools to prematurely sort out students on the basis of their "ability" as established by tests, and to direct them into "learning" or "achievement" tracks from which it can be difficult to escape.

The bureaucratic imperative to appear efficient can become so institutionalized that teaching innovations—team teaching, televised instruction, "new" types of lesson plans, ungraded learning, and achievement rather than age groupings of students—are rendered less effective in realizing goals of individual creativity and innovativeness. For example, John Goodlad (1969), in summarizing the findings from a study of 100 kindergarten and first-grade classrooms in 13 states, found little evidence that the reform movement of the 1950s and 1960s had made a significant impact on the way schools were administered. He and his researchers found that a single teacher tended to lead all instruction, with students passively responding, usually one by one, in a controlled classroom; pupils rarely did individual, self-sustaining work; standard textbooks were the most conspicuous learning instruments; small groups of students in the pursuit of knowledge were rarely found.

These obstacles in implementing less structured school programs are supported by external and internal pressures. From outside the school, it is clear that parents, who in a decentralized school system are capable of exerting much influence, value order and discipline over student self-inquiry and experimentation. For example, a Louis Harris poll on parental attitudes conducted for *Life* magazine, notes that two-thirds of high school parents believe that "maintaining discipline is more important than student self-inquiry."

Much like their parents, students themselves often come to accept the emphasis on control as proper and normal. For as parents are likely to emphasize, getting through "the system" and into college or into a good job are the keys to success. For some, this process of "getting through" becomes one of avoiding work and involvement; for others, it involves giving the teacher what is wanted; and for still others, it means compiling an impressive academic record. But for all students, survival involves suppressing emotion, subordinating their interests to the larger organization, regulating and regimenting themselves, forfeiting privacy and intimacy, and duly absorbing what can be a bland, standardized curriculum. High school students show some signs of resisting such a system, but most accept it and actually believe that it is right and correct.

There is no inherent "rightness or wrongness" in this situation. Much of the emphasis on control appears inevitable. Moreover, many intellectual tasks, such as spelling and the fundamentals of math and reading, appear to be efficiently learned by most students in structured environments. Additionally, children may indeed need to learn control if they are to be ready for participation in the work force where most jobs are highly regulated. Thus, the dilemma becomes one of implementing control and innovativeness within a mass bureaucracy that has become, and will remain, vocationally oriented. While most parents explicitly seem to prefer control and order, others still desire that the schools encourage curiosity, creativity, and spontaneity. Many schools do appear to realize both goals, but in most, values of conformity appear to dominate.

CENTRALIZATION VERSUS DECENTRALIZATION. In America, as in no other modern industrial nation, education is decentralized. The task of financing and administering lower education has been given to the states, which in turn delegate much to the local communities.

SOCIOLOGICAL INSIGHTS

FREE SCHOOLS AS AN ALTERNATIVE
OR A PERMISSIVE NIGHTMARE?

In recent years the "free school" or "new school" alternative to current school structures has been advocated and implemented. What are the principles of free schools? Below the ideology of free schools is summarized as a means of highlighting the conflict in America over how to educate.

In the new schools of American lower education, the administration must actively seek to find ways to promote freedom of movement, contact, and discussion among students and, most of all, it must abandon the mania for the clock and the crushing routine typical of both elementary and secondary schools. Additionally, the social partitioning of students by age levels, as well as the partitioning of the school's physical plant, must be abandoned. Age stratification can be one of the most destructive forces in education, for it circumscribes the number of contacts and relationships possible among students, while imparting a compartmentalized view of the world. By making the physical plant more open and by eliminating, at least some of the time, age, grade, and sex restrictions on the use of facilities, more creative use of the school's plant will ensue. The current system of grading in American schools must cease to be an end in itself and become a diagnostic tool indicating a child's weaknesses and strengths. Coupled with changes in the grading system, state and national math, reading, and IQ tests must be used to evaluate school and teacher performance, not to categorize and stratify students prematurely into ability groupings.

The new school classroom can be a place where students talk, discuss, argue, and get involved in what they are doing. In such an environment, the teacher is the facilitator of learning that can involve both gentle prodding and drill. The new classroom will be noisier (and appear more chaotic), but the noise will reflect the excitement that comes with learning. If the classroom is to meet the intellectual and human potential of its students, it must become a relaxed, informal, comfortable place filled with interesting things to do.

The new school should have a curriculum because there are certain things that all students must know. Informal classrooms do not necessarily imply a "flabby" educational process. Elementary school students must be made aware that they are expected to learn certain materials, but the *manner* in which this awareness is generated does not have to be formally stated. Informal prodding, drilling, and even testing can communicate the teacher's expectation without imposing a rigid lesson plan and regular graded examinations.

In the informal system of new schools, an enormous burden falls upon the teacher. The teacher must be more alert and constantly ready to respond to a student, while not being able to fall back on the lesson plan or school routine. What is commonly misunderstood about informal teaching is that teachers do not abandon their authority. Teachers enforce rules concerning good conduct; but in an informal system rules can be enforced more effectively because authority is based on respect. Another misunderstanding about the teacher's role revolves around the belief that teachers abdicate teaching and instructing to the students. This is not the case, for certain subjects—reading at the elementary level and certain complex subjects at the secondary level —cannot be acquired without some direct teacher-to-student instruction. But the manner of this instruction should deemphasize the "chalk talk" at the front of the room, with students sitting quietly and passively. The teacher must be willing to engage smaller groups of students informally—cajoling them, reacting to their inquiries, and yet imparting necessary substance. Another mistaken assumption about informal teaching is that it takes an exceptional teacher to be effective. But, it can be argued that it is in the formal educational approach, with all its emphases on order, control, routine, silence, and scheduling, that teachers must be exceptional to ever reach the students.

Such is the ideology of free schools. Can it be implemented? What constraints will be imposed in mass education structures? At present, there appears to be little movement within public education to implement the free school approach, thus it is likely to become primarily a concern of select private schools.

While some funds flow into the states and communities from various federal agencies, state income and sales taxes, plus local community property taxes, provide the resources to support most lower public education. The consequences of such decentralization are far-reaching.

1. Decentralization generates enormous inequality in school facilities from state to state, as well as within any state or local community. As long as the financing of schools remains tied to state and community taxes, poor states and communities cannot afford the same physical facilities or quality of teachers as can more affluent areas. The result is that those who are most in need of educational opportunities—the poor—are the least likely to get them.

In 1971 the California Supreme Court ruled that the use of local property taxes to finance education "discriminates against the poor . . . [and] makes the quality of a child's education a function of the wealth of his parents and neighbors." If this landmark decision is upheld by the U.S. Supreme Court, statewide financing of education will become more equitable. Although disparities in the quality of schools between states would remain, at least one source of inequality through decentralization will have been eliminated.

2. The decentralized profile of American lower education often prevents the federal government from implementing desirable nationwide policies, such as school integration. Since schools are more financially dependent on local than federal funds, they are more responsive to local public sentiment. While the federal government has some financial leverage, it does not have as much as the states and communities. Equally important, the federal government has no centralized and clearly articulated administrative linkage with the states and local communities, except the Office of Education, which is a subdivision within the Department of Health, Education, and Welfare and which has only vague and shifting administrative and fiscal responsibilities.

3. With unclear fiscal and administrative linkages to the states and local schools, federal funds flow into the schools from many diverse agencies. While the Office of Education does coordinate these expenditures to a limited extent, much financial and administrative duplication occurs, resulting in the inefficient use of federal tax dollars.

4. Financing schools from local property taxes and state revenues has created a financial crisis in the schools. It is increasingly difficult to finance lower education with property taxes or limited state revenues. To do so has raised property taxes to such an extent that taxpayers are now consistently rejecting school bonds and tax-override elections, even in the more affluent suburban districts. And in the large cities, which are already on the edge of financial chaos, the lack of revenue has caused a decline in the quality of educational facilities.

5. Finally, administrative and fiscal decentralization exposes the schools to the fads of public opinion and political manipulation in a community. In virtually all communities in America, education is a political issue, with the result that schools become politicized. Therefore, administrators and teachers must always be attuned to public opinion and the political climate of the community. Under these conditions it is more likely that a conservative educational process will ensue, for to initiate new or controversial programs invites public criticism and political intervention.

Centralization of education initially might seem like the easy solution to most of these problems. The schools could be administratively centralized into a cabinet-level Department of Education and financed by increased federal income taxes. Correspondingly, increases in federal taxes would be countered by a lowering of state income and local property taxes. Transforming American education in this way would give it a centralized profile similar to that in other modern nations. However, whether such a change is desirable is questionable; while partially resolving one set of problems, it may create new problems. The centralized school systems in large cities such as New York can offer some clue as to the dangers involved in centralization (Rogers, 1968).

First, centralization establishes a long chain of command and authority that can make teachers and administrators upward-oriented rather than student-oriented. Level upon level of subordinates could, under some circumstances, make educators just as conservative as they sometimes become under political pressure from the local community.

Second, large bureaucracies tend to evidence fragmentation of administrative units from one another, resulting in much duplication of effort. Whether such waste would be any less than that in the current system cannot be known. But if previous experience with large federal agencies can serve as a guide, considerable fragmentation, isolation, and duplication might well be expected.

Third, fragmentation and isolation of administrative units creates a situation in which they spend most of their energies attempting to consolidate their power with respect to other units. In turn, strong informal norms emphasizing self-preservation are likely to emerge within administrative units, deflecting further attention away from organizational goals (such as educating students). These processes result in the bureaucracy's increasing insulation from, and ignorance of, it clients. Internal politics and personal career ambitions of bureaucrats could conceivably begin to take precedence over the goals of education and service to the children of a community.

As David Rogers (1968) points out, teacher professionalism and unionization, which are typical of highly centralized systems, can compound this trend toward bureaucratic isolation. While professionalism keeps competence high, it can isolate teachers and administrators from students. As the national profession assumes prominence, implementation of its latest fads, techniques, and formulas can take precedence over concern with the unique needs of diverse groups of students. Similarly, unionization can give teachers needed wage increases, but at the same time it can enslave teachers to just one more bureaucracy (the union) and thereby limit choices in dealing with their clients, the students. Thus, while centralization can perhaps reduce educational inequalities, resolve the current fiscal crisis, allow for more implementation of national policy through the schools, and make educators less vulnerable to local political pressures, it can potentially result in the waste of resources, isolation from students, and bureaucratic rigidity—making centralization versus decentralization an enduring dilemma in American education.

QUESTIONS OF EDUCATIONAL EQUALITY

Mass education in America was to become a democratizing influence increasing the capacities for mobility among people who lived in and migrated to America. Public schools, in Thomas Jefferson's words, were to ". . . bring into action that mass of talents which lies buried in poverty in every country for want of means of development. . . ." To some extent, mass public education has increased the overall abilities and talents of Americans, but it does not appear to do so equally.

This situation is of great importance in modern America, for the United States is now a credentialed society. One's chances for money and prestige in the occupational sphere are directly related to educational credentials and only indirectly to desire, ability, and performance on the job. While credentialing is a convenient and perhaps necessary way to assess qualifications, it grants the educational system the power to be society's gatekeeper. Those who conform to the system get the appropriate diplomas; those who, for various personal, cultural, and socioeconomic reasons, cannot conform are more likely to be placed at the bottom of the labor pool.

American education reinforces social-class boundaries. While supposedly established to help the disadvantaged, public schools were not an important path to upward mobility among early immigrant generations. More frequently, mobility was achieved by forcing children into the work force so that they could contribute to the family's total income—thereby sacrificing the younger generation's education (Thernstrom, 1964). Today, despite a conscientious effort in many areas, schools have not promoted equality. For example, by most statistics, the educational gap between nonwhites and whites has remained roughly the same. Absolute gains in years of schooling for blacks and other minority groups have been paralleled by similar grains in the white population, hence preserving the gap. In the credentialed society, such educational gaps translate into income differentials, thus maintaining the

American system of inequality. This failure of the schools to be an equalizing force can be attributed to two forces: (1) the structure of public education, and (2) the traits that lower-class children, especially minority poor, bring with them to school.

STRUCTURAL DISCRIMINATION IN PUBLIC SCHOOLS. Some critics have argued that, historically, public schools have had the consequence of imparting to the lower classes the habits of "obedience and submission necessary for public peace, a docile labor force, and the protection of property" (Silberman, 1970:60). While such a charge is certainly an overstatement, it does appear that many of the bureaucratic rigidities of schools have operated, usually in a de facto way, against children from non-middle class backgrounds. Even in the face of an educational ideology and well-intentioned programs emphasizing equality for the poor, the structure of the schools has built-in racial, ethnic, and social-class biases.

First, the very formality of the school system, with its frequent emphasis on the clock, scheduling, routine, silence, and restriction of movement, can potentially discriminate against children from lower-class cultures, in which physical aggressiveness, noise, and spontaneity are more likely to be valued (W. Miller, 1968). Forced to sit quietly and follow routines, lower-class children frequently become alienated from a school system dominated by values of order and control.

Second, the teachers of public schools tend to be from the middle class. While most have a desire to reach lower-class students, the subtle attitude or expectation that these students will have learning problems can set up a false prophecy that teachers themselves fulfill. By expecting so little of their lower-class students, they impart to them their middle-class prejudice—not necessarily intentional or malicious—that their students are inferior and cannot do well (Rosenthal and Jacobson, 1968; Silberman, 1970:83–86). The effects of open prejudice by teachers are obvious, but more pervasive is the conveyance of a subtle, middle-class attitude toward lower-class children that perpetuates the very learning problems that teachers decry. This bias, and the self-fulfilling prophecy that it generates, will persist as long as a large proportion of teachers—regardless of their good intentions—come from the middle class.

Third, the testing and grading system discriminates against students from the lower classes. Whether an IQ test, a national achievement exam, or an in-class quiz, the very fact that a competitive and timed test is being given favors students from middle-class homes, where the importance of test-taking and verbal competition is more likely to be emphasized. Furthermore, although some changes have been made on standardized national examinations, tests remain verbal and written, again giving children from the middle class, where greater stress is placed on words, a competitive advantage. Also, national achievement and IQ exams frequently portray a middle-class world. For example, a typical question from a standardized IQ test reads (Havighurt and Neugarten, 1967:78–79):

A symphony is to a composer as a book is to what?
□paper □sculptor □author □musician □man

Because symphonies, sculptors, authors, and musicians are more familiar to middle-class children, they are likely to do better than their counterparts from the lower classes. Doing well on tests is crucial for survival, for it is on the basis of national achievement and IQ examinations, as well as classroom grades, that students are labeled, channeled, and counseled into college prep or vocational programs (Cicourel and Kitsuse, 1963). Furthermore, since it is test performance that determines success, one's educational self-concept as a good, bad, or mediocre student is internalized on the basis of these examinations. Since such self-concepts determine not only performance but also educational aspirations, the current system of test-taking often serves to discriminate against the poor by convincing them, at a very early age, that they cannot survive in the competitive world of the middle classes.

The biases of the schools operate against all lower-class children, especially those who evidence distinctive cultural patterns that deviate sharply from the middle-class cultural ambience of the schools. It is for this reason that most studies of school achievement find that family background and neighborhood have more influence on a student's test scores than the quality of school facilities or teacher qualifications (Coleman, 1966; Jencks, 1969). When researchers originally discovered this they were surprised. They had truly expected to find that inequality in school facilities suppressed achievement and accounted for the learning problems of students from poor backgrounds. Instead, variations in family background appeared to explain why students did not achieve in school. It cannot be doubted, of course, that certain family characteristics can impair learning and, hence, school achievement. But these researchers (Coleman, 1966) probably did not devote sufficient attention to another fact: school environments. Further studies into school environments that are so loaded against lower-class cultural patterns will inevitably force researchers to the conclusion that underachievement is caused by the family background and neighborhood of the student. It should not be surprising that children of lower-class parents who can approximate middle-class patterns are the ones who achieve, by *the middle-class yardstick*, in middle-class schools located in impoverished areas. Conversely, those lower-class parents who cannot make this cultural transformation are likely to inhibit their children's adjustment to the middle-class ambience of schools. These researchers' acceptance of the measuring instruments of schools—IQ tests, national achievement tests, and grades assigned by middle-class teachers—could be *expected* to expose deficiencies (or is it deviations?) in lower-class families. It would be difficult to contend, however, that these researchers have not isolated a key force in retarding educational achievement—the family. Current assessment techniques do have *some* validity and, thus, it is necessary to understand how family and school interact to reduce educational attainment for lower-class children.

BACKGROUNDS OF STUDENTS. The traits that children bring with them to the schools will obviously affect their performance. The school rewards some traits and punishes others; and a school system dominated by a middle-class, mass culture will be more likely to reward the traits of students who display middle-class rather than lower-class attributes. However, such a portrayal is too simple. The fact remains that many lower-class homes and environments are not conducive to success in schools, even if schools were structured along ungraded and noncompetitive informal lines and were to have lower-class teachers and administrators.

Although it is difficult to establish culturally free criteria, it is likely that lower-class backgrounds do not lead to the cultivation of certain motives (McClelland, 1961), attitudes and values (Rosen, 1956), language patterns, and cognitive style (Silberman, 1970:80) that will facilitate learning in *any* type of school. Attribute deficiencies are perhaps not as great as many educators imply, but some preschool training may be necessary for children from some lower-class backgrounds. Unfortunately, most current preschool programs not only attempt to overcome these basic deficiencies, but also attempt to indoctrinate students into more general behavior styles that will help them survive in middle-class schools. Such a program places an enormous burden on the individual student rather than on the school. For indeed, it is equally necessary for the school to become more flexible and adaptable to lower-class cultural patterns. While preschool programs initially raise IQ and achievement scores of students, the gains are only temporary and fall off in subsequent grades unless there is continued, direct intervention in the schools and the children's lives. A more equitable solution, and one that is less degrading to lower-class students, might be to abandon most preschool programs (except where *real* deficiencies, such as malnutrition and clearly deprived or unstable home life, in children's backgrounds are evident) and restructure the schools so that they can adjust themselves to the diverse and unique features of children from lower-class homes and neighborhoods. Were the cultural biases of the schools eliminated, the differences in IQ and achievement scores of middle- and lower-class children might recede.

Charles Silberman (1970:98–112), in discussing several "successful" slum schools, documents some of the conditions necessary for such success: (1) a warm and sympathetic school environment (most readily achieved, he argues, by more informal schools); (2) a school staffed by ordinary teachers who *expect* their students to do well; (3) administrators who will not allow teachers to fail and will hold the teacher—not the student—accountable for failure; and (4) schools that also educate the parents and expect the parents to help in their children's education.

Changes allowing for the implementation of these general goals might help reduce educational inequality. "Deficiencies" in lower-class families cannot be changed dramatically unless poverty and inequality are reduced. It is the schools, then, that must seek to change, not just their students, but also themselves, since in their present profile they reinforce and perpetuate the learning problems brought to the school. And as the society's gatekeeper, perpetuation of the present system of education is likely to maintain inequality in America.

HIGHER EDUCATION IN AMERICA

THE DILEMMA OF SIZE AND SCOPE

By 1973, there were over 2500 institutions of higher education in America. And in this same year one survey reported that 6.4 million students were enrolled in four-year colleges, with another 1.7 in two-year colleges. These figures, however, are conservative since they come only from institutions answering a survey questionnaire. Since World War II, state-supported universities have grown most rapidly, culminating in extensive "multiversity" systems in many states. The growing size of colleges and universities is a reflection of how much America has become a credentialed society. For in order to get a "good" job, formal education credentials are increasingly considered necessary, with the result that close to one-half of college-age youth have entered the credentials race. This figure is just about doubled that of fifteen years ago— underscoring the rapid growth of higher education. While college enrollments have begun to level off in recent years, the problems associated with size and growth still pose a number of dilemmas that have yet to be resolved.

Expanded enrollments have increased the size of many college and university campuses. In turn, increases in size have led to even more bureaucratization: the ever-escalating specialization, compartmentalization, and neutralization of college life. Processing the masses of students entering American universities has resulted in a shortage of funds for faculty, hence, larger classes, an increased reliance on centralized records, advance registration, and other impersonal but cheap and efficient ways of processing students.

However, increases in the size of universities have also resulted in the development of large libraries, excellent laboratory facilities, and concentrations of highly skilled faculties. Just how to reconcile these advantages of large size with the impersonality of the accompanying bureaucratization represents a major dilemma for America's large state and private universities (Sewell, 1971).

SOCIOLOGICAL INSIGHTS

EDUCATION AS BIG BUSINESS?

With over 8 million students attending universities and colleges, it can be expected that education has become a "big business," involving the expenditure of billions of dollars each year. For example, the expenditures for the staff of universities and colleges is enormous. The 266,913 teachers listed by the American Association of College Professors (a voluntary organization) in only 1,242 colleges receive salaries totalling $4.38 billion. Coupled with the remaining teachers and support staff, a considerable segment of the population works directly in higher education. And of course, many work in the construction trades that build and expand the physical facilities of colleges and universities. Moreover, colleges and universities keep 8 million potential workers out of the job market each year, thus increasing their impact upon the economy. As a result, higher education is intimately involved in economic processes, and this involvement extends well beyond its function of training the young in various intellectual and vocational skills.

To the extent that the university's most important goals are the initiation of students into the life of the mind, the instillation of a commitment to use reason in the resolution of problems, and the development of both technical competence and intellectual integrity, the current system of mass education is only partially successful. And yet, it appears difficult to organize mass education on other than a large university and multiversity format since the costs involved in building and maintaining smaller campuses are high—a fact of economic life that threatens the solvency of many small, private colleges. Such mass organization, however, involves high levels of bureaucratization and all the attendant problems experienced by students and professors caught in organizational restrictions of large bureaucracies.

THE DILEMMA OF RESEARCH VERSUS TEACHING

In all large universities the dilemma of teaching versus research prevails. This dilemma is a reflection of the dual functions performed by universities: to impart knowledge to students and to expand the existing body of knowledge in society through research. Both are proper and necessary functions of the university, yet to emphasize one appears to require a deemphasis of the other. To promote research requires the diversion of university funds into research facilities, a large pool of graduate students to perform research legwork, and time off for professors from undergraduate teaching. To concentrate on undergraduate education requires more teaching time from professors, less subsidy of graduate students, and large amounts of university funds for a wide variety of programs.

Part of the trouble in reconciling these two functions stems from the expectation that the same people—professors—must perform both functions: teaching and research. Too often students and professors have been led to believe that a good researcher is likely to be a good teacher because research keeps one up-to-date in their field. In reality, given the high degree of specialization within academic disciplines, it is more likely that researchers are behind in all areas except their narrow field of interest. Furthermore, in addition to a breadth of knowledge, good teaching requires that professors spend time with students outside the classroom. Thus, except in rare instances, the same person cannot be both an excellent teacher and researcher. Excellent researchers can often be exceptional lecturers, but rarely do they have out-of-class time to spend with students. Conversely, teachers who must keep up in their fields, prepare lectures, and spend time with students cannot become overly involved in research.

In the abstract, the solution to the dilemma is obvious: Strike a division of labor between research and teaching. Some professors could be primarily teachers; others could concentrate on research, giving occasional lectures. Maintaining such a division of labor has proven difficult for several reasons:

1. Research productivity is more easily measured than is quality teaching. Since all bureaucracies, including universities, require evidence of efficiency and performance, research is more likely to be rewarded than teaching.
2. Professors' mobility from university to university depends on their reputation outside the local bureaucracy. A reputation as an excellent teacher rarely goes beyond the local campus and it rarely extends even beyond the classroom. For professors to establish a reputation, therefore, requires them to have articles published in trade journals. Professional prestige stems from the quantity and quality of these publications. Even within academic departments, prestige is established by one's non-teaching activities: research, publishing, and consulting.
3. Similarly, a university's prestige relative to other colleges is established not by the quality of its teachers as teachers, but by the quality of its teachers as researchers. Most administrators of universities, as well as most students and their parents, are concerned about reputation and prestige—thus unwittingly encouraging the very faculty research that can dilute an undergraduate teaching program.

The rewarding of research over teaching aggravates trends evident with bureaucratization—increasing distance between professors and students, large classes, and a general lack of intellectual community. Yet, just how to transform the reward system in universities so as to encourage good teaching in addition to quality research is difficult. Few professors are willing to give up their mobility or suffer a loss of prestige in the eyes of their colleagues. Few administrators, parents, and students wish to allow a school's national reputation to decline in the name of good teaching, especially in a credentialed society where the reputation of the school from which one gets a degree is initially more important than one's actual capabilities. For these reasons, the dilemma of teaching versus research will be one of the enduring problems of structure in American higher education.

THE DILEMMA OF INSTITUTIONAL COOPTATION

Since World War II the federal government has increasingly funded university research. Such funding has proven financially beneficial to America's large universities: Research funds have allowed them to increase their graduate student populations; to assemble excellent faculties; to construct large-scale and expensive research facilities, from computers to whole buildings; and, by taking as much as 40 to 50 percent of research grants for overhead costs (accounting, providing offices, etc.), to add to their general funds. In fact, to maintain the elaborate research facilities of most large universities (and a growing number of smaller campuses) now requires a constant flow of federal research funds and contracts. Large research projects involving elaborate equipment and extensive personnel cannot be conducted without federal funding —making the research enterprise and much of the graduate and undergraduate education dependent on the federal monies, much of which comes from the military (see Chapter 8).

Research is expensive and to the extent that it must be a university function, funds must come from somewhere. The magnitude of university research makes it inevitable that the majority of the funds come from the government. There are, however, a number of dangers involved in such a financial liaison (Maccoby, 1964; Orlans, 1962; Lapp, 1962):

1. Government-financed research can become narrow and confined to the specific purposes of federal agencies. Fiscally confining the purview of university research violates the purpose of such research within the university: to expand knowledge in all spheres of human endeavor.
2. Large-scale, government-financed research tends to be bureaucratized, increasing the potential for a conservative, rigid, and efficiency-oriented administrative apparatus that could, at times, stifle creative research. In fact, bureaucratized research can become banal because incumbents within both the federal and the university research bureaucracies are more likely to seek to avoid controversy (Maccoby, 1964). Bureaucratic preferences for safe, predictable, and noncontroversial findings can, of course, run counter to basic university goals revolving around the free expansion of knowledge. Furthermore, bureaucratized research tends to be atheoretical since theoretical work cannot be easily measured and recorded by bureaucrats concerned with demonstrating output and efficiency for each research dollar. Routine, atheoretical, and applied experiments are thus highly functional for research bureaucracies, but are often less useful from the standpoint of developing science.
3. In accepting money from the federal government—a good deal of which comes from the Pentagon—the university accepts and

supports the current ranking of national priorities. The university as a place of free inquiry, where assumptions of all kinds should be explored, can thus be put in a position of implicitly supporting the very societal conditions that it must, ideally, skeptically analyze. Under these conditions some researchers might be reluctant to speak out on issues—even when they have considerable expertise—because they fear the loss of lucrative and prestigious research contracts or because of their inability to see through the bureaucratic maze to the potential dangers of their work. As Robert Lapp (1962:21) notes, for researchers involved in work on "gyro-mechanisms, on miniaturized electronics, on plasma physics . . . [it is] easy to forget the monstrous machines of destruction to which their work is contributing."

4. Research funded to meet current national priorities indirectly shapes the programs and structure of the university with respect to "the kind of staff it hires, the types of buildings and laboratories it builds, the space it assigns to different activities, the types of academic programs it permits to grow fastest, the distribution of its faculty efforts between research and teaching, and the attention its faculty gives to university affairs" (Sewell, 1971:115). While the dangers of open political manipulation are obvious, these kinds of subtle alterations of the university's direction by the lure of the federal dollar could potentially pose a danger to academic freedom and inquiry.

In addition to direct federal funding of research, the university maintains many other ties to its institutional environment: Universities own stock in corporations, many of which are primary defense contractors; universities are often large landholders and, in some instances, slum lords; they compete for lucrative research contracts, much like business corporations; their faculty members often act as consultants for both government and business; and members of their boards of trustees are usually prominent businessmen, frequently from the companies with whom the universities do business (Ridgeway, 1968). Many of these connections are financially necessary to maintain the solvency of the university. To sever them completely would require a drastic increase in tuition at private universities and an increase in taxes for state campuses.

This financial dependency of the university on its institutional environment—from government research to stockholdings—presents a preplexing dilemma: What kinds of institutional connections should universities have, and which ones can it sever without biting the hand that feeds it? To cut itself off completely from the government and business would destroy the university. Universities cannot survive on tuition and the benevolence of foundations, as many critics advocating total withdrawal into the ivory tower fail to realize. One "solution" to the dilemma is for the university to make explicit all external connections and for students, faculty, and administrators to decide which ties should be broken. The intemperance of radical and liberal elements of the university community could be mollified by coalitions of conservative administrators and faculty, while the tendency of conservatives to underemphasize ethical and educational integrity will be partially overcome by coalitions of liberal-to-radical students and faculty. Out of such compromises in committees where students, faculty, and administrators have representation and voting power, the university can maintain those financially necessary linkages that do not undermine academic freedom while also maintaining a commitment to undergraduate education, humane and moral principles, the university's function as a free and broad-based research institution, and its function as skeptic and critic of policies in the broader society.

No permanent solution to the dilemma is possible. However, the university community will probably have to accept a *continual* conflict and dialogue over the issue of its affiliations. This dialogue must be institutionalized so that it takes the form of dialogue and compromise among conflicting factions rather than the confrontation politics so evident in the 1960s.

RESOLVING THE PROBLEMS OF HIGHER EDUCATION: THE DILEMMA OF PRIORITIES

Universities have five principal functions:
1. They are charged with the socialization of general skills and knowledge.
2. In doing so, especially in a credentialed society, they place and allocate people in the broader society.
3. They store and preserve the culture of a society—its history, lore, technology, and general fund of knowledge.
4. They expand the cultural storehouse in a society through research in a wide variety of fields.
5. They are involved in transforming the society on a broad front, whether through research innovations, criticism of existing governmental policies and priorities, or special educational programs.

All of these are proper functions for universities and colleges. However, which ones should have priority is currently in dispute

SOCIOLOGICAL INSIGHTS

WHY DID STUDENTS REVOLT?

In the 1960s, and briefly in the early 1970s, college and university campuses were often scenes of confrontation and violence between students and forces of social control. Why did this revolt occur? Many scholars have sought to answer this question. Below, the general profile of their findings are summarized.

The complaints of students in the 1960s were well known: Universities are too impersonal; they emphasize narrow specialization; they underemphasize undergraduate education in favor of graduate education and research; they interfere in students' private and personal lives; they have been co-opted by government and industry, while remaining indifferent to major social problems; and they have actually contributed to these problems in their admission, personnel, and financial policies (Sewell, 1971). Since these conditions existed for decades, it was not just the dilemmas of university structure that caused the revolt. Rather, a new kind of student entered this structure in the late 1960s, and these students were less tolerant of university and societal structure.

Most studies of student activists indicate that they come from affluent, middle-class backgrounds. Student leaders tended to come from families in which both parents were well educated and in which moral and ethical issues were taken seriously. Activist leaders, then, were much like their parents: questioning, skeptical, and critical of the society in which they lived (Flacks, 1970a, 1970b, 1967; Keniston, 1970, 1969a, 1969b, 1968).

Youths from affluent, liberal backgrounds where middle-class values and life-styles were questioned eventually confronted the realities of the broader society. Their values and occupational aspirations were deviant and had little place for expression and realization. There were few notches in either the economy or government bureaucracies for such youth, for almost all job alternatives were visualized as too authoritarian, too constraining of self-expression and human dignity, and too irrelevant to, if not supportive of, society-wide problems of injustice, discrimination, and inequality. Events of the 1960s made students even more aware of how few alternatives they had. Because of the war in Vietnam, male students had to choose among fighting, leaving the country, going to jail, or hiding in the impersonal university structure.

Aggravating this situation was the status of students as a minority caught at the juncture of postadolesence and preadulthood (Horowitz and Friedland, 1970:118–148). Physically, intellectually, and psychologically students are adults, and yet they are dependent for resources on their "more adult" parents. Students thus remained disconnected from the broader society, while being concentrated in what were often exploitive student housing ghettos and impersonal university structures that often operated as heavy-handed *in locus parentis* institutions.

The modern university increasingly approximates, to use a polemical phrase, a "knowledge factory" (Horowitz and Friedland, 1970). It is heavily bureaucratized and often appears, from a student's perspective, concerned as much with the efficient processing of students as with their education. For students committed to values emphasizing humaneness and freedom for self-expression, the rigidities of the university bureaucracy were difficult to tolerate.

Students have always grumbled about the impersonality of large, bureaucratized universities. But for the sons and daughters of educated, affluent professionals who have instilled an ethic of education for its own sake, the factory-like university system—stamping out properly credentialed "cogs" to be fed into a bureaucratized society—became, for some, the symbol of the mass society and culture they deplored; it became a part of the "corrupt" society that must be either changed or destroyed. The latter sentiment was especially likely in large, research-oriented universities where the connections among the university, government, and industry were so extensive as to give the appearance of one large "establishment."

Three conditions—the perceived incongruity between what affluent students thought should be and what was; the situation of being an exploited minority; and, the bureaucratized, factory-like university—interacted, in ways not fully understood, to generate student unrest in the 1960s. These same conditions no longer appear to generate violent protest, yet their persistence poses an interesting question: Could a revolt occur again?

and is at the core of most problems confronting higher education in America. The dilemmas of teaching versus research, of university involvement with government and industry, of student dissatisfaction with the academic bureaucracy, and of the failure of universities to address many social problems are all a reflection of the failure to establish priorities. Since universities and colleges are always short of funds, it is not possible to perform all functions equally. Priorities must be established, and discussion and conflict are inevitable.

In making the hard choices in the coming decades, a number of critical questions will be asked: First, can the university educate a near majority of the population? The education ethic has created a situation where all youths and their parents feel they must go to college. Compounding this compulsion is the fact that employers often require college credentials as a condition of employment. Should both the education ethic and the concern with credentials be deemphasized, and should the university cease being society's gatekeeper? For indeed, is a college education critical for most jobs in the American economy?

Second, should the university continue to engage in basic research while cutting back on some of the applied research it currently undertakes? As long as the university is dependent on applied research funds, does it run the danger of being co-opted by those agencies and enterprises that pay its bills?

Third, can the university transform society? Or, can problems of poverty, racism, urban decay, and inequality only be resolved by changes in the broader society? Do university personnel have an obligation to speak out on these issues, to address them in the classroom, and to consult with and criticize policy makers? But, can universities be staging areas for political protest?

While universities appear tranquil in the mid 1970s, they must operate under difficult financial problems. These physical problems will make questions of priorities and function even more important as colleges and universities begin to adjust to leveling student enrollments and severe economic difficulties.

PART TWO
PROBLEMS OF STRATIFICATION IN AMERICA

The existence of inequality has been a fact of social life ever since human technology first allowed for the creation of a surplus above and beyond bare subsistence needs, and once a surplus had been created, humans have competed and fought for a share (Lenski, 1966; Turner and Starnes, 1976). Human affairs are now dominated by such protein questions as: Who gets how much of the surplus? Are there vast inequalities in its distribution? Can people improve their chances at getting more surplus in their lifetime?[1] The answers to such questions can reveal a great deal about the structure of a society. And as will become evident, inequality is the result of how basic institutions are structured. For people's access to valued resources is determined by the structure of the basic institutions of economy, government, law, family, and education (Turner, 1972b). Therefore, in analyzing the causes of inequality, and its consequences for social problems, an understanding of how basic institutions operate to limit or open people's access to resources is necessary.

Part Two will be divided into three interrelated topics, all of which pose problems of structure for America: (1) the overall system of inequality, (2) the creation of a vast pocket of poverty from this system, and (3) the maintenance of racial and ethnic discrimination by this system of inequality.

INEQUALITY

Various cultural and social forces have perpetuated a system of inequality in the United States, a system that has changed little over the last 25 years. While there is affluence among the large middle classes, the lowest ranks and those in minority categories are not much better off, relative to the rest of the population, than they were immediately after World War II. Thus, despite a War on Poverty and widely publicized ameliorative legislation, there has been little if any change in the pattern of inequality in the United States. Such stability in the resource distribution can either be viewed as a problem or seen as an index of the respective abilities of individuals. But, as will become evident in Chapter 7, inequality in resource distribution has little to do with the ability and merit of individuals in American society. Rather, inequality in America reflects powerful economic and political forces that are legitimized by dominant cultural beliefs that serve to maintain a consistent pattern of inequality.

POVERTY

One of the results of the current system of inequality in America is a vast pocket of poverty in the midst of the most affluent land in the world. Historically, poverty has periodically been rediscovered in America.

[1] Obviously, such a conceptualization of stratification is extremely simple and narrow, but it is sufficient for the purposes of the chapters in this part. For more detailed, analytical discussions of stratification, see Parsons, 1953; Hodges, 1964; Lenski, 1966; Heller, 1969; Mayer and Buckley, 1970; and Williams, 1970:99–165; Turner and Starnes, 1976.

In the 1960s, for example, one such rediscovery occurred, and as will be discussed in the chapter on poverty, two contrasting conceptions of why people are poor emerged. These two concepts, in turn, dictated entirely different programs of how to eradicate widespread poverty in the midst of affluence (Skolnick & Currie, 1970:19–22).

One conception viewed poverty as a failure of certain segments of the population to become modernized. Poverty was seen as a separate and deviant culture, transmitted from generation to generation, that kept the poor from access to the mainstream of American life. From this viewpoint, poverty could only be eradicated by a massive assault on the habits, life-styles, values, beliefs, and aspirations of the poor in order to "bring them into line" with those of the middle class. Government programs, then, were to be directed at the impoverished young in an effort to resocialize and retrain them so that they could fit into the American way of life (Gans, 1969).

A second conception of poverty emerging in the 1960s held that the plight of the poor was not the result of their cultural deficiencies, but of how the wealth was distributed in America. The poor were poor not because of their cultural shortcomings, but because of a well-institutionalized and established system of inequality that consistently favored the wealthy and affluent. To eradicate poverty would therefore involve more than intervention in the life-styles of the poor, it would encompass an attack on the basic institutions and cultural beliefs supporting the system of unequal resource distribution.

RACIAL AND ETHNIC DISCRIMINATION

Inequality and poverty are compounded by a third dimension in America: race and ethnicity. In addition to the conditions maintaining the current system of inequality and impoverishment of millions, there are a series of discriminatory forces that operate against certain racial and ethnic groups. The widespread poverty among racial and ethnic groups is not the result of biological inferiority, nor is it just a matter of cultural deprivation. Rather, it is social institutions such as the economy, the law, the government, and the educatonal system that, by favoring the white majority, discriminate against members of the minority.

Chapter 6

INEQUALITY IN AMERICA

Money and wealth determine people's access to prestige, power, health, and other valuable resources. Since so much of modern life revolves around money, one of the most important questions to be asked about a society is *who* holds and controls *how much* of the money and wealth? An answer to this question will offer much insight into a society and its people. For if a few control most of the wealth, others may suffer. And if the same groups of people consistently maintain their privilege over several generations, while other groups live in permanent poverty, a society is likely to reveal restrictive and discriminatory social patterns. Thus, not only does the distribution of wealth affect people's life-styles, but it also has implications for virtually all activity in the society. Indeed, the existence of poverty, the nature of racial and ethnic discrimination, the rates of crime, the administration of justice, the political process, the quality of education, the operation of the economy, and the profile of communities are all influenced by the degree of inequality in a society.

THE PROFILE OF INEQUALITY

How much inequality exists in America? There are two types of statistical indicators of inequality that can give a tentative answer to this question: income distribution and asset (wealth) distribution. Income distribution refers to how much of the total income in a given year different segments of the population command, while asset distribution concerns what proportion of all the valuable assets—money, cars, stocks, bonds, homes, and the like—are held by different segments of the population. More is known about income than asset distribution primarily because the government has been collecting data on people's incomes through the Census

Bureau and Internal Revenue Service. The government, however, has not collected recent data on how and where wealth has been accumulating—thus forcing reliance upon data that are over a decade old.

In Table 5, the distribution of family income for the last 25 years is reported.[1] To read the table it is necessary to know what an "income fifth" is. Basically, income fifths are statistical groupings and are constructed by rank ordering every family in America by its total income for a given year—from the wealthiest to poorest

[1] There are numerous studies of income distribution; for example, see Kolko, 1962; H. Miller, 1964, 1965, 1968; MacDonald, 1968; Lampman, 1965, 1967; Department of Labor, *Manpower Report to the President*, 1969; *Social and Economic Conditions of Negroes in the United States,* Current Population Reports, No. 24, 1967; Schaffer, Schaffer, Ahrenholz, and Prigmore, 1970: 28–66; Solow, 1967; S. Goldsmith, 1967; Turner and Starnes, 1976. For a defense of inequality and a critique of these studies, see Kristol, 1974.

TABLE 5 PERCENTAGE OF TOTAL INCOME RECEIVED BY DIFFERENT INCOME GROUPS, 1947 TO 1972

Income Rank

Year	Total Percent	Lowest fifth	Second fifth	Third fifth	Fourth fifth	Highest fifth	Top 5%
1972	100.0	5.4	11.9	17.5	23.9	41.4	15.9
1971	100.0	5.5	12.0	17.6	23.8	41.1	15.7
1970	100.0	5.4	12.2	17.6	23.8	40.9	15.6
1969	100.0	5.6	12.4	17.7	23.7	40.6	15.6
1968	100.0	5.6	12.4	17.7	23.7	40.5	15.6
1967	100.0	5.5	12.4	17.9	23.9	40.4	15.2
1966	100.0	5.6	12.4	17.8	23.8	40.5	15.6
1965	100.0	5.2	12.2	17.8	23.9	40.9	15.5
1964	100.0	5.1	12.0	17.7	24.0	41.2	15.9
1963	100.0	5.0	12.1	17.7	24.0	41.2	15.8
1962	100.0	5.0	12.1	17.6	24.0	41.3	15.7
1961	100.0	4.7	11.9	17.5	23.8	42.2	16.6
1960	100.0	4.8	12.2	17.8	24.0	41.3	15.9
1959	100.0	4.9	12.3	17.9	23.8	41.1	15.9
1958	100.0	5.0	12.5	18.0	23.9	40.6	15.4
1957	100.0	5.0	12.6	18.1	23.7	40.5	15.8
1956	100.0	4.9	12.4	17.9	23.6	41.1	16.4
1955	100.0	4.8	12.2	17.7	23.4	41.8	16.8
1954	100.0	4.5	12.0	17.6	24.0	41.9	16.4
1953	100.0	4.7	12.4	17.8	24.0	41.0	15.8
1952	100.0	4.9	12.2	17.1	23.5	42.2	17.7
1951	100.0	4.9	12.5	17.6	23.3	41.8	16.9
1950	100.0	4.5	11.9	17.4	23.6	42.7	17.3
1949	100.0	4.5	11.9	17.3	23.5	42.8	16.9
1948	100.0	5.0	12.1	17.2	23.2	42.5	17.1
1947	100.0	5.1	11.8	16.7	23.2	43.3	17.5

SOURCE: Census Bureau, *Current Population Reports*, Series P-60, 1973.

—and then dividing this rank-ordered list into five equal categories from the top to the bottom fifth. Each income fifth is equal in size, and represents 20% of the population, but its proportion of the total income in a given year will vary. By reading down the columns of Table 5 for each income fifth, it is evident that the bottom fifth of the population has derived only about 5 percent of the total income in a given year, while the top fifth has received about 40 percent. The second, third, and fourth income fifths have, respectively, derived around 12 percent, 17–18 percent, and 23–24 percent of the total income. Two features of these government figures are noteworthy: First, income distribution has remained constant over the last twenty-five years; there has been virtually no redistribution of income in the United States. Second, close to one-half of all income goes to only one-fifth of the population, signaling enormous inequality in income for families in America.

The total wealth distribution in 1962, by income fifths, is reported in Table 6. By referring back to Table 5 for the year 1962, it is possible to compare the percentage of the income earned in that year and the total wealth held for comparable statistical groupings. It is important to caution, however, that such a comparison does not reveal the degree of wealth inequality, because wealth is computed for income fifths, and it is likely that some very wealthy families did not earn high incomes in a given year.

This fact becomes immediately evident when "wealth fifths" are computed. Wealth fifths are computed in the same manner as income fifths, except that it is wealth—that is, a family's total assets—that is rank-ordered and then grouped into five equal categories. In Table 7, wealth fifths are reported. As can be seen, one-fifth of the families controlled about 76 percent of all the assets for the year 1962. Phrased differently, the bottom three fifths, or 60 percent of the population, held less than 9 percent of all assets

TABLE 6 1962 DISTRIBUTION OF WEALTH BY INCOME FIFTHS

Income Fifth	Percent of Total Wealth Held
Highest fifth	*57.2*
Fourth fifth	*15.6*
Middle fifth	*11.4*
Second fifth	*8.6*
Lowest fifth	*7.2*
Total	*100.0*

SOURCE: Board of Governors of the Federal Reserve System, *Survey of Financial Characteristics of Consumers, 1962*, Washington, D.C.: Government Printing Office, 1962.

TABLE 7 1962 DISTRIBUTION OF WEALTH BY WEALTH FIFTHS

Wealth Fifth	Percentage of Total Wealth
Highest fifth	*76.0*
Fourth fifth	*15.5*
Middle fifth	*6.2*
Second fifth	*2.1*
Lowest fifth	*0.2*
Total	*100.0*

SOURCE: Department of Commerce, "Social Indicators," Washington, D.C.: GPO, 1973.

in 1962. Such data, despite the fact that they are over a decade old, reveal considerable inequality in America. No systematic data on wealth inequality have been collected since 1962 which, by itself, is a somewhat curious situation since income distribution data have been consistently collected. But it is evident that considerable wealth is concentrated among a comparatively few families.

Table 8 reports the percentage of total wealth held by the wealthiest 1 percent of the population. These data span a greater period of time and have been collected up until 1969, and they give a more comprehensive and complete picture of wealth concentration among the richest people in America. It should be cautioned, however, that these data are not completely comparable from year to year (see Note on Table 8), but they do give a rough —and only a very rough calculation is possible—of wealth concentrations at the very top. In general, it appears that about 25 percent of all assets in America have been held by 1 percent of the population.

While the data are not complete, they do provide an approximate picture of inequality in America. There is considerable income inequality which, over time, has accumulated in vast wealth inequalities. The critical question now becomes: What social and cultural forces have caused, and now perpetuate, such a high degree of inequality? It is to answering this question that the remaining pages of this chapter are devoted.

THE STRUCTURE OF INEQUALITY

THE ECONOMY AND INEQUALITY

The American economy is often defined as a free enterprise system, but in actual fact, it is a "mixed" economy involving intensive governmental intervention, regulation, and control of enterprise and industry. Such intervention and control has been necessary to preserve economic and social stability, but it is hypothesized here that this mixing of government and private industry has tended to be selective: The wealthy and affluent have been able to benefit more from governmental policies than the poor. Such a statement should not imply that the poor receive no benefits from governmental intervention, but only that they are less likely to receive substantial economic benefits than the more affluent sectors.

One way to visualize how economic processes can promote inequality is to ask: What happens to the poor (bottom income fifth), the more affluent (middle three fifths), and the wealthy (top one fifth) in their economic dealings? How does government help or hurt the economic participation of members in these three categories? And why do the economic advantages and disadvantages of the poor, affluent, and rich persist over substantial periods of American history?

TABLE 8 SHARE OF WEALTH HELD BY
THE RICHEST 1 PERCENT, UNITED STATES

Year	Percent of Wealth Held	By 1% of:
1810	*21.0*	*U.S. families*
1860	*24.0*	*U.S. families*
1900	*26.0–31.0*	*U.S. families*
1922	*31.6*	*U.S. adults*
1929	*36.3*	*U.S. adults*
1933	*28.3*	*U.S. adults*
1939	*30.6*	*U.S. adults*
1945	*23.3*	*U.S. adults*
1949	*20.8*	*U.S. adults*
1953	*27.5*	*U.S. adults*
1956	*26.0*	*U.S. adults*
1958	*26.9*	*U.S. adults*
1962	*27.4*	*U.S. adults*
1965	*29.2*	*U.S. adults*
1969	*24.9*	*U.S. adults*

SOURCES: For 1810, 1860, and 1900, Robert E. Gallman, "Trends in the Size Distribution of Wealth in the Nineteenth Century," in Lee Soltow, ed., *Six Papers on the Size Distribution of Wealth and Income*, New York: National Bureau of Economic Research, 1969, p. 6. For 1922, 1929, 1933, 1939, 1945, 1949, and 1956, Robert J. Lampman, *The Share of Top Wealth-Holders in National Wealth, 1922 1956*, New York: National Bureau of Economic Research, 1962, p. 204. For 1953, 1958, 1962, 1965, and 1969, James D. Smith and Stephen D. Franklin, "The Concentration of Personal Wealth, 1922–1969," *American Economic Review* 64:2 (May, 1974):166.

NOTE: Smith and Franklin report that data for 1962, 1965, and 1969 were adjusted to achieve statistical comparability with the earlier 1953 and 1958 data. The result sacrifices their best estimates for the later years in the interest of consistency and, they note, produces a downward bias in their best estimates of wealth concentration. The bias is, itself, estimated to be 10–15%. Thus, the actual concentration of wealth in the years 1962, 1965, and 1969 could run as high as 27.8%, 29.6% and 25.3%, respectively.

THE ECONOMICS OF POVERTY. Along with its enormous productive capacity, the American economy has frequent periods of economic recession. It is during these recessions that some of the ways that the economy can promote income inequality become evident. The first to be fired and laid off will tend to be those who can least afford to be out of work—the unskilled, uneducated, and poorly paid. For these workers all that is available is welfare and temporary unemployment insurance, as is revealed by the fact that one-fifth of those on welfare in a given year are the heads of families who have been laid off because of economic cutbacks (Seligman, 1970). For example, if a factory, business office, or any organization organized to earn a profit in the market is threatened with decreased profits, they are most likely—although not always—to lay off some of their "least essential" personnel who will tend to be the nonunion, uneducated, and low-paid employees such as janitors and low-level clerical staff. These workers are then forced to seek unemployment compensation and eventually welfare. Naturally, if a recession becomes severe, as in 1974 and 1975, then many employees, including unionized and professional white collar workers, are laid off. But in contrast to the uneducated and nonunion poor, these workers have more financial resources, better types of unemployment compensation, and most important, better alternative job prospects.

The problems caused by these inevitable economic cycles are aggravated by a labor market that places the poor in intense competition with each other. In a modern economy in which automation can at times displace unskilled jobs, the uneducated can be thrust into severe competition for the few remaining menial opportunities left on the open job market. The existence of a surplus of unskilled labor tends to keep wages down and place workers in a situation of having to compete aggressively for low-paying jobs. Coupled with the fact that the labor market has been increasing at a rate of over 1.5 million persons per year, the low-income worker, who does not enjoy the increased protection that union membership or education affords, is constantly faced with job insecurity.

Competition in a labor market subject to disruptive economic cycles has kept wages paid to the poor extremely low. Since the New Deal, the federal government has encouraged collective bargaining between organized unions and management. This encouragement has kept the wages of skilled and semiskilled workers belonging to unions sufficiently high to provide a well-above-subsistence income. However, for the protection of unskilled workers for whom unionization is a long way off, only a federal minimum wage exists. This wage cannot provide even a subsistence living for the unskilled, nonunion worker who works 40 hours a week all year long. For example, maids, busboys, dishwashers, some farm laborers, many custodians, institutional laborers like hospital order-lies and industrial handymen, waitresses, low-clerical and sales workers, ambulance drivers, and many other categories of non-union, uneducated, and poorly paid workers cannot earn enough to support a family of four above government-established sub-sistence levels. Many of these workers must seek welfare supple-ments, and others must hold two jobs. Government has been reluctant to maintain the minimum wage above subsistence levels, primarily because of the increased "costs" of such action to con-sumers, as well as business and industry, who constitute a large majority of the voting public. For instance, the most recent increase in the minimum wage to an average of $2.00 per hour in 1974 (the actual minimum varies somewhat in different occupations) was delayed for three years because in 1971, when an increase was first proposed, President Nixon declared that it was "inflationary" and that the increase should be gradual. In contrast, in the same year, auto workers, steelworkers, and many other categories of industrial union workers negotiated substantial wage increases over the same three-year period—increases that were declared inflationary but which were tolerated nevertheless. Hence, unlike many of their skilled counterparts who belong to a union, many unskilled workers do not have assurance from a union contract or from the federal government that even if they work full time they can earn a suffi-cient living to stay off the welfare rolls.

THE ECONOMICS OF AFFLUENCE. In present times of inflation many union and white-collar workers have suffered a decrease in their standards of living, but in contrast to the poor in the bottom income fifth, middle-income groups do enjoy some protection from economic vicissitudes. Unionized blue-collar and white-collar workers of large industries, for example, are more likely to be pro-tected from economic cycles, intense competition in the labor market, and the resulting low wages. For union workers, the union provides some benefits during unemployment, but equally impor-tant, large unions have the political power to pressure government to subsidize industries where large numbers of union members work. Thus, should economic recession cause widespread unem-ployment in heavily unionized industries, pressures are brought to bear that can force government to directly subsidize the industry, to make large purchases in the relevant market, or to impose import-export restrictions in order to cut down competition from other countries. For example, workers in the slumping auto industry have received a number of subsidies in recent years, from devaluation of the dollar, which acts to raise the prices of import autos, to an outright import tax on some foreign cars. Such policies have made the prices of American cars "competitive" and thus kept production, employment, and wages at higher levels than they would be otherwise. The necessity for this kind of governmental action cannot be questioned, but the fact that governmental subsidy of the poor's income has not been so immediate attests to the comparative powerlessness of the poor to force government to intervene in economic processes affecting them. Similar subsidies from the government exist for virtually all "essential" industries that have large numbers of unionized workers. For example, Congress voted and the President signed an income tax bill in March, 1975, that provided purchasers of newly constructed homes with a tax credit of up to $2,000. This same bill provided substantial tax rebates for the poor and affluent, and this fact should be emphasized, but it directly sought to stimulate the housing industry and the union workers it employs, while at the same time subsidizing those who could afford to purchase a home. And while the cash benefits and tax rebates to the poor should not be ignored, no such *job* or *housing* subsidy went to the less organized and apparently "less essential" poor.

White-collar workers also benefit from union pressures, but they are afforded additional protections: (1) Their skills usually make them less in supply, and hence, more in demand in the labor market; (2) they perform much of the "brain work" for the wealthy who possess political power to keep their investments prospering; and (3) the large organizations and professional associations of white-collar workers display considerable political power. Hence, government is more likely to be pressured by the wealthy and large organizations and associations of the affluent to subsidize either directly or indirectly the jobs and income of certain classes of workers. For example, the $250 million loan guarantee to the Lockheed Corporation was only unusual because of its size, but it illustrates a general tendency of government to assist industries with high proportions of professional and managerial personnel. Whether through a "loan," a new government contract, or a tolerated "cost overrun," white-collar industries are often subsidized by the government with the result—sometimes intentional, sometimes inadvertent—that white-collar (and of course blue-collar) jobs are preserved and wages are kept high. The poor rarely have this type of intervention on their behalf.

THE ECONOMICS OF WEALTH. The super-wealthy or top 1 percent own about one-quarter of all assets in America—stocks, bonds, real estate, and utilities (see Table 8). American corporations are thus under a disproportionate control by wealthy investors who naturally have a clear interest in favorable government policies. And they clearly have the assets to finance campaigns, to bribe officials, to lobby, and to exert other forms of political influence as individuals and as directors of big corporations. Their efforts benefit not only the workers of their corporations, but also their profits. By protecting profits, the wealthy can be assured of maintaining their high levels of income. For example, it is not surprising that the exposed campaign financing abuses in the Nixon administration came from large corporations such as Gulf Oil and American Airlines, and trade associations like the Milk Producers Advisory that are subject to federal regulation and subsidy. Indeed, the corporations themselves and their wealthy stockholders have a vested interest in maintaining profits and have thus been willing to use profits and wealth to exert political influence.

In looking at the poor, the affluent, and the rich in relation to economic processes, then, the conclusion appears inescapable—the affluent worker and rich investor are better able than the poor to pressure government into selective economic intervention. Such intervention has less impact for the uneducated and the nonunion poor who are marginal participants in the economy and who do not have the wealth or collective organization to exercise political influence proportionate to their needs. It is these differences in the political power of different economic groupings that *appear to have structured* a political-economic system favoring the rich and affluent, while subjecting the poor to some of the unfortunate instabilities of the free enterprise system and a labor market which has less demand for their services than for the services of the more affluent. Inequality is structured not just in the economy, but also in the political system.

GOVERNMENT AND INEQUALITY

In America, as in almost all other societies, economically advantaged segments of the society have greater capacity than the less advantaged to exert the political influence that maintains their advantage. For once some members of the society have some privilege, it is in their interest to maintain their position; and since they have financial and organizational resources not always available to the less affluent, they are in a position to better realize their interests. Naturally, all segments of a society have some political power, but the critical questions in analyzing how power influences inequality are: How much power do different segments of society possess? And what is the type of power that they hold?

There are many problems in analyzing power, for the concepts and phenomena it denotes are most illusive. Power is usually defined as the capacity to realize one's goals, even in the face of resistance. But there are many different types of capacities, many diverse goals, and many different types and degrees of resistance. Also, many capacities remain hidden and are not easily seen, as is the case, for example, when lobbyists informally, over a long period of time, convince legislators of the "rightness" of their cause. Furthermore, goals are not always clearly articulated or understood, nor are they always uniform and without contradiction. Resistance can take many forms including, for example, conflicts among interest groups, technical difficulties in achieving goals, lack of sympathy among political decision makers, and so on. Another problem in analyzing power is isolating "power groups." While it is sometimes easy to visualize discrete interest groups such as the American Medical Association, the Milk Advisory Board, General Motors, and the like, it is sometimes difficult to visualize the poor, affluent, or rich as a "group," for indeed there is considerable diversity and oftentimes conflicts of interest among subsegments of these rather broad categories.

It is with these analytical problems in evidence that the analysis of political influence and inequality begins. They are not easily resolved; and for the purposes of this volume, they are emphasized as points of qualification for what must be a somewhat oversimplified portrayal of how different segments of the society exert different degrees of political power, and thereby perpetuate the pattern of inequality outlined in Tables 5, 6, 7, and 8. In previous discussions, the poor (bottom income and wealth fifth), the affluent (middle three fifths), and the wealthy (top fifth, and at times, top 5% or 1%) have been isolated as groupings in the American straticiation system. These groupings are not social classes in the traditional sense of the term—that is, groups with common economic interests, basis of power, life-styles, and cultural symbols. Rather, as emphasized in Tables 5, 6, 7, and 8, these are *statistical categories* that group families and individuals in terms of their share of the income and wealth. Yet, because they involve a rank ordering of families, they are a good indication of the relative degree of access to scarce resources possessed by people in America. And while the top of the bottom fifth in a given year may resemble the bottom of the lowest middle fifth in terms of economic interests, life-style, and culture, it may still be convenient to treat these statistical categories as real groupings, and perhaps, even as social classes. It is important, of course, to recognize that such treatment is a simplifying assumption, but for the purpose of analyzing the overall pattern of inequality in America, this is a useful assumption.

With these necessary qualifications, then, attention is now drawn to Table 9 where estimates of the power of different groups are made. It should be emphasized that these are estimates; there is no way to accurately measure the power of the bottom income and wealth fifths, or that of any other statistical grouping. Table 9 provides only rough estimates of the relative degree of power among (1) the poor, (2) the more affluent blue- and white-collar workers, and (3) the highly paid professional as well as the super-rich 1%. It should be recognized that the large middle category—the affluent —embraces people such as auto workers, carpenters, sales clerks, and the like, who may not consider themselves well off, and the wealthy category includes people, such as lawyers, dentists, doctors, college professors, military officers, and the like who are usually defined as only "upper-middle" class. While this categor-

TABLE 9 ECONOMIC GROUPS AND POLITICAL POWER

	Poor	Affluent	Wealthy
(1) Size	Large	Very large	Small
(2) Distribution	Rural and urban; high concentrations in cores of large cities	Urban; large masses in suburb	Rural, urban, suburban; much dispersion
(3) Degree of Organization	Low; few effective national organizations	High; unions, professional and trade associations; the corporations where they work	High; corporations they own and manage; trade associations of their corporations
(4) Nature of Organization	Fragmented; often in conflict; loose organization at national level	Highly centralized, tightly coordinated national confederations with clear goals	Highly organized; covert and overt confederations
(5) Financial Resources	Meager	Great	Vast
(6) Lobbying Tradition	Short	Long; at least 100 years; more effective since 1940	Long; over 100 years; always been effective
(7) Tradition of Influence	Little	Much, especially since 1940	Much, always been effective
Sum Total of Power	Low	High	Very High

ization is certainly an oversimplification, it does reflect meaningful —in terms of relative access to resources—differences among segments of the population. The poor live very marginal lives, the affluent must sometimes scrape and save, but they are able to meet most or all of their material and many of their psychological needs, and the wealthy have little difficulty meeting all needs.

Table 9 does not address inequality as a social class issue, nor does it focus on traditional class distinctions such as poverty, working-, middle-, and upper-classes. Rather, it addresses the issue of who gets resources, leaving the question of how these resources are spent—whether on campers or large cars—to those who wish to distinguish, for example, working-class cultures and life-styles from middle-class life-styles. In terms of income and wealth, the middle- and working-classes overlap to such an extent that they can often be distinguished only by life-style and cultural variables. Such variables do not point to inequality, merely to different preferences for how money is spent. Thus, the affluent in America constitute a rather diverse group whose family incomes range from $10,000 to $20,000, and whose values, beliefs, and life-styles vary. Those earning less are poor in terms of current standards of living in America, while those earning more are wealthy.

In Table 9, seven dimensions affecting the respective ability of the poor, affluent, and wealthy to exert political power are listed (Turner and Starnes, 1976). Each column lists the current situation of the poor (bottom fifth), affluent (middle fifths), and rich (top fifth) for each of the seven dimensions. At the bottom, the cumulative amount of power for these three income groups is hypothesized. As can be seen, the poor do not fare well on these seven dimensions of power, the affluent do much better, and the wealthy do very well.

From (1) and (2) on Table 9, it might initially seem that the poor's size and concentration in the cores of cities and in rural areas might help them consolidate power. However, the affluent represent an even larger group who are also concentrated in urban and suburban areas; and as dimensions (3), (4), (5), (6), and (7) of Table 9 reveal, it is the degree of political organization that can be decisive in influencing political decisions. The poor are not organized; they have few financial resources to support organizations; they have, therefore, never developed a lobbying tradition or effective channels of political influence. In contrast, the affluent are represented by many organizations such as unions, professional associations, and the corporations in which they work; the resources of these organizations are great; and they have a longer lobbying tradition as well as more developed influence channels.

The rich possess all of these characteristics and thus exert enormous political influence. The poor are outnumbered, outorganized, outfinanced, and outlobbied by the affluent and rich. The result has been for the government to establish and implement economic policies favorable to the affluent and rich.

It is not necessary to assume corruption in government to visualize just how the size, organization, and resources of different income groups create a set of political pressures supporting the present profile of inequality. While illicit practices undoubtedly occur, reform legislation would not necessarily alter this present balance of power. The affluent represent a majority, and their organizations have effectively pursued their interests. Because of their ownership of key industries, the wealthy and governmental officials usually cooperate to assure the economic stability so necessary for keeping the large affluent groupings content. While the rich's hoarding of income and wealth deprives both the poor and affluent, the middle-income group's short-run interests—economic stability, steady work, and an above subsistence income—drive them to form an uneasy coalition with the wealthy. The long-run interests of the affluent probably lie with the poor because the wealthy control most of the wealth and a disproportionate amount of yearly income (see Tables 5, 6, and 7). But as long as people are reasonably content with their life-style, and most affluent Americans are, then the political, economic, and social disruptions necessary for redistributing the wealth in America are likely to be perceived as undesirable by the majority. For indeed, people are not likely to seek change in a system that gives them at least some degree of comfort, especially when such change and the resulting disorder might temporarily threaten the continuity of affluence.

It is these fears of the affluent that help the wealthy maintain their wealth, while keeping the poor economically dislocated. Such a distribution of political power has become structured into a dual governmental system for perpetuating inequality. One system is the well-known welfare system which subsidizes the poor, but which also helps maintain poverty. The other, less understood system is the "wealthfare system" which operates to maintain the respective shares of wealth and income for the other four-fifths of the population (Turner and Starnes, 1976). It would be speculative to argue that these two systems are the result of a "conspiracy." Much more likely is the operation of the dimensions of power listed in Table 9 in many specific contexts and for many specific political decisions over a long period of time; and over time, a legacy of decisions favoring the affluent and wealthy have accumulated and now give the appearance that "conspiratorial" forces have been at work. While the super-rich are powerful, especially since the affluent tend to support them, it has yet to be documented that the rich are so organized as to deliberately and in concert establish a dual wealthfare and welfare system. More accurately, this system is the result of more gradual political processes, but its impact is nonetheless profound: the perpetuation of vast inequality.

THE WELFARE SYSTEM. The welfare system in America will be subjected to more detailed analysis in the next chapter on poverty, but it is necessary, at this point, to mention its most salient feature. Welfare payments are always kept low and provide only the most minimal form of subsistence. By keeping welfare payments low, people are often forced to take jobs that offer an income that is only slightly above welfare support levels, since even a small increase in income can represent the difference between subsistence and severe deprivation.

This traditional feature of welfare keeps people in marginal economic conditions and perpetuates their poverty, but equally important, welfare is sometimes a form of wealthfare since a cheap labor pool is maintained for industries in need for seasonal labor or individuals in need of temporary or permanent labor. For example, upper-income groups are able to secure low-cost maids, gardeners, and handymen; all Americans enjoy inexpensive fruits and vegetables planted and harvested by the labors of migrant workers; and all people enjoy inexpensive meals at restaurants staffed by poorly paid workers. Much of this exploitation of the marginally employed is justified by the recognition that they can get welfare when laid off; and even when they are working, some can have their incomes supplemented by welfare payments and programs. Such justifications only highlight the fact that welfare is a form of wealthfare—the more affluent are getting goods and services at costs considerably below what they would be if the poor were paid an above subsistence wage. Thus, government welfare enables the poor to survive when not needed in the marginally paid work force, but induces or forces them to work for low wages in menial jobs without many fringe benefits. Such a system is designed for the "poor's own good," but when viewed from the perspective of overall inequality, it also seems to work as a government subsidy for the affluent and wealthy who need inexpensive labor. This form of government subsidy is but another reflection of the respective political power of different income groups. But it is also one of the many subtle ways a wealthfare system operates to perpetuate inequality. For indeed, it is through wealthfare that inequality in America is maintained.

THE WEALTHFARE SYSTEM. The term *wealthfare* has polemical overtones, but is the simplest way to summarize how government subsidizes the more affluent and wealthy segments of the society. Perhaps the term is inappropriate, since it is intended to cover subsidies to not just the rich, but also to middle-income Americans. It should also be emphasized that such subsidies are not necessarily "bad" or "unnecessary"; on the contrary, they may be desirable and even necessary for economic stability and people's well being. What must be recognized, however, is that in contrast to a welfare system that is highly abusive of the poor, the wealthfare system is highly benign and considerably more generous. And since it is the middle-income groups who most often complain about the high cost of welfare and the welfare "cheater" (Feagin, 1972), it is necessary to document the way government spends billions for their benefit each year. It is this differential in welfare and wealthfare expenditures that is, in large part, responsible for vast inequality in America.

Government subsidizes the well being of the affluent and wealthy in many ways, but in contrast to welfare payments to the poor, the subsidies are not so obvious, nor are they as carefully monitored. There are at least four basic forms of government wealthfare:

1. government contracts
2. government price supports
3. government export-import programs, and most importantly
4. federal tax expenditures

1. When the government grants a civilian or defense contract to industry, it is subsidizing the salaries of workers and the profits of owners. Much of this subsidy is necessary to provide vital products and services as well as to maintain economic stability. But as was noted earlier, these contracts are nevertheless subsidies and can be considered as a type of government "make work" for the affluent. The major difference between this "make work" and the forced labor of the welfare recipient is that the wages, fringe benefits, length of tenure, and working conditions of the job are considerably better than those in the work performed by the poor.

2. Government controls the price of many commodities in the market, as is the case, for example, with many agricultural and dairy products. While wage and price controls make regulation at times most explicit, it is the more subtle forms of regulation that

contribute to wealthfare. The actual mechanisms for these more subtle forms of wealthfare are complex, but they involve (1) indirect attempts to manipulate supply and demand, and hence prices, in the open market or (2) direct efforts to set the price of goods and commodities. When indirect programs to manipulate supply and demand are employed, production is either encouraged or discouraged through taxation, massive government purchases, and export-import programs designed to regulate the flow of competitive goods in and out of the country. When prices are directly set by government, they can be established above or below what their open market price would be. If the price is set artificially high, owners, managers, and workers receive a clear subsidy in the form of increased profits, heightened job security, and higher wages. And if prices are kept low, then government usually (not always, of course) makes up the difference with a cash subsidy.

Government price regulation is designed to affect "basic" industries that tend to employ large numbers of unionized employees (with agriculture the most notable exception) and that tend to have heavy capital investment by the rich. Such price regulation is undoubtedly essential, but it is selective: the industries of the affluent and rich are more likely to be subject to price regulation. Wages for more marginal workers outside big industry, such as those for maids, gardeners, dishwashers, seasonal agricultural workers, and other categories of poor, remain unaffected by price policies except, of course, to make these poor pay higher prices.

3. Export-import policies are designed to control the impact of exported and imported goods on prices in the domestic market. To allow the excessive exportation of a good will drive its price down, since supply will increase relative to demand. By allowing some companies to export and by protecting others from imports (through quotas and taxes), government keeps prices high and thus maintains the salaries of workers and the profits of owners. In a world economy that is clearly influenced by international politics, export-import regulation is critically necessary. But again, this regulation has a selective impact: the large industries which are owned by the wealthy and in which the more affluent work are the most likely to be affected. Lumber, steel, cars, chemicals, aerospace products, computers, textiles and many other basic industries are the most affected, and while in some of these industries poor workers benefit, the subsidy more typically assists the already affluent worker and the rich investor. It is in this way that the export-import policies can be seen as a form of wealthfare.

4. Probably the most obvious form of wealthfare is through the tax system, making its operation in need of considerable elabo-

ration. Federal income taxes in America are supposed to be progressive, which means that the more the net income, the higher the tax. On paper, individuals are supposed to pay from 0 percent to 70 percent of their net income in taxes, depending on how much they make. Corporate taxes on net profits are not progressive, since on paper, all net profits are to be taxed at a 48 percent rate. These tax rates are rarely maintained in practice because of conspicuous loopholes which undermine the progressivity of individual taxes, and which reduce the rate of corporate taxation. As will be discussed shortly, these loopholes are justied in two basic ways: (1) They are needed to encourage investment in big industries. (2) They actually benefit everyone, since more investment means more economic growth which, in turn, creates more jobs for people at all income levels. But whatever their justification, loopholes represent a subsidy because they allow some people and corporations to avoid taxes, and unpaid taxes represent lost revenue to government. The extent of the revenue loss is enormous, and by conservative estimates is over $65 billion per year. In contrast the federal government spends less than $10 billion on welfare per year.

There are five basic types of loopholes, all of which help the rich, some of which assist the affluent, and few of which benefit the poor: (1) exclusions from income, (2) deductions from income, (3) tax credits, (4) special tax rates, and (5) tax sheltering.

1. *Exclusions.* Some types of income are not counted for tax purposes and are excluded from net income. Income from an expense account, income earned abroad, sick pay, welfare payments, exercise of stock options, employer contributions to medical insurance, the first $100 on stock dividends, the interest on life insurance savings, and the interest on local and state bonds are but conspicuous examples of a general practice to exclude some forms of income from taxation. Some of these exclusions are helpful to the poor, such as welfare payments, but most favor the affluent and rich who own stocks, bonds, and large life insurance policies and who work in jobs where expense accounts, medical insurance, and stock options are fringe benefits. These loopholes violate the progressivity of the federal income tax structure because they prevent the fair and progressive taxation of income earned by the more affluent and wealthy sectors of the society. They are thus "tax expenditures" for the affluent and rich, accounting for about one-third of the entire wealthfare budget in a given year.

2. *Deductions.* Individuals and corporations are allowed to deduct income-related expenses from their taxable net incomes. But some individuals and all corporations are allowed to deduct much

more than expenses, thus signaling another form of tax expenditure or wealthfare program. The deduction of 50 percent of all capital gains income (the major source of income for the rich), the accelerated depreciation allowed for real estate, oil wells, cattle, or orchards, and the deduction of depletion allowances are conspicuous ways the rich and their corporations protect income by amassing deductions that bear little relationship to costs incurred in making money. For the less affluent and poor, interest on home mortgages and other purchases can be deducted, as can state income, sales, and gasoline taxes—small wealthfare payment when compared to those available to the more affluent and super-rich.

3. *Tax credits.* Some forms of income are given tax credits, that is, a percentage of income from certain areas goes untaxed. For example, the elderly receive tax credits for retirement income, but more significantly, corporations receive tax credits of 7 percent of the cost of machinery. Such credits allow companies and individuals to avoid taxation, and hence, keep their income. While credits give some benefits to small companies and poor individuals, they provide enormous benefits to the rich and large corporations. It is this kind of credit that represents government subsidy for the companies of affluent workers and rich owners, thereby assuring their favored position.

4. *Special tax rates.* Some types of income are taxed at a special rate. The most conspicuous example of this wealthfare is the capital gains tax which allows a maximum tax rate of only 50 percent of that for other types of income. This means that as much as 50 percent of all capital gains income could be deducted (not counted) for tax purposes. And now, the remaining 50 percent is taxed at one-half the rate of ordinary income. Some relevant figures reveal just who the recipients of this wealthfare payment are: 65–70 percent of all capital gains income goes to those who make over $25,000 per year; and among those who make $1 million or more a year, 82 percent of this income is capital gains. Thus, the very affluent and super-rich have their own special tax rate which costs the federal government more money in uncollected income than all expenditures for welfare to the poor in a given year.

5. *Tax sheltering.* Various combinations of tax laws allow people and corporations to defer (sometimes almost forever) paying their taxes. By allowing massive paper deductions, credits, and exclusions from gross income, people and corporations can "shelter" their real income. For example, by using accelerated depreciation— that is, depreciating the entire amount of an item such as a piece of equipment in the first years of its purchase—plus tax credits for purchasing the equipment, a corporation can show a paper

"loss" and pay no taxes, even though they may have earned huge profits. To take another example, rich investors who put their money in cattle ranches, orchards, and real estate, can then take both accelerated depreciation (on items whose value is appreciating) and depletion allowances (on items that are not always depleting) and thus show a paper loss that they then deduct from income derived in totally unrelated areas. In these ways, the rich shelter and protect their income and avoid paying taxes. Allowing the rich to do this is but another form of wealthfare.

How much does welfare and wealthfare cost the government? About $10 billion is spent by the federal government on welfare, while $65 to $80 billion is spent on wealthfare. Some of this money goes to the less affluent, but much of it goes to the affluent and rich. If all these uncollected taxes were collected in accordance with principles of progressivity, and then distributed in accordance with national priorities, then the public could see just how their tax monies are spent. As it stands now, the beneficiaries of tax wealthfare remain hidden and obscured by the complexity of tax subsidies and by the indirectness of the tax wealthfare payment. One meaningful way to visualize just who the beneficiaries of wealthfare are is to compute the average tax expenditure, or wealthfare payment, to people in different income groups. In Table 10, this is done for the year 1972. People making a medium income of $11,000 receive a tax wealthfare payment of about $400; those making over $500,000 get over $200,000; and those earning over $1 million are on the government dole for $726,000. And the poor get virtually nothing from wealthfare.[2]

[2] For a more detailed analysis of taxes and tax expenditures, see Turner and Starnes, 1976; P. Stern, 1974; and Surrey, 1973.

TABLE 10 "WEALTHFARE" PAYMENTS TO DIFFERENT INCOME GROUPINGS IN 1972

Income in 1972	Average Tax Wealthfare Payment
Under $3,000	$ 15
3,000–5,000	*143*
5,000–10,000	*286*
10,000–15,000	*411*
15,000–20,000	*600*
20,000–25,000	*871*
25,000–50,000	*1,729*
50,000–100,000	*5,896*
100,000–500,000	*29,503*
500,000–1 million	*216,751*
1 million and over	*726,198*

SOURCE: S. S. Surrey, *Pathways to Tax Reform*, Cambridge, Mass: Harvard University Press, 1973, p. 71.

SOCIOLOGICAL INSIGHTS

A TAX EXPENDITURE BUDGET

If uncollected taxes were viewed as expenditures, a tax expenditure budget could be constructed. Recently the treasury department has begun to draw up a tax expenditure budget. Below are listed some of the major items on this budget. This is where uncollected tax revenues are being "spent" in 1972. Note how many of these expenditures are likely to go to the highly affluent and wealthy. The items on the budget are listed under five headings: (1) individual consumers, (2) individual investors, (3) wage earners, (4) recipients of government welfare and assistance, and (5) expenditures on industry and corporations. This is the *most conservative* way to compute the budget:

(1) Individual consumers:
        standard deduction
        support of philanthropy tax break
        home ownership interest and tax deductions
        governmental tax (state and local) deductions
        medical deductions
        deductions of interest on purchases
        deductions for educational expenses
        deductions for casuality losses
        deductions for home services
Total: $20.7 billion

(2) Individual investors:
        exclusions on stock dividends
        exclusions of interest on bonds
        favorable capital gains treatment
        exclusions of interest on life insurance
        real estate capital gains treatment
        shelter investments
Total: $13 billion

(3) Wage earners:
        exclusion of pensions, insurance, sick pay, and unemployment compensation
        expense accounts
        exclusions for armed service employees
        workmen's compensation exclusions
        exclusions for income earned abroad
        favorable employee stock option treatment
Total: $9.4 billion

(4) Recipients of welfare and government assistance:
  provisions for elderly
  exclusion of welfare assistance
  exemption for blind
  veteran's benefits
Total: $4 billion

(5) Expenditures on industry and corporations:
  investment credits
  depreciation deductions
  capital gains treatment
  depletion allowances
  exemptions on bonds
  exclusions of foreign income
Total: $15 billion

Grand Total: $62.1 billion

In sum, the differences in the political power of different income groups have created a dual wealthfare and welfare system which maintains the profile of inequality in America. This profile reveals that a large number are kept poor, a majority maintain some degree of affluence, and a few enjoy massive privilege. This system is tolerated because wealthfare is not easily seen because it is hidden and often indirect, whereas welfare is highly visible and direct. But no social pattern persists by deception and invisibility alone; it must be justified by dominant cultural beliefs.

THE CULTURE OF INEQUALITY

Welfare and wealthfare are legitimized by a series of cultural beliefs. Indeed, all societies have a set of cultural orientations that, on the one hand, guide concrete behavior and institutional arrangements and, on the other hand, are created and maintained by these arrangements. It would be difficult to document how inequality is woven into the fabric of a society without, at some point, examining some of the cultural beliefs that justify and legitimize such inequality. Without these cultural beliefs, inequality would persist only by the blatant use of force and coercion. Such legitimization in America occurs through two related processes: (1) Cultural beliefs make current inequality seem correct and proper. (2) Some of these beliefs divert the majority's attention away from the privilege of the rich and focus it upon the poor, thereby giving indirect support for wealthfare to the wealthy, while making the majority suspicious of welfare to the poor.

Four basic beliefs legitimizing the welfare and wealthfare systems appear to operate in America (Turner and Starnes, 1976): (1) "national interest" beliefs, (2) "trickle-down" beliefs, (3) the work ethic, and (4) the charity ethic. These beliefs should not be viewed as entirely negative, for indeed many of the benfits enjoyed by Americans are partially the result of people's mobilization by these beliefs. Yet, despite the benefits ensuing from these four beliefs, they do have the consequence of legitimizing vast inequality in America, and thus, it is this particular consequence that will occupy the present analysis.

1. "NATIONAL INTEREST." Tax expenditures and government subsidies in the economic marketplace are often defined as in the national interest, because they allow the society to pursue and meet its goals. For instance, cost overruns to defense contractors are defined as regrettable but necessary to maintain a strong military deterrent; tax expenditures on wealthy investors are deemed necessary to encourage investment in the economy and thereby achieve the goal of continued economic growth; and tax loopholes for corporations are seen as necessary to encourage certain economic activities necessary to meet national goals. By reading a newspaper on any given day, wealthfare programs are justified as in the national interest, because they maintain vital industries, keep jobs open, reduce hardships, stimulate the economy, and maintain the national defense. To some extent, of course, these beliefs in national interest are accurate and do justify programs having beneficial consequences, but at the same time, they promote vast inequality and exacerbate all the tensions associated with such inequality.[3]

2. "TRICKLE-DOWN." There is a strongly held belief that tax expenditures and market subsidies "trickle down" to all segments of the society, even the poor. While this belief implicitly acknowledges that subsidies are initially bestowed on the wealthy, it is argued that the money is ultimately invested, causing economic expansion and creating jobs for all segments of the work force. To a limited extent, some money does trickle down to the more affluent workers in large industries, but very little reaches the really poor and a great deal stays in the hands of the rich. And yet, a cursory

[3] For an argument as to how these beliefs result in more net "harm" than "good" and get in the way of achieving national goals, see Turner and Starnes, 1976.

reading of a newspaper will reveal the extent to which this belief is used to justify wealthfare.

In sum, national interest and trickle-down beliefs legitimize wealthfare. As will become evident, the work and charity ethics justify the current welfare system; and in so doing, they help perpetuate a welfare system that stigmatizes the poor, while keeping them impoverished. Furthermore, unlike national interest and trickle-down beliefs, these two "ethics" bear little relationship to actual conditions, and in fact, they effectively divert the affluent majority's attention away from both the plight of the poor and *wealth*fare abuses of the wealthy.

3. THE WORK ETHIC. One of the most pervasively held beliefs in America is that income should come from work and the job. Such a belief is partly responsible for the efficient and energetic work of labor in America's successful corporations, but it also distorts people's perceptions about the availability of decent work for the poor, while deluding the majority that the wealthy "work" for their income. For the poor, decent paying jobs with some security and fringe benefits are not available; and yet, because they too hold to the work ethic, their failure to secure work is often defined by them and by the affluent as their own fault. For indeed, the work ethic enables the affluent to view the poor's plight as the result of inadequate desire and motivation to work their way out of poverty, ignoring the fact that the pay and tenure of most jobs available to the poor will perpetuate impoverishment.

4. THE CHARITY ETHIC. The work ethic makes the bestowing of welfare subsidies highly conditional in that they should be given only when there is no work alternative. Thus, if someone is disabled, old, and *temporarily* out of work, then they should be assisted. But their ability to work, even at the most menial, low paying, and ungratifying jobs, should be constantly monitored in order to force adherence to the work ethic.

The work and charity ethics divert a considerable amount of public attention to the poor, especially those who receive welfare. Payments are kept low in order to induce/force the poor to work; recipient's life-styles and availability for work are constantly monitored; and people are often subjected to abusive practices by the guardians of the work and welfare ethic (see Chapter 7 on poverty). Newspaper headlines will expose welfare "cheaters" and other welfare "abuses," and in so doing, they will occupy a considerable amount of public attention and foster false stereotypes about the character of the poor. These beliefs, as supported by the media, will justify low welfare payments and other practices that keep the poor poor. But they also divert attention away from the $70 billion or so given away in tax expenditures and the many unknown billions in market subsidies. Moreover, these beliefs not only divert attention away from the existence of wealthfare, but they make many people oblivious to wealthfare cheaters and wealthfare abuses.

In sum, then, inequality is the result of the disproportionate power of economic groups to exert political power. This disproportionate power has created both a welfare and wealthfare state, one of which preserves privilege and the other of which perpetuates poverty. This dual system is legitimized by at least four dominant cultural beliefs: "national interest," "trickle-down," the work ethic, and the "welfare" ethic. It is in this sense that inequality in America is a problem of structure, because it is built into economic and political arrangements as well as key cultural premises.

IS INEQUALITY INEVITABLE?

Except in a few instances of very simple societies, inequality appears to be endemic to human organization (Lenski, 1966; Turner, 1972b). The dynamics of power always appear to operate to allow those with privilege to preserve their wealth; and while revolutions have often bestowed privilege on new sets of elites, inequality itself has not been eliminated. Inequality appears to be an inevitable part of modern societies, but it is meaningful to ask: Could there be less inequality in America? The answer to this question is clearly yes, for American society exhibits vast inequalities (see Tables 5, 6, 7, and 8). Many other modern societies reveal much less income and wealth difference between the richest and poorest citizens.

Thus, while inequality itself is not a problem, the amount of inequality can become a problem. It is argued here that the degree of inequality in America represents an important social problem, primarily because it creates many tensions, conflicts, and inequities in the society. It contributes little to general affluence since Americans could be highly, and perhaps even more, affluent without such vast inequality. Inequality aggravates many social problems because it gives a comparative few control over resources that could be used to address problems in, for example, education, pollution, housing, transportation, crime, drug control, and health care. Further, independent of depriving the government of needed revenues, the possession of vast wealth by individuals and corporations gives them a degree of political influence which often prevents the reordering of national priorities so that many problems affecting the majority of the population can be addressed by government.

In the specific context of stratification, inequality directly aggravates two major problems in America—poverty and racial and ethnic tensions. Poverty in general, and the plight of racial and ethnic minorities in particular, is intimately connected to the forces producing and maintaining inequality in America. And while inequality has consequences for all phases of social life, it has its most direct impact on the persistence of poverty in the most affluent society in the world and on enduring racial and ethnic tensions in the "melting pot" democracy. It is to these topics that an analysis of inequality must eventually turn.

Chapter 7

POVERTY IN AMERICA

Inequality in America has created a large poverty sector. Through economic and political processes, culminating in the dual welfare and wealthfare systems, millions of Americans live at or below current standards of subsistence. The plight of these Americans has periodically been a topic of concern by the more affluent, but this concern has yet to be translated into a series of programs or social readjustments that would eliminate widespread poverty in the most affluent land in the world. Poverty is one of America's most enduring problems of structure.

There are at least two levels of poverty: (1) being deprived and (2) being impoverished. Each of these levels is determined by how far below an established level of subsistence a family or individual lives. Establishing a national level of subsistence for individuals and families in different regions is never easy, but presently an income of about $7,500 can be considered the national subsistence level for a family of four. Naturally, this level is lower for smaller families and single individuals. Deprived families or individuals fall somewhat below this subsistence level, where the impoverished are considered to have less than half that needed for subsistence. A deprived family is constantly pinched to make ends meet; should a crisis hit the family—such as an unexpected medical bill or a period of unemployment—it would be unable to survive without public assistance. An impoverished family, on the other hand, has a perpetual and chronic need for assistance; it is among the impoverished that widespread hunger and starvation occur (Kotz, 1971).

How much deprivation and impoverishment exists in the United States? Has the number of the poor increased or decreased? Such questions cannot be answered in absolute terms because standards of bare subsistence have escalated over the last 30 years. It is therefore difficult to compare the present with the past in terms of a fixed line of poverty. The poor, like anyone else in America, are not going to be satisfied with a fixed standard of living when the level of those around them has, until recently, been going up at a rate of about 2.5 percent per year. If the poverty line were not constantly adjusted upward in accordance with increasing affluence in the society, electricity, flush toilets, automobiles, and television sets would be luxuries. What was once a luxury quickly assumes the status of a basic necessity in a constantly expanding economy.

Using the standards of deprivation and impoverishment in each of the last four decades, two conclusions concerning trends in poverty emerge:[1] (1) The proportion of the population that can be classified as *deprived* has remained about the same over the last 25 years—hovering at about 20 percent of the population. (2) The proportion of *impoverished* has decreased over the last 25 years from around 15 percent to 10 percent of the population. Thus, while abject poverty has decreased somewhat, a below-subsistence living is still common for many families and individuals.

Depending on whether deprivation or impoverishment is used as the criterion and depending on whose figures are used to establish a subsistence level of living, estimates of the number of poor range from a low of 25 million to a high of 50 million. Even using the low figure, it is clear that poverty is not just an isolated problem in the most affluent society in the world.

THE PROFILE OF POVERTY

Some common myths about the poor include:

1. The poor are the lazy and shiftless who do not want to work.
2. The poor are composed primarily of single males out of a job or unwilling to work.
3. The poor are "social leeches" who live off welfare and exploit its benefits.
4. The poor are composed mostly of blacks and other minorities.
5. The poor are isolated in just a few places: the cores of large cities and in the rural South.

Each of these statements is incorrect, and yet many affluent Americans would probably agree with them. In reality, the poor

[1] There are numerous sources that document trends in poverty. For example, see Ornati, 1964; Harrington, 1971; H. Miller, 1965; Orshansky, 1965, 1968; MacDonald, 1968. These figures must be viewed as approximations of the actual numbers of deprived and impoverished because, depending on whose figures are used, the percent of deprived and impoverished varies. This discrepancy in estimates stems from the fact that there is no agreed upon subsistence and poverty level among analysts.

are located in all regions and in all sizes of cities; nearly 80 percent of the poor are white; they are poor not so much because of inadequate motivation, but because of few opportunities; most poor work and want desperately to work if they are unemployed; most poor are heads of families; and the majority of the poor receive no welfare of any sort. Although data are imprecise, the poor can be categorized in the following way (H. Miller, 1965; Harrington, 1963, 1968, 1971; Seligman, 1965, 1970; Turner and Starnes, 1976):

1. About 8 million families and 5 million unattached individuals can be considered poor in that their incomes are below established subsistence levels. Of these individuals and families, around 78 percent are white, although minority populations are overrepresented (in comparison with their numbers in the general population) among the poor.
2. About one-fourth of the poor families in America are headed by females.
3. Another one-fourth of these poor families are headed by persons who work full time, but whose wages are insufficient to meet subsistence requirements. This figure indicates that low wages are still a major cause of poverty and that the poor are willing to work.
4. Over 1.5 million family heads work full time, but are laid off during the year—indicating that another large group of the poor want to work, but are at the mercy of economic cycles.
5. Nearly one-fourth of the poor families have an aged head whose retirement income is not sufficient to meet subsistence needs.
6. A majority of the single poor are young, uneducated, and unskilled and want to work, but cannot find the jobs because of their lack of job skills.
7. Of all the poor, only around 40 percent receive public assistance. Many are too proud to receive it; others are bewildered by the complex welfare system; still others do not know that they are eligible; and many do not qualify under the frequently arbitrary rules of welfare agencies.
8. One-half of the nation's poor live in rural areas, but receive less than one-twentieth of the federal funds made available to the poor. These rural poor are concentrated in Appalachia (extending from southern New York to central Alabama and Georgia), California, the Ozarks, Wisconsin, and Minnesota—revealing a broad geographical profile of rural poverty.

While some individuals and families move in and out of the major poverty categories listed above, most Americans born poor are likely to stay deprived or impoverished. Unlike rural migrants and immigrants of previous generations, the current population of poor appear to have less chance for movement to a better standard of living. In Michael Harrington's words (1968:vii), these poor are the "internal aliens in this affluent country," because unlike previous generations of migrants, they have little hope for upward mobility. They are the farmland refugees, the unskilled worker who has been replaced by a machine, the old and infirmed, mothers of dependent children, high school dropouts, farm and menial workers whose wages cannot keep up with the costs of living. Because these poor and their offspring are likely to remain in poverty categories, a search for the reasons why this should be so have been undertaken by both social scientists and political decision makers.

One of the most prominent explanations invokes the concept of a *poverty cycle*—a circular chain of events that perpetuates poverty from generation to generation. Daniel P. Moynihan (1969:9), who is both a social scientist and political figure, has schematically summarized this notion as presented in Figure 7.1. Limited income results in poverty; poverty somehow creates a physical and cultural environment that suppresses the poor's aspirations, motivation, and capacity to achieve; without these, the poor do not acquire

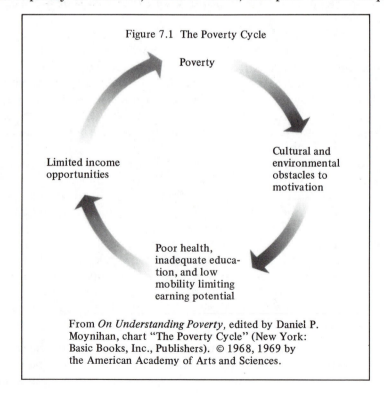

Figure 7.1 The Poverty Cycle

Poverty

Cultural and environmental obstacles to motivation

Poor health, inadequate education, and low mobility limiting earning potential

Limited income opportunities

From *On Understanding Poverty,* edited by Daniel P. Moynihan, chart "The Poverty Cycle" (New York: Basic Books, Inc., Publishers). © 1968, 1969 by the American Academy of Arts and Sciences.

sufficient education, resulting in limited earning potential; with little earning potential, there are limited earning opportunities; hence, poverty is inevitable.

This vision of poverty is incomplete because it tends to under-emphasize the broader cultural and institutional forces within which this cycle operates. For example, it would be difficult to address the issue of limited income opportunities without focusing on the political and economic processes in the broader society that limit opportunities. Limited income is not solely the result of a poor education, but of governmental reluctance to redistribute income, to attack the tax structure that favor the affluent, to finance decent schools in poverty areas, and to provide jobs for those who cannot find them in the private sector. Obviously, most investigators, including Moynihan, recognize the importance of these society-wide forces; but in referring to the cycle of poverty, they have inadvertently diverted attention away from the forces in the broader stratification system that perpetuate poverty. The result of such diversions is for attention to be drawn to piecemeal solutions (Fernbach, 1965). For example, if poor children are seen to have inappropriate values and low aspirations, then a separate school program is initiated; if the poor require skills, then a hastily implemented job training program is established; or if racial dis-crimination is involved, then a new civil rights law or "affirmative action" program are developed. All such programs are no doubt necessary, but rarely have they been coordinated or guided by a true understanding of the deep-seated cultural and structural forces perpetuating poverty. For as will become evident, poverty is not a phenomenon so easily eliminated by superficial laws and programs which change the life-styles and presumed pathologies of the poor or which suddenly give the illusion of equal opportunities.

Thus, the real causes of and solutions to poverty can only be discovered by exploring in more detail the cultural and social forces of the broader society that maintain poverty. Rather than being a cycle of poverty, it is more appropriate to refer to a national "cycle of inequality," of which poverty is the result at the lower ranks. In this way, attention is drawn not just to the life-styles of the poor, but also to the political, economic, legal, and cultural forces that allow a cycle of poverty to persist.

THE STRUCTURE OF POVERTY

GOVERNMENT PROGRAMS AND POVERTY

While consistently inadequate in their efforts, all levels of gov-ernment in the United States have attempted to cope directly with poverty. Urban renewal, public housing, the War on Poverty, and the giant Office of Economic Opportunity bureaucracy, divisions in the Department of Health, Education, and Welfare, and the sprawling welfare system all document the involvement of the federal government and state and local agencies in eliminating poverty. While the data on the poor reveal that various programs have cut the percentage of people in abject poverty or impoverishment from around 15 percent to 10 percent, the percentage of deprived individuals and families who must live below subsistence has remained about the same over the last 25 years. Overall, it must be reluctantly admitted that the government has failed to reduce significantly the numbers of the poor in the United States.

There are several reasons for this failure: (1) Federal programs have often been based upon questionable cultural premises; (2) the programs have been typically underfinanced; (3) federal programs have been piecemeal, overlapping, and fragmented; and (4) none of the current programs confront the real source of poverty—the persisting pattern of society-wide stratification and inequality.

CULTURAL PREMISES OF GOVERNMENT PROGRAMS. Government programs proceed from several premises, embedded in basic American cultural orientations, that undermine their effectiveness. One cultural premise revolves around the sanctity of private enterprise and competition, and is justified by what was, in the last chapter, called the "trickle-down" belief. For example, even the New Deal of Franklin D. Roosevelt and the New Frontier of John F. Kennedy held a vision that economic prosperity would somehow filter down to the poor. However, in light of the institutional forces that maintain inequality, this seems to be a dubious assumption. Instead of directly subsidizing the poverty sector, a typical governmental approach, as in the New Deal and New Frontier, has been to pour billions of tax dollars into the economy in order to stimulate private enterprise and competition and then wait for the ensuing prosperity that will presumably be of benefit to both the affluent and poor. Most typically, however, it is the rich and affluent who have benefited, with poor receiving little aid.

Another way in which this cultural emphasis on private enterprise constrains federal programs for the poor is by assuming that private incentive and open competition must be left intact (Dentler, 1967:101–124). Such a belief does not allow the government to create jobs for the poor that might compete with those in the private economy, and it restrains the federal government from seriously regulating those industries that employ the poor. Since open competition is now greatly mitigated among big companies, and since government regulation and subsidy have become commonplace for large economic interests, it is curiously contradictory to suggest that anything but incentives and open competition for the poor will violate basic American values (Harrington, 1968; Fernbach, 1965).

Another cultural belief inhibiting government programs is the charity ethic which maintains that government assistance, whether through welfare or public works, should be only temporary and custodial. To have permanent public assistance is considered to undermine people's desire for achievement. However, in a society with about 35 million poor, rapid automation, and an economy incapable of sustaining full employment (due to periodic recessions) and unable to provide subsistence wages for much of its work force, this cultural premise emphasizing the temporary and custodial nature of federal assistance is inappropriate. It is more realistic to recognize that certain categories of the poor, such as the aged, unwed mothers, and the handicapped, will have to be permanently supported by government subsidies. Currently, almost all government programs spend millions of dollars and create monstrous bureaucratic entanglements to ensure that government subsidies for the poor are not permanent and that individual achievement is not undermined—a questionable assumption about human motivation that can damage even the most promising federal programs.

A related cultural premise is that a person's income can come only from work and that esteem and moral worth are degraded if income comes from other sources.[2] This work ethic has been translated into provisions, in almost all federal assistance legislation, that require people to work after a certain time period or when they meet certain conditions. For example, in the recent legislative proposals for a guaranteed annual income for the poor, there is an argument over a requirement that unwed mothers work once their children reach school age. Thus, in Harrington's (1971) estimate, by some current beliefs it is considered more dignified for an unwed poor mother to perform menial labor for a below-subsistence wage than to be at home, raising her children. Menial labor is considered work and hence highly worthy, whereas raising one's children is not work, and hence not as worthy. Such provisions do little to eradicate the cycle of poverty, because they force people to work

[2] In 1971, echoing this cultural premise, President Nixon was moved to proclaim that "scrubbing floors or emptying bed pans" is as dignified as any other job including the presidency. Apparently impressed by his own words, Nixon went on to say that: "If a job puts bread on the table and gives you the satisfaction of providing for your children and lets you look everyone else in the eye, I do not think it is menial."

at subsistence wages *and* neglect their families—conditions that are not conducive to breaking the cycle outlined in Figure 7.1.

A final cultural obstacle to eradicating poverty is the pervasive belief in local community autonomy and control, as opposed to direct intervention by the federal government. Such a belief has sometimes allowed local political and economic interests to subvert the good intentions of many federal programs. This belief in local community autonomy has also made it difficult to have a national program and plan for eliminating poverty (Harrington, 1968, 1971). While most Americans firmly believe that federal programs are inefficient and wasteful (Gans, 1964), they fail to grasp that one of the reasons for this inefficiency is that these programs are usually channeled through local community agencies, where the potential for corruption and patronage are higher.

In sum, government programs are often undermined before they are even initiated. Until the cultural premises guiding thought and action are changed, they will continue to be less effective than would be desired. In a way, a counterproductive cycle has been initiated: federal programs start off on the wrong foot; they are, therefore, ineffective; ineffectiveness supports people's conceptions that the government cannot really do the job and/or the poor are simply motivationally deficient and do not deserve assistance; and thus, it is easy to justify terminations and cutbacks in programs designed to help the poor.

THE FAILURE OF THE WAR ON POVERTY. There has perhaps never been a more ambitious program than the War on Poverty, begun in 1964. Conceived in great haste and rapidly pushed through Congress, this program, with its many diverse projects, was to eradicate poverty in the midst of affluence. In many ways, the failure of this massive "war" epitomizes the mistakes consistently made in ameliorative federal legislation for the poor;[3] and thus, its structure is worthy of more detailed discussion.

The War on Poverty and its administrative agency, the Office of Economic Opportunity (OEO), were with the wisdom of hindsight, poorly conceived. In 1963 President Kennedy began to conceive an antipoverty program, spearheaded by a kind of domestic Peace Corps (later to become VISTA). When Lyndon Johnson became president, the public and Congress had rediscovered poverty and were receptive to antipoverty legislation. In the haste to take advantage of such public receptiveness, the program was

[3] For more extensive discussions of the War on Poverty, see Moynihan, 1969: 3–35; Seligman, 1970: 161–218; Levitan, 1967.

rapidly drawn up and pushed through Congress. Ideally, the War on Poverty was to be a broad frontal attack on poverty, encompassing income tax cuts, civil rights, regional development, youth programs, vocational training, and hospital insurance (Seligman, 1970:162–163). The broad scope of the program greatly contributed to its demise, because it encompassed, duplicated, and overlapped with specific programs in the Departments of Labor, Agriculture, and Health, Education, and Welfare (HEW). Supposedly, the OEO was to consolidate and coordinate the diverse programs that were set up, ranging from juvenile delinquency prevention to job training. But in reality, the OEO was automatically placed in a situation that inevitably generated squabbles with other executive departments over priorities and program funding.

Furthermore, the OEO chose to bypass state governments and the local welfare establishment, with the result that the program immediately came under attack from senators, congressmen, and social workers. Additionally, the program was to encourage "maximum feasible participation" of the poor, but laws enacted by Congress and the guidelines of the OEO did not specify clearly what this meant and it soon became, in Moynihan's words, a "maximum feasible misunderstanding." One consequence was for local governments to seek control of each program for purposes of consolidating political power while excluding the poor from decision making. Under these conditions, the OEO soon was in the middle of struggles over control of poverty funds among leaders of the poor, local political officials, and local welfare agencies. Also, despite its lofty claims as a comprehensive program, the War on Poverty became oriented primarily to urban blacks, even though half the poor lived in rural areas and four-fifths of the poor were white. And when the urban riots of the 1960s emerged, the Congress and the public suddenly became unwilling to support programs geared primarily to "ungrateful" blacks. Finally, unlike other types of war efforts in American history, the War on Poverty was grossly underfinanced considering the magnitude of the problem.

In addition to administrative problems, the War on Poverty failed to confront the real issue of income distribution in the United States.[4] Although a guaranteed annual income was entertained, serious action along the lines of direct subsidies to the poor were considered too radical. The result of this major constraint was for

[4] Experimental guaranteed annual income programs have been initiated by the OEO. Since President Nixon proposed a guaranteed annual income, the OEO has become bolder on the issue of income redistribution; but, during the initial phases of the War on Poverty, OEO was conspicuously silent on this issue.

a piecemeal attack on poverty, with poverty workers isolating single "causes" of poverty and then constructing separate programs to eliminate each cause. In Ben Seligman's words (1970:164–165), "If the poor are untutored, they should be trained; if they withdraw from society, their attitudes must be altered." Unfortunately despite the good intentions of the program's framers and backers, the result was a fragmented and piecemeal program with a Job Corps (to train the unskilled); Community Action Programs (to generate new attitudes and political awareness); a massive Head Start program (to start children off "right" in school); a Neighborhood Youth Corps (to provide jobs in the summer); an Upward Bound program (to get blacks into college); and a VISTA program (to encourage general involvement in the War on Poverty). Since each of these programs was underfinanced, chaos resulted as the proponents of each program in the OEO, in local community government, in the target community, in the welfare establishment, and in state government fought over limited funds. Because programs in the OEO and other executive departments overlapped and duplicated one another, additional chaos stemming from fragmentation resulted. For example, a high school dropout could find himself in the position of not knowing whom to turn to: the Office of Juvenile Delinquency sponsored by the Department of Labor, the Office of Education of HEW, the Neighborhood Youth Corps or Job Corps of the OEO, or the local welfare bureaucracy (Seligman, 1970:109).

Although the failure to directly confront the pattern of income distribution can be understood in light of American cultural values and economic institutions, it is remarkable that the program did not seriously approach the issue of job creation. What blacks in ghettos wanted were jobs rather than training in a Job Corps center for nonexistent work. The poverty program's indirect approach of training the young, as in the Head Start or Job Corps programs, tended to ignore the needs of adults with large families; they needed immediate income, if not in the form of direct income subsidies, at least through jobs with above-subsistence wages. It was only late in the War on Poverty that this failure to provide jobs became evident. But by this time, public and congressional support of the program had turned to either disillusionment or apathy.

Considering the handicaps—financial, administrative, and conceptual—of the War on Poverty, it was inevitable that it could not meet the high hopes and expectations placed upon it in 1964. Almost from the beginning months its demise was inevitable, for even by liberal estimates it reached only 15–20 percent of the poor. Furthermore, the OEO was unable to offer proof, even after several years of the program's existence, that it had changed the lives of the poor that it did reach. Congress wanted this proof, and even today, no such proof exists.

As the Vietnam War began to expand in the late 1960s, coupled with increasing disillusionment with the War on Poverty's results, federal funding declined; programs were cut back or absorbed by other executive departments, such as Labor, Agriculture, and HEW, and obscurity began to cover the once prominent Office of Economic Opportunity. It would be incorrect to assume, as many have done, that the Vietnam War, with its demands on the budget, destroyed the War on Poverty. Like so many federal programs, the War on Poverty had many inherent weaknesses that made fulfillment of its goal impossible:

1. The goal of the program was vague and far too broad.
2. Insufficient attention was paid to how monies would be administered and how local and state governments, the target communities, the local welfare establishments, and the OEO were to coordinate their activities and resolve their power struggles.
3. It duplicated programs in other executive departments, creating waste and inefficiency as well as power struggles.
4. The program was underfinanced at all stages.
5. It failed to address the fundamental cause of poverty—income distribution. In so doing, it became fragmented into a series of loosely integrated programs revolving around socialization and training for the young. It therefore bypassed all the really significant institutional and cultural causes of inequality.

WELFARE. In addition to the special programs designed to "break the poverty cycle," the federal government, in conjunction with state and county bodies, has bestowed welfare on the poor. Such welfare consists of cash and "in-kind" subsidies (usually medical care, surplus food, and food stamps) to certain categories of the poor. These subsidies are designed to enable "deserving poor" to survive at a marginal level of existence, while inducing them to "better themselves" through work or participation in various governmental programs, such as those of the War on Poverty. Much of the current structure of welfare can only be understood by examining the history of "charity" in America, for indeed, the present welfare system, or as politicians and citizens alike exclaim, "the welfare mess," is the result of a series of historical events.

These events require elaboration in order to visualize how the "welfare mess" is a problem of American culture and social structure (Turner and Starnes, 1976; Piven and Cloward, 1971).

The history of welfare in America has been shaped by several dominant beliefs which traditionally have reduced perceptions of viable alternatives in relief-giving. One constraining belief is the work ethic—that income should come from work and that nonwork income is undesirable. Another belief reducing alternatives to relief-giving is the charity ethic that views welfare as appropriate only for the "deserving" poor who, if they could, would seek their income through work. A third belief dictates that charity is a local community affair and that welfare should be, in large part, controlled by local officials who know and understand the particular problems of "their poor."

Early relief-giving in America represented a literal application of these beliefs, with local communities and private agencies solely responsible for welfare and with the "indolent" poor subjected to the vicissitudes of the community workhouse. Not until the Great Depression in the 1930s did the federal government begin to assist states and communities in relief-giving, and even then, the federal government intervened most reluctantly. In 1931, for example, President Hoover proclaimed: "I am opposed to any direct or indirect government dole . . ." and even in 1935, after years of massive federal welfare, President Roosevelt maintained that "the federal government must and shall quit this business of relief." Shortly after 1935 the federal government did begin cutting back on its programs, but at the same time the passage of the 1935 Social Security Act was to forge the profile of the contemporary welfare system. Under this act, the federal government would provide "grants and aids" to states for certain "categories" of poor, such as the aged, blind, orphaned, and dependent children (absence of parent). The "able-bodied poor" were left out of the federal government's "categories," despite the fact that work was unavailable. Between 1935 and 1939, most states took at least some of the "grant and aid" money and created the profile of the present welfare system:

1. States were allowed to set their own grant levels, thereby assuring state and regional differences in welfare assistance.
2. State and county governments were left to structure their own offices in any manner they preferred, with only the most general federal guidelines constraining the organization of local welfare bureaucracies.
3. Since the federal government made no provisions for the "able-

bodied," the states rarely made their own; and only with re-
vision of the Social Security Act in 1961 were families with an
unemployed father included in grant and aid categories.
4. In all states "work requirements" for the poor who "could
work" once their "temporary" need for charity passed were
enacted and enforced.

It is this structure, legitimized by beliefs in the work ethic, the
charity ethic, and local control, that was to regulate relief-giving
in America for 25 years, and even today, only a slightly modified
version of this structure is in operation. There have been many
problems with the welfare system since its inception in the late
1930s, but two stand out as most important: (1) the system has
been highly abusive of the poor, and (2) it has perpetuated
poverty.

During the years between 1940 and the early 1960s, the welfare
system has worked against as much as for the poor. At the state
and local levels, there are elaborate and excessively complex conditions for securing welfare, for recipients must be more than
impoverished, they must also be morally "worthy" and eager to
work.

Besides the elaborate conditions imposed upon recipients, they
also must *continually* prove their need for welfare. The welfare
bureaucracy—unlike the social security and veterans' bureaucracies—does not seek out the poor; on the contrary, the poor
must seek out the welfare agencies, fending for themselves in a
labyrinth of overlapping offices, rules, and administrations. Then,
once recipients are on welfare, the bureaucracy continually surveys
and evaluates their qualifications, or "worthiness." In the past,
some surveillance methods violated the recipients' constitutional
rights. For example, social workers at one time periodically raided
unwed mother's homes, without a search warrant, to check to see
if a man was living with her—thereby disqualifying her for welfare.
Fortunately, such violations of the recipients' legal rights, such as
equal protection under the laws, due process, and immunity from
unreasonable searches, are not as prevalent today as in the past
(Ten Broek, 1968). Yet, the constant surveillance continues and
consumes much of the manpower and money allocated to the welfare bureaucracy. If this concern that recipients might be "cheating" were lessened, the size of the welfare bureaucracy would be
drastically reduced.

In addition to the injustices and abuses inherent in the surveillance activities of the welfare bureaucracy, local administrators
are often given too much discretionary power in interpreting wel-

fare laws. More than any other body of laws, welfare laws are vague and fail to specify the conditions under which they apply. This vagueness has become license to bureaucratic administrators to implement policies arbitrarily. Until very recently, with the emergence of the National Welfare Rights Organization and various legal groups devoted to helping the poor, these abuses were excessive and there were no channels of appeal for those against whom abuses were leveled.

In the early 1960s, the various groups representing the poor were able to have the most abusive welfare practices stricken by the federal courts. For example, the "no man in the house rule" for mothers with dependent children (AFDC) was struck down by the Supreme Court in 1968; also in 1968, a three-judge panel struck down laws requiring that AFDC mothers be willing and able to work; midnight raids to welfare recipients' homes were declared unconstitutional; and in 1970, the Supreme Court ruled that welfare recipients have the right to appeal termination of their benefits. While many of the abusive features of the welfare system have been eliminated or mitigated, poverty persists. And in many ways, the current structure of welfare promotes persistent poverty.

As presently constituted, the welfare system maintains poverty by providing subsistence or below-subsistence payments to recipients. In turn, the remaining work requirements and below-subsistence benefits force/induce the poor to enter the job market where, for the vast majority, only the most low-paying and menial work is available. The decentralized structure of welfare, which allows states to set their own grant and aid levels, operates to keep welfare benefits below low wages. For example, one study recorded that there was a very high correlation between agricultural wages (usually the lowest in an area) and welfare benefits in all regions of the country, leading to speculation that benefits are deliberately kept low in order to induce the poor to work in any job that pays above-subsistence wages (Piven and Cloward, 1971). Such a system also operates as wealthfare for the affluent employer who requires inexpensive and seasonal labor, since workers can be pulled off of welfare when needed and then returned to the welfare roles when the need for their labor subsides. In this way, the welfare system maintains a large unskilled labor pool that can be forced/ induced to enter an economic system that perpetuates poverty. These practices are legitimized by beliefs in the appropriateness of local control over the relief-giving and by beliefs in the importance of work and in the temporary nature of public assistance.

While few would argue that the present welfare system is good, there are several cultural obstacles to its restructuring. First, economic interests and the affluent have a "vested interest" in a system that maintains a cheap labor pool; and while it is difficult to know exactly if, or how, local political and welfare officials are pressured to maintain the system, some influence undoubtedly must occur because the needs of some economic organizations for seasonal and inexpensive labor correspond too closely to the way the welfare system operates. Second, once structured, the welfare system becomes an "establishment" that lobbies actively to maintain its current operation, despite the recognition that it is inefficient and does not improve the plight of the poor. And third, dominant beliefs in local control, the work ethic, and the charity ethic make the public fearful of abandoning a system that personifies basic cultural orientations. Thus, the obstacles to welfare reform are many, but the growing recognition that the system is both abusive of the poor and inefficient has led to speculation about possible alternatives. The most likely of these alternatives to be implemented is the guaranteed annual income.

THE GUARANTEED INCOME ALTERNATIVES. A guaranteed annual income would establish an income floor for all individuals and families. The federal government would simply subsidize the income of those who fall below this floor. Many current welfare programs, with their conditions, surveillance, and arbitrary administration could (theoretically at least) be subsumed under one national welfare program. The result of such a program would be to cut back the size of the welfare establishment, eliminate its duplication at the local, state, and federal levels, and simplify administrative procedures. If the income floor were set at the subsistence level and constantly adjusted upward with inflation, abject poverty would be eliminated. The cost of such a program is difficult to estimate, but a figure of $35 billion annually is probably close to realistic. If income tax expenditures were cut, some observers believe that such a program could be financed without seriously affecting the rest of the federal budget.

In late 1974 President Ford "circulated" a tentative draft for a guaranteed income, and at present, this plan is the most likely direction of welfare alternatives. Basically, the plan would completely abolish the traditional grants and aids approach to welfare by taking much of the financing and administering of welfare out of the hands of state and local governments. Instead of food stamps, surplus food, and conditional cash stipends, the tentative program would bestow a cash subsidy of $3600 on a family of four with *no* other source of income. While details of the program are not available at present,[5] some income supplement would be available to families that earned outside income, but at a total income level of $7200, income supplements would cease.

Many questions about this program remain to be answered if it is to pass Congress. First, will there be a work requirement? Will some people be forced to work for low wages in menial jobs when they become available? Second, will the $3600 supplement rise with increases in the cost of living? Or, will the poor be forced to live on a fixed income supplement in times of rapid inflation? Third, and perhaps most important, why is the income guarantee so low, when official government figures in 1974 placed subsistence for a family of four at around $7000? Would not such a low income supplement force the poor to enter an exploitive job market in much the same way as the current welfare system?

The fate of President Nixon's previous guaranteed income program in 1972 can probably offer the best clues as to how these questions will be answered when and if the Ford plan is ever subjected to Congressional discussion and debate. If the President does not do so, Congress will probably add a work requirement, despite the fact that such work requirements are unnecessary in a guaranteed annual income proposal. For example, in a major study of the effects of a guaranteed income in a program without a work requirement, there was no perceptible withdrawal of those on income guarantees from the work force.[6] Rather, without the threat of economic disaster over their heads, workers tended to hold out for better paying and more permanent jobs—behavior that is highly conducive to breaking the poverty cycle. Further, the current welfare bureaucracy will be likely to maintain its monitoring or "watchdog" function and thus subject the poor to many of the abuses of the present system. Coupled with work requirements, local welfare bureaucracies could continue to revoke benefits if they perceived work to be available to a recipient. Moreover, the fact that the income guarantee is set at about one-half the subsistence level, the poor would be forced to seek work, virtually any work, to supplement meager welfare benefits. The result of these features would be for the new welfare system to

[5] Unfortunately, this book is being written at a time when this plan is only under consideration. Currently, there appears little chance for such a program. In several years, the guaranteed annual income program that eventually might emerge may deviate somewhat from the one discussed here.

[6] See Office of Economic Opportunity, *Further Preliminary Results of the New Jersey Graduated Work Incentive Experiment,* Washington, D.C.: Government Printing Office, 1971.

still maintain a cheap labor pool that the more affluent could draw upon when they need cheap or seasonal labor.

Thus, for the Ford Plan, or any subsequent income guarantee plan, to avoid the problems of Nixon's previous proposal and for the income guarantee concept to represent a real alternative to the present system,[7] it is, first, necessary to enact an adequate guarantee of at least $7500 per year (in current dollars) for a family of four. Second, work requirements should be abolished. Third, to prevent the proliferation of yet another welfare bureaucracy, watchdog functions should be assumed by the Internal Revenue Service, which would spot-check recipients of this "negative income tax" in the same manner as it does those who pay income taxes. In this way, welfare payments would approximate wealthfare payments through the tax system and subject both groups to similar forms of subsidy. It would be preferable, of course, to eliminate welfare and wealthfare through the tax system and simply make welfare and wealthfare direct expenditures. In this way, the $35 billion or so spent on income guarantees would not seem so large when compared to the $60–$70 billion spent on wealthfare. But, realistically, wealthfare through tax loopholes is not likely to be eliminated, and thus, equity would dictate that the poor's income guarantee should be no more carefully monitored than the affluent and wealthy's wealthfare payment.

ECONOMIC PROCESSES AND POVERTY

In Chapter 6, the job market and wage plight of the poor were documented, and it was noted that the poor are in the most competitive of the job markets and that they must compete with each other for very low-paying jobs. As was noted, the federal government has not attempted to intervene in this situation by providing government jobs and/or by raising the minimum wage. In contrast to the government's willingness to intervene in big industry with wealthfare, this reluctance might seem amazing. But, as was discussed, the affluent are better organized and able to exert more pressure on the government than are the poor.

Aside from these economic processes, another discriminatory situation has become evident: The poor pay more than the more affluent in the market for what they get (Caplovitz, 1963). Because their incomes are low, the poor automatically pay a higher proportion of it than do the more affluent for basic necessities such as

[7] For discussions of the guaranteed annual income, see Harrington, 1971; National Welfare Rights Organization, 1969; Rainwater, 1969; Vadakin, 1968; Gans, 1964; Miller and Roby, 1969; and Rossi and Blum, 1969.

SOCIOLOGICAL INSIGHTS

Below is an article released by the Associated Press in December of 1974. The information in italics marks improvements in the current system; boldface type identifies danger areas that will undermine some of the proposed improvements.

FEDERALLY OPERATED WELFARE PLAN PROPOSED BY CONGRESSIONAL PANEL

WASHINGTON (AP)—A new congressional study describes existing welfare programs **as antiwork and** *antifamily and recommends replacing most of them with a federally administered system.*

The report Wednesday by a panel of the Joint Economic Committee urges that the aid to families with dependent children, **food stamp,** and other programs be scrapped. The Ford administration is studying similar changes in the welfare system.

The program of supplemental security income for the aged, blind, and disabled should be retained, the report says. Welfare eligibility rules that withold benefits from families headed by males should be scrapped, it said.

The proposal recommends replacing the terminated programs **with a system of tax credits and subsistence payments that would be reduced by 50 cents for every dollar earned by recipients.**

In addition, states would be required for at least two years to supplement the proposed new program with payments to families that received benefits under the aid-to-dependent-children program as of December 1976, if the families were worse off under the new system.

The congressional study's recommendations are very similar to proposals put forth by Caspar W. Weinberger, secretary of health, education and welfare, earlier this year. The Ford administration currently is studying the Weinberger proposals.

Subcommittee chairman Rep. Martha D. Griffiths, D-Mich., who released the three-year study and its recommendations Wednesday, said the report's proposals would provide more money for most of the nation's 35 million welfare recipients, while providing incentives to work and keep families together.

The report recommended starting the new program in 1977.

The report says current welfare programs are uncoordinated "with gaps, overlaps, cross-purposes, inequities, administrative inefficiencies . . . and wasted taxpayers' money."

The proposed program, to be administered by the Internal Revenue Service, "Will assure a higher level of benefit accuracy

at *lower cost than relying on separate state agencies,"* the report states.

Griffiths said the proposal would cost the federal government
only $15.4 billion more than the estimaed $142 billion that will be
spent this fiscal year for what was called income security programs.

These include federal payments for such items as welfare,
housing, social services, and food stamps. The Agriculture department announced Wednesday that food stamp recipients will pay
30 percent of their monthly income for stamps, beginning
March 1. They now pay an average of 23 percent.

**The subcommittee said the total value of grants and tax credits
would amount to $3,600 for a "penniless two-adult family of four,
$3,000 for a penniless one-adult family of four."**

**The report said the current welfare programs tended to dampen
work incentives for beneficiaries by reducing net gain from work
to as low as 25 or 15 cents on the dollar in some cases.**

**"Our program is not going to give them that much money.
You're going to be encouraged to work," Rep. Griffiths said.**

She said the program would encourage families to stay together
by doing away with regulations that keep families headed by males
from receiving benefits.

"We are destroying family life in America with these welfare
programs," she said. "If you are only going to help women with
children, then the obvious way to get help is to get rid of your
husband."

The study was conducted over three years. Among its findings
were that the largest gap in welfare coverage was for low- and
modest-income workers, especially men and their families and
that benefits varied greatly from state to state.

food, clothing, and housing. What is more significant is that the
poor are more likely to get inferior quality merchandise, dollar for
dollar, than the nonpoor. For example, the rent paid by the poor—
especially racial and ethnic minorities—tends to be exorbitantly
high, for even a slum dwelling. It has also been clearly documented
that the poor pay much more for food of inferior quality than do
those in the suburbs (P. Jacobs, 1970). Since the poor, trapped in
cities or in rural backwashes, are not mobile, they cannot shop
around as can middle-class buyers, with the result that they are

subjected to the monopolistic practices of local food and clothing stores. Furthermore, since the poor have little surplus, they cannot take advantage of food and clothing sales by buying in quantity. Another economic bite on the poor comes from sales taxes which hurt the poor far more than those at higher income levels. For example, a 5 percent sales tax cuts deeply into a $3000 income, whereas it is just an annoyance to those with incomes from $10,000 to $15,000. (Also, the more affluent can use the sales tax as a tax deduction and thus not really pay 5 percent.)

Probably the most prevalent economic problem faced by poor are the various "credit traps" (P. Jacobs, 1970). Because the poor have low incomes, they are considered greater credit risks and hence they must pay higher interest rates on the money they borrow. Such a situation might be understandable except for the fact that loan companies *actively solicit* the poor's business, since the high risks are not as great as the high profits to be derived from charging high interest rates. Credit managers in poor neighborhoods make little effort to check on the credit of the poor. All that is required is that the applicant have a place of residence and a fixed income. If the borrower cannot meet the payments, the company forecloses, resells the product, and then attaches the borrower's paycheck for the difference. Even in the face of recent truth-in-lending laws, merchants in ghetto neighborhoods are equally ruthless about extending credit. They entice the poor to buy goods—radios, television sets, furniture, and so forth—by offering "easy payment" credit deals. By merely paying "so much per week" (not by the month, as with middle-class buyers), the poor are seduced into buying items with little understanding of monthly costs or high interest rates. One of the principal goals of these merchants is to keep the poor permanently on the credit hook. This goal is realized in a number of ways, the most prevalent of which is to have the borrower come into the store each week to make a payment and then entice him to buy something else on "easy credit."

Paul Jacobs (1970) estimates that the poverty market includes 35 million people having a total income of $28 billion. This market, in the aggregate, is thus "big business," and the poor are simply overwhelmed by merchants and loan companies who, for the most part, take a large part of the poor's income out of the community. Unlike middle-class Americans, who are now "consumer conscious" and very likely to complain about the quality of merchandise, the poor rarely complain and are usually unaware of their consumer rights.

A CULTURE OF POVERTY?

Some of the cultural, governmental, and economic forces in the broader society that have perpetuated inequality and poverty have been examined. Now attention is drawn to a cultural force that has been presumed to exist *only* among the poor. Many authors have noted that distinct cultures exist among various social strata (W. Miller, 1958, 1969; A. Davis, 1952) and that, among the poor, a distinct *culture of poverty* exists (Lewis, 1968). This culture of poverty is presumed to suppress aspirations and success motivations. Oscar Lewis (1968), who has been the most persistent advocate of this position, argues that the culture of poverty is not only an adaptation but also a reaction of the poor to their marginal position. Their culture allows them to cope with feelings of hopelessness and despair that emerge from their realization of the "improbability of achieving success in terms of the values and goals of the larger society." What is crucial to this notion is that, once created, the culture of poverty is *transmitted from generation to generation*. Such transmission puts each new generation in a state of cultural and motivational "unreadiness" to achieve and aspire— even should opportunities for success become available. Included in various culture-of-poverty conceptions are lists of additional behavior patterns among the poor that further inhibit their adjustment to a middle-class, success-oriented society. These include patterns of promiscuousness (unwed mothers, common law marriages), physical aggressiveness, unstable family life, and so on. These patterns are also passed down from generation to generation and inhibit social and economic mobility.

Reaction against the culture of poverty hypothesis has been extensive. Authors falling into this camp can be labeled *situationalists* (Gans, 1969) because they argue that while the poor evidence distinctive life-styles, these styles are not transmitted in a kind of inexorable and mechanical way from generation to generation. Rather, they argue that these distinctive patterns of thought and action among the poor are recreated by each generation as it adjusts to being poor, isolated, discriminated against, and trapped in rural and urban ghettos (Rossi and Blum, 1969; Rainwater, 1969; Valentine, 1968). Furthermore, desires for success and achievement are not absent among the poor; instead they are modified and/or repressed as the poor attempt to cope with their economic and social plight (Rodman, 1963).

The distinction between the culture of poverty hypothesis and this situationalist viewpoint is far from trivial. Depending upon the position taken, solutions to the problem of poverty will vary (Rain-water, 1969). If the culture of poverty is the guiding perspective for a government program, then the solution to poverty is per-sonality change and resocialization of the young because it is necessary to interrupt the transmission of lower-class culture from one generation to another. If the situational view guides ameliora-tive efforts, government programs should be directed toward income guarantees and other subsidies that will remove people from the situation of being poor. Further, if the poor are deemed to hold the same success values as the affluent (only somewhat modified or latent), then programs will be directed toward providing oppor-tunities for the poor to realize these values.

Most federal programs have used either the culture of poverty perspective or a position that incorporates at least some of its tenets. For example, War on Poverty programs such as Head Start and Upward Bound have been geared to resocializing the poor. Other program that recognize at least some of the situationalist's arguments have been geared to providing opportunities in the eco-nomic, political, and educational spheres (e.g., Job Corps, voting rights legislation, and other civil rights programs). However, criti-cisms of such programs are that they do not focus on the broader system of stratification and the structural and cultural forces maintaining the society-wide pattern of inequality. One way to make this critique is to assert that federal programs end up by blaming the poor for their cultural inadequacies, such as low achievement motivation, rather than attacking the real roots of the poverty problem—the present nationwide system of income distri-bution (Valentine, 1968).

Since it is only recently that all the tenets of the situational view have gained prominence, programs derived from its premise appear somewhat revolutionary. Most notable of these programs is the guaranteed annual income, which would subsidize people's income to the point of removing them from the "situation" of being poor. Unfortunately, as noted earlier, the currently proposed in-come guarantees are not sufficient to pull people out of poverty and thus will have little impact in changing their impoverished station in life in either a cultural or situational sense.

Who is right in this debate over the culture of poverty? At this point answers are not available. In all likelihood, each position is accurate for different groups of impoverished at different times and in different places. The poor do not represent a homogeneous population. As Herbert Gans notes, "Despite a middle-class in-clination on the part of researchers to view the poor as homogene-ous, all available studies indicate that there is as much variety among them as the affluent" (1969:206). Some of the poor may be culturally impoverished, others may be realists about their chances in life, and still others may have high aspirations that must lay dormant. Many may need "cultural rehabitation," others special opportunities, and some just an income that allows a subsistence living.

There is an often quoted conversation that supposedly took place between F. Scott Fitzgerald and Ernest Hemingway. Fitzgerald is reported to have argued that the affluent are, in terms of ability, temperament, and other psychological states, basically different from the poor. To wit, Hemingway replied: "Yes, they have more money." This discussion has been duplicated again and again by social scientists who have debated whether or not the poor are basically different by virtue of a culture of poverty or are simply adjusting to poverty in ways that could easily be changed with more money. If Hemingway and social scientists of the situationalist persuasion are right, then an adequate guaranteed annual income, coupled with real opportunities for success, would reveal the superficiality of differences between poor and affluent, as the poor quickly assumed the cultural patterns of the affluent. If Fitzgerald and social scientists who argue that a true culture of poverty exists are correct, then programs directed as resocialization of the poor should be pursued. Currently, it is impossible to know which position is the most accurate since an *adequate* guaranteed annual income has never been tried and since programs based on Fitzgerald's premise have rarely been sufficiently well financed to determine if, indeed, resocialization works. Both opinions are probably valid to some extent for *different* groups and segments of the poor. But until adequate action, using both assumptions, is taken, poverty will remain one of America's most enduring problems of structure.

Chapter 8

RACIAL AND ETHNIC CASTES IN AMERICA

Inequality and poverty are compounded by a third force in American society: racial and ethnic discrimination. Such discrimination has perpetuated a quasi-caste system with various minority groups such as blacks, Mexican Americans, Cubans, Puerto Ricans, and Indians at its bottom rungs. Although Anglo whites constitute a majority of those in poverty, members of certain racial and ethnic minorities are overrepresented in poverty groupings and are more likely than whites to stay in poverty over several generations. The perpetuation of minority poverty is thus one of the enduring problems of structure in American society.

INSTITUTIONALIZED DISCRIMINATION

Discrimination is more than a person-to-person process. It has been institutionalized and built into the structure of the American stratification system. Specific events occurring within the basic institutions of economy, government, education, and law have often had the consequence of denying entire racial and ethnic categories —particularly blacks, Chicanos, and Indians—access to scarce and valued resources in the society. Since there are nearly 22 million blacks, over 5 million Mexican Americans, and perhaps as many as 600,000 Indians in the United States, a very large segment of the American population has been exposed to *institutionalized* discrimination. This situation is reflected in data on income, education, housing, mortality, disease, and life expectancy of these three minority populations.[1]

---

[1] In this chapter attention will be drawn only to blacks, Chicanos, and Indians. This selection is not meant to underemphasize the discrimination experienced by other large minority groups: Cubans, Puerto Ricans, and

1. The average yearly income for blacks, Chicanos, and Indians is, at best, only around 65 percent of that for whites; Chicanos earn somewhat more than blacks, and Indians earn only a very small percentage of the white income. This income gap has been closing at a very slow rate and has changed little since 1960; and in fact, it has dropped for blacks over the last years.
2. These income differences are reflected in the fact that members of these minorities are from three to five times more likely to be in a poverty situation than whites.
3. Members of these minorities are all underrepresented in skilled blue-collar and white-collar occupations.
4. In terms of total years of education, blacks lag the least behind whites; the average educational attainment of Chicanos and Indians lags behind that of blacks.
5. The life expectancy for members of these minorities averages around five years less than that for Anglo whites. Infant mortality rates, while declining, are still considerably higher than those for whites.
6. Members of these minorities are three times more likely than whites to live in housing classified as dilapidated.
7. Among these minorities, death due to disease (especially influenza, pneumonia, and tuberculosis) and accidents occurs at a much higher rate than among Anglo white.

While there are differences in income, housing conditions, education levels, and health among blacks, Mexican Americans, and Indians, the similar plight of these groups is more striking than the differences.[2] The exact institutional forces that have promoted this situation are somewhat different, and the interacion between each minoriy population and the broader institutions of American society has also varied. But the end result has been the same: relegation to the lowest positions in the stratification system.[3]

Asians. However, the growing political protests among young blacks, Chicanos, and Indians make these groups currently more visible than the others and, hence, more likely to be considered a social problem. Also, blacks and Indians are the two largest racial minorities, and Chicanos comprise the largest ethnic group in the United States.

[2] For information on income and education levels for these minorities, see *Census of the Population, Characteristics of Population,* 1960 and 1970, vol. 1. For a secondary analysis of statistics on the characteristics of these minority populations, see Moore, 1970; Pinkney, 1969; Miller, 1964; Brophy and Aberle, 1966; Spicer, 1962; Special Subcommittee on Indian Education, 1968; Knowles and Prewitt, 1969.

[3] For more theoretical analyses of such relegation, see Turner and Singleton, 1976; Blauner, 1972; Newman, 1973; and Daniels and Kitano, 1970. The analysis offered here is more of a description of "what happened." Only partial answers as to "why" it happened are given.

MEXICAN AMERICANS[4]

THE ECONOMIC CONQUEST OF MEXICAN AMERICANS

Mexican Americans settled in the Southwest long before white Anglos began to move westward in the nineteenth century. In the early 1800s, there were approximately 5,000 Mexicans in Texas, 7,500 in California, less than 1,000 in Arizona, and close to 60,000 in New Mexico (McWilliams, 1949:52). Most of these settlers owned land and engaged in ranching and farming. However, with the initial westward migrations of Anglos in the 1800s, and with the extension of the railroad into the Southwest in the 1850s with its resulting flood of migrants, Mexican Americans were "hopelessly inundated by the tide of Anglo immigration, reduced to landless labor, and made politically and economically impotent" (Moore and Cuéllar, 1970:20). Thus, initial relegation of Mexican Americans to the bottom of the stratification system in the United States was a reflection of economic and demographic changes of the last century.

The change from independent rancher to landless laborer occurred first in Texas, where the fencing off of large cattle and sheep ranches destroyed the open range upon which smaller Mexican (and Anglo) ranchers depended. One by one Mexicans were forced off their land; and as the cotton industry first moved into Texas and later into the rest of the Southwest, the displaced rancher and his descendents were forced to become the tenant farmers or the cheap labor of the emerging "plantation" system. In New Mexico a similar process of displacement of small ranchers by large enterprises occurred, although Mexicans were able to retain considerable political power because of their large numbers. In Arizona, where few Mexicans resided, the Anglo economic takeover was quick and resulted in a new pattern of economic exploitation of Mexicans by Anglos. Because the indigenous Mexicans constituted only a small labor pool, it was "necessary" to import cheap labor from across the border to maintain the large ranching and farming enterprises. This process initiated the first of many subsequent waves of immigration that were to place both the indigenous Mexican settler and the new migrant into a subordinate economic position.

In California Anglo economic domination of Mexicans occurred first in the northern part of the state, where large Mexican landholdings were broken up, initially, by the waves of prospectors during the gold rush and, later, by a steady flow of settlers and

[4] For basic reference works on Mexican Americans, see Stoddard, 1973; Moore and Cuéllar, 1970; Burma, 1970.

squatters. In southern California, Mexicans maintained their land-holdings and political power for some time; but with the drought of 1862, followed by a devastating flood, many Mexican landowners were placed in economic jeopardy. Then, as taxes began to rise and cattle prices dropped, the large Mexican estates were broken up. And when Anglos began to flood into the southern part of the state, the now landless Mexicans were used as cheap labor for the large, Anglo-owned agricultural enterprises that began to dominate the state.

In all these states, the railroad was of particular importance in subordinating the Mexican resident and immigrant. First, the rail-road brought in thousands of Anglos who began to push Mexicans off the land. Second, the railroads required large work gangs of inexpensive, mobile labor, that was gotten by encouraging the immigration of impoverished workers from Mexico. As these mi-grants poured into the Southwest in search of new opportunities, the social image of the Mexican Americans who had lived in the Southwest for generations was altered from that of independent landholders and entrepreneurs to one of unskilled, migrant laborers.

The early part of the twentieth century saw an extension of the economic forces that were relegating Mexicans to the bottom of the stratification system. The emergence of mass, capital-heavy, labor-intensive, irrigated farming in the Southwest assured that no small farmer could afford either the capital investment or the labor pool necessary to farm melons, grapes, citrus fruit, sugar beets, cotton, and vegetables. The result was that the last of the remaining Mexi-can ranchers and farmers were forced off the land (Moore and Cuéllar, 1970:20–21). Furthermore, the need for a large, migratory labor force to harvest the crops of these new farms stimulated even more migration of unskilled labor from across the border. And the expansion and extension of the cotton industry west of Texas served as a similar stimulus for Mexican migrations (Waters, 1941). The proliferation of railroads in the Southwest continued well into this century and was also a major force behind the esca-lated migration of Mexican laborers, who were shipped around in boxcars much like cattle.

By the 1920s Mexican Americans constituted a migrant prole-tariat who could harvest crops and work on the railroads. During the same decade small groups of Mexican Americans began to appear in the factories of Michigan, Ohio, Indiana, and Pennsyl-vania. Many Mexican Americans acquired nonfarm skills and settled in large urban areas, initiating the urbanization of Chicanos.

The depression undermined the gains made by these urban, working-class Mexicans and further impoverished the migrant agricultural workers. During the 1930s many Mexican Americans fled from depressed rural conditions in search of employment in cities, but only with the onset of World War II did large numbers of Mexican workers eventually find employment. Many others enlisted in the army and acquired skills there. While the offspring of indigenous Mexican ranchers and early migrant workers were urbanizing during the war, the importantion of *bracero* (temporary and alien) Mexican labor for work in the wartime agricultural boom was again accelerated. When the demand for bracero labor receded in the postwar period, illegal immigration continued, culminating in the mass deportation of millions of Mexicans during the 1950s. Of those who avoided deportation, many became the current migratory work force that harvests the crops of the massive agri-businesses in Texas, Arizona, and California. Even under pressures for unionization by Cesar Chavez and the United Farm Workers, this labor force works at low wages (yielding only a poverty-level living) and frequently under unsanitary and unsafe conditions. For those who escape to the cities to join the already large urban concentrations of Chicanos in California and Texas, few economic opportunities are available (Kramer, 1970:171; Heller, 1966; Madsen, 1964).

Today urban Chicanos, who constitute a majority of the Mexican-American population, suffer from severe economic discrimination (Moore and Cuéllar, 1970:60–65; P. Bullock, 1964; Ramirez, 1967). Chicanos get lower pay than Anglos for the same kind of work. They are grossly underrepresented in highly unionized occupations because of union discrimination. Their lack of formal education is apparently used to keep them from even those jobs that do not require extensive education. Even with education, Chicanos receive less pay and lower job status than Anglos with equivalent education.

In sum, the economic forces operating against Mexican Americans display a unique pattern. Initial agricultural development displaced the early Mexican settler. Further economic development and the extension of railroads into the Southwest created a demand for cheap and mobile labor, which in turn stimulated massive migration from Mexico. During the twentieth century Mexican Americans have become highly urbanized and now constitute a large underemployed urban proletariat that is predominantly poor. Like the Indians, Mexican Americans have suffered the economic abuses directed against a colonized, indigenous population; and like the black slaves, Mexican Americans have suffered abuses directed against an immigrant people brought in to perform cheap agricultural labor. The economic exploitation of Chicanos has not been as great as it has been for either blacks or Indians; and yet, the fact that Chicanos have had to endure *both* forms of exploitation has pushed them into the bottom rung of the American stratification system.

POLITICAL DISCRIMINATION

Except in New Mexico, and for a period in southern California, Mexican Americans have suffered from political discrimination. The original Mexican-American settlers became politically disfranchised when they lost their land to the large agricultural, ranching, mining, and railroad interests that controlled state legislators and sought to keep Mexicans in an economically and politically subordinate position. These efforts were promoted by the fact that many migrant Mexicans were aliens and had no voting rights. Over time, as both indigenous and migrant Mexicans became defined as one social category, the Anglo majority established a variety of procedures—from a poll tax to open primaries—to keep impoverished Mexicans out of the political arena. And while these political tactics are no longer legal, Chicanos are now only beginning to enter the political arena which for so long was openly discriminatory.

Early Mexican settlers and migrants also suffered from the lack of a well-developed political structure in the Southwest (Moore and Cuéllar, 1970:33). Unlike the early European migrants in the Northeast, Mexican migrants confronted a loosely organized political system since there were few large cities to support political machines and since party organization within the southwestern states or territories was only in its incipiency. There were simply no political opportunities, and thus Mexican Americans were not able to acquire training in either big-city or state politics—a condition that had greatly facilitated the social mobility of early European ethnic groups. In Texas and California, where the political structure was most developed, large economic interests controlled the state legislatures and kept Mexicans confined to migrant shantytowns where they remained politically isolated.

The prolonged border dispute between Mexico and the United States further isolated Mexican settlers and migrants from Anglo political institutions. The open war between the United States and Mexico in 1846 placed Mexican Americans in the unfavorable position of being identified with a political enemy. Even after the Treaty of Guadalupe Hidalgo, which ended the war, border raids and skirmishes between Anglos and Mexicans persisted for nearly 60 years. Mexican Americans remained politically isolated for fear of arousing Anglo resentment stemming from these prolonged border skirmishes.

This legacy of political disfranchisement has followed Chicanos as they have migrated into the growing urban areas of the Southwest over recent decades. Many urbanites have not even had citizenship status. And the rate of naturalization of migrants has been very low because migrants have tended to retain political loyalties to Mexico, while harboring a distrust of the American political system (Grebler, 1966). This distrust was justified in the 1950s during "Operation Wetback," when over 3 million alien Mexicans were apprehended, without benefit of a court-issued warrant of arrest, and expelled from the country. Aside from illegal apprehension, expulsion was often done illegally, without any attention to due processes of law (a court hearing, the right to a lawyer and to plead a case, etc.). Furthermore, hundreds of thousands of American citizens who "looked Mexican" were stopped, searched, and forced to prove their citizenship—a practice that would not be tolerated by the Anglo population (Moore and Cuéllar, 1970:43).

The distrust of American governmental agencies arising out of Operation Wetback persists to the present day. Although there has been a growing participation of Mexican Americans in state legislatures and Congress, they are still underrepresented in most local, state, and national bodies. This situation is reflected in the lack of federal programs directed at Mexican *barrios* (slums) in the large cities of the Southwest; especially notable is the absence of Mexican-American programs in the War on Poverty. While various economic and political organizations of Chicanos have emerged over the last 20 years, these groups do not exert the political pressure proportionate to the size of the Mexican-American population —the nation's second largest disadvantaged minority. The burgeoning Chicano movement and the rise of national leaders, such as Cesar Chavez, to positions of political prominence have so far done little to balance the historical legacy of political discrimination against, and isolation of, Mexican Americans.

EDUCATIONAL DISCRIMINATION

While their average educational attainment varies from state to state, from a low in Texas to a high in California, Mexican Americans as an aggregate lag behind most other minorities in the number of years of schooling completed (Miller, 1964; Grebler, 1967; Stoddard, 1973). Despite a large increase over the last 20 years in the number of school years completed, Mexican Americans are still far behind blacks, Anglos, and Orientals, even in the 14 to 24-year-old group where dramatic changes in educational achievement would be most evident (Grebler, 1967).

One reason for such low educational attainment has been the

resentment of Mexican Americans against their confinement, as outsiders in a community, to segregated, inferior schools. Originally and even today in rural communities, Mexican Americans have been forced into labor camps; as the children of farm laborers became resentful of their segregation into inferior schools, they tended to drop out and subsequently find themselves in the same jobs as their immigrant fathers. Considerable residential and educational segregation persists in urban areas; Chicano youths must endure inferior teachers, dilapidated school facilities, and a white Anglo curriculum. While these urban students go further in school than their rural counterparts, many still drop out of high school and less than 10 percent go to college.

In addition to de facto school segregation stemming from patterns of residential segregation, Chicano youths are often deliberately segregated from Anglos. Such segregation, especially in Texas, is justified by a series of outdated stereotypes. Teachers and administrators tend to assume that the bilingual student will automatically have learning problems and that the Mexican-American student, as a member of a traditional, peasant culture, will not be highly motivated to achieve. It is then assumed that Chicano youths cannot compete with Anglo children, and until they are assimilated, they must remain segregated "for their own good." The fact that segregation persists through secondary school, where language problems and cultural obstacles would have lessened, reveals the real intent behind school segregation. More importantly, the stereotypes used by teachers and administrators are self-fulfilling in that they are used to justify placing Chicano youths into inferior programs that, in turn, probably lessen aspirations and educational achievement.

Within these segregated schools, cultural assimilation into a white Anglo world is supposed to occur. Often students are punished for speaking Spanish in the playground; the white Anglo curriculum is rigidly imposed; and Anglo dress and behavior codes are tightly enforced. While in some places, such as urban California, the schools are more flexible and accommodating to the cultural uniqueness of Mexican-American youths, a suppression of Mexican culture remains widespread throughout the Southwest. Faced with such suppression, Mexican-American youths simply leave school at the earliest possible age—thus decreasing their job opportunities.

LAW AND MEXICAN AMERICANS

Mexican Americans have long been subject to extensive surveillance by local, state, and federal enforcement agencies. Because Mexican Americans constitute an impoverished, physically distinguishable minority living in high-crime rural and urban barrios, local police are more likely to be "suspicious" which increases the probability that they will "watch" and perhaps "question" residents—a practice which may at times be necessary in a high crime area but which is deeply resented. For it must be recalled that it was not long ago that Mexican Americans were subject to vigilante law enforcement initiated by ranching, fruit-growing, and mining enterprises in efforts to "resolve" labor disputes. This legacy of vigilante law, coupled with current police practices, has created a "culture of suspicion" of Anglo institutions that has contributed to a Mexican-American withdrawal into ghetto areas in both rural and urban areas (Lohman, 1966:55). In some states, particularly Texas, Mexican Americans have had to confront special state units, such as the Texas Rangers, who were originally established to deal with the "Mexican problem" (Moore and Cuéllar, 1970:89). It was only recently, after the abuses of the Rangers were exposed, that the Rangers were reduced to a token force.

The most unique feature of Mexican-American relations with the police revolves around the issue of their citizenship. Since many Mexican Americans were imported as alien labor and then deported *en masse* by the federal government during the 1950s, Mexican Americans have always been subject to regulation by the federal border patrol. The officers of the border patrol have wide authority under federal law and it is often used to check up on the citizenship status of Mexican-American families. For example, officers can stop families on highways, go to their homes, enter their places of work, and engage in extensive questioning. Realizing the power of the border patrol to disrupt the lives of Mexican Americans, some local and state police officers have threatened to call the border patrol to achieve compliance (sometimes illegally) to their demands, such as search, seizure, and detention. Thus, Mexican Americans are subject to a kind of triple jeopardy from federal, state, and local police forces that have the power to intrude into their lives and demand proof of not only innocence to a crime, but also of their citizenship.

NATIVE AMERICANS[5]

ECONOMIC EXPLOITATION OF AMERICAN INDIANS

By 1871 all the various Indian nations had been conquered and these native Americans were confined to reservations as wards of the state. While the confinement of Indians to reservations repre-

[5] For recent commentaries on and analyses of the situation of native Americans, see de la Garza et al., 1973; Levitan and Hetrick, 1971; Jacobs, 1972; and Brophy and Aberle, 1966.

sented an obvious form of economic and political dominance, additional economic exploitation began with the Dawes Act of 1887. Under this act, reservation lands were divided up among family heads and individuals in an effort to make each Indian an independent and self-supporting farmer. Most Indians had little knowledge of farming technology and little desire "to plow up nature." Furthermore, the small independent farmer represented a white rather than red ideal because the Indian was more likely to have lived in an economic and social system where there was little capital, no permanent ownership of land, and in which hospitality and free giving were dominant themes. Reconciling this system with notions of the small, independent, ruggedly individualistic farmer was to prove impossible. As a consequence, most Indians simply leased or sold their land to whites and forever lost control over much of their own domain. By 1939 Indians possessed only 86 million of the 138 million acres they had before the Dawes Act, and much of what remained was semiarid and incapable of supporting the growing Indian population (Kramer, 1970:195).

Recognizing the economic plight of Indians, the Indian Reorganization Act of 1939 attempted to encourage tribal corporate ownership and management of Indian land. Many tribes incorporated and have since attempted to develop farming, mining, ranching, and even industrial enterprises. Unfortunately, Indians have had little corporate management experience, and, therefore, well over one-third of those businesses have failed (Brophy and Aberle, 1966:77). Also, numerous tribes did not incorporate; the result was that during the 1950s, many individual Indians who were tired of attempting to farm poor and arid land, "sold" their holdings to whites. Thus by 1960, Indian landholdings had shrunk to 53 million acres (Brophy and Aberle, 1966:68). In less than 100 years after their confinement to reservations, Indians have been forced to give up nearly two-thirds of their greatest economic asset: land. And the remaining 53 million acres of the original 138 million was not capable of supporting the Indian population.

Today most Indians on reservations work as seasonal wage labor on farms and in light industries. Their unemployment rate ranges from 30 percent to 50 percent; and the employment picture is getting worse as mechanization has displaced the Indian from the cotton, sugar beet, and potato fields. Currently, Indian income is the lowest in the nation, with a near majority of Indians receiving over half their income from welfare payments. The worst slums in America are found on reservations; and the young, landless, uneducated, isolated, and unskilled Indian population now faces a severe economic crisis. Because their remaining lands are less fertile than those that were "bought" by whites, tribal farms and ranches are not able to compete with large, white agri-enterprises, and thus, are not able to provide economic relief. Also, because most Indians still lack farming skills, capital, or management experience, a great portion of irrigated farmland goes unused. Perhaps the most successful economic ventures of certain tribes are in mining and timber enterprises, which have yielded high royalty rates; but these resources are not evenly distributed and benefit only a small proportion of the impoverished Indian population.

Since 1950 Indians have been encouraged, with promises of financial support from the government, to leave the reservation and settle in urban centers, with the result that approximately one-half the Indian population now lives in urban areas (Kramer, 1970: 196). The lack of job skills, which has impeded economic development on reservations, has greatly handicapped Indians as they have attempted to enter the urban labor force. Because of job and union discrimination and the cultural differences between whites and Indians, little economic integration of Indians into white society has occurred (Kitagawa, 1965).

Thus, the legacy of economic exploitation, especially the great "land grabs" by whites in this century, has forced Indians into urban areas because they can no longer support themselves on their depleted reservations. Yet the legacy of isolation on the reservation prevents many Indians from making the cultural and psychological transition to urban, industrial life. And the burden of change has been placed upon the *individual* Indian, for white institutions—from factories to labor unions and welfare agencies—display little flexibility in adjusting to Indian patterns. The contemporary Indian is therefore faced with impoverishment no matter what course of action he chooses: to stay on the reservations results in poverty, but to leave the reservation and encounter a white-dominated economic system in urban areas also results in poverty.

BUREAUCRATIC ENCIRCLEMENT

The history of the relations of the Indian tribes with the federal government reflects their status as conquered nations. It was well into this century before military forces had left Indian reservations. Even with the departure of the military, colonization of American Indians was initiated by the Bureau of Indian Affairs (BIA). Steiner (1968:83) has aptly summarized: the tribes were more than conquered nations, they were wholly surrounded by their conquerors, who, guided by their Puritan ethic, set out zealously to "convert the heathen" and "civilize the savage." Indians must therefore become wards and the government must be their guardian. This ward-of-the-government status may have been more injurious psychologically to the tribes than their military defeat.

Because of their ward-of-the-state status, the government was "justified" in regulating, through the BIA, almost all Indian activities and services. No other category of citizens, except perhaps federal prison inmates, have had their lives so comprehensively regulated by the federal government. While the establishment in 1824 of the BIA may have been necessary and even desirable, it forced the Indian population into a state of dependency on the federal government.[6] In doing so, the BIA undermined the Indian culture and their self-respect while relegating them to the bottom of the stratification system in America.

Currently, the BIA continues to thwart Indian self-determination. As Brophy and Aberle note: ". . . the BIA has kept company with many European nations who have failed to meet the needs for developing promising individuals in undeveloped colonial nations so that eventually new formed governments might have trained leaders to achieve political stability" (1966:188). This failure has often been used to justify the maintenance of the Indians' dependency on the BIA. Even in the face of growing Indian militancy, Indian leaders are kept out of the higher administrative positions in the BIA. When Indians do occupy positions in the BIA, they have tended to be subordinate to white administrators and supervisors.

In addition to the failure of the BIA to utilize its control of Indian affairs to encourage Indians to develop their own self-governing and administrative potentials, the very structure of the BIA as a highly centralized bureaucracy also inhibits Indian self-determination. From central offices in Washington, D.C., the BIA fans out into 10 area administrative offices; then into around 60 major field installations, such as boarding schools and irrigation projects; and finally into 400–500 minor installations. One of the persistent problems with this structure is that too much authority resides in the hands of white administrators in Washington and in the 10 area offices. Those superintendents in the major and minor field installations, who are closest to Indian problems and needs, have the least authority; all major decisions must go up to at least the appropriate area administration. This situation has been demoralizing for both well-intentioned superintendents and Indians desirous of responsive action by the BIA.

Another source of incredible inefficiency in the BIA bureaucracy is the myriad of tribal rules, archaic legislative acts, and judicial

---

[6] It is of interest to note that the BIA was initially in the War Department—underscoring the Indians' conquered status. In 1849 the BIA moved to the Department of Interior, where it is currently located.

precedents through which decisions must be sorted. For example, it has been noted that there are 384 Indian treaties, 5000 statutes, 2000 federal court decisions, over 500 attorney-general opinions, hundreds of Interior Department and solicitor rulings, 95 tribal constitutions, 74 tribal charters, and untold mazes of BIA administrative procedures (Brophy and Aberle, 1966:123). In the face of this panorama of constraints, decisions are made very slowly and given an unnecessarily detailed review. More important, perhaps, is the administrative indecisiveness generated by the existence of so many rules, for some BIA administrators have become ritualists who lose sight of their client, the Indian. As is frequently the case with bureaucracies, "the BIA has tended to develop a view that the Bureau and the Indians have opposing interests" (Brophy and Aberle, 1966:130).

EDUCATION

The cultural differences between Indians and Anglos make Indian education a delicate and difficult task.[7] For example, the language and thought patterns of Indians are often much different from those of whites. Indian cultures did not have written languages, and so the connection between the spoken and written word (which Anglos take for granted) may be alien to the Indian child; the way time and verb tenses are handled in Indian languages is vastly different from those in English. In addition to language and thought styles, the behavior patterns of Indians and Anglos can be widely divergent. For instance, the competitive and aggressive behavior considered appropriate in Anglo classrooms can be alien and frightening to individuals of certain Indian tribes.

These cultural differences obviously require an educational program specially suited to the cultural patterns and needs of Indians. However, Indian educational experience has more often reflected their subordinate status to the surrounding white society, for Anglo school patterns have typically been imposed upon the Indian population. The result has been a kind of "educational imperialism" that has often humiliated, degraded, and alienated Indian students, the majority of whom do not finish secondary school. Because Indians were geographically dispersed, the young were often shipped to dormitories in small communities adjacent to reservations and sent to public schools. They endured the multiple miseries of dormi-

---

[7] For basic references on Indian education, see Brophy and Aberle, 1966: 138–159; Coombs, et al., 1958; *Indian Education,* Branch of Education, BIA, No. 423, 1965; McGrath, et al., 1962; *Indian Education,* Committee on Labor and Public Welfare, U.S. Senate, Part 2, 1969; Levitan and Hetrick, 1971: 28–61; and Feldstein, 1972.

tory confinement, community discrimination, and harassment by Anglo teachers and students. Somewhat less degrading were federally run boarding schools where students lived in dormitories and attended all-Indian classes. Yet, the isolation from family and the typically sterile and sometimes substandard dormitory conditions have made federal schools highly unpleasant. Even federally financed state schools *on the reservations* have been degrading to Indians because administrators and teachers tend to be non-Indians who frequently have little understanding of Indian culture.

Whether a public school on or off the reservation, or a federal Indian school, the curriculum has usually reflected Anglo cultural patterns. Usually only English is allowed; classroom conduct is supposed to resemble that of white children; Indian history is often ignored; and teachers are white. Some Indians whose family backgrounds include an awareness of English and white cultural patterns can cope with this kind of school situation, but many are simply not prepared to deal with the structure of the Anglo educational system. It is the ravages of their educational experience that have prevented Indians from acquiring those minimal skills that will be necessary for their own self-determination and economic mobility.

LEGAL ISOLATION

Indians exist under three types of law: They can be subject not only to state and federal laws, but also to tribal law. Moreover, official tribal action is not restricted by constitutional guarantees of freedom of worship, speech, the right to assemble and protest, due process of law, or the safeguard of indictment for infamous crimes by a grand jury (Brophy and Aberle, 1966:42). While many tribes have enacted their own "bill of rights," the potential for abuse of the basic freedoms enjoyed by most Americans still remains. Since much of tribal culture has been lost under past BIA policies, it is curious that this restrictive feature of Indian culture remains so strongly entrenched.

State and local police, laws, and courts have rarely been non-discriminatory to Indians off the reservations. Arizona and New Mexico have only recently allowed Indians to vote, and in many states Indians are never called for jury duty. Frequently, state laws benefiting the general population, such as those for health and education, do not apply to the reservation—unless consent is given by the tribes and the BIA. While this situation does protect Indians from "harmful" legislation, it isolates them from the legal processes of the broader society and deprives them of the benefits of full participation in and protection of the law. For it seems likely that as long as Indians remain in legal isolation on the reservation, they will not be able to engage in their own self-determination or press effectively for their rights in the broader society.

Over the years the vast body of BIA administrative rules has taken on a "legal" character and has often constrained Indians' activities to the point of limiting their freedom. Indians are thus subject to "administrative laws" that are often benevolent, but which also isolate Indians from the broader society. This insulation has worked against Indians when they have left the reservation, for in the face of unsympathetic communities, police, and courts, they fail to assert their legal rights, primarily because they are often ignorant of them. Thus, while a certain amount of legal and administrative insulation from the broader society may have been necessary at one time, the continuance of such legal isolation will inhibit the mobility of Indians out of poverty.

In sum, the institutional forces confining Indians to the bottom rungs of the stratification system are a curious mixture of benevolent paternalism and malevolent exploitation that has isolated native Americans, disseminated their tribal cultures, taken their economic resources, and forced their dependence upon the federal government. While the BIA has undoubtedly performed some valuable services, it seems that, until the BIA actively works to break down this dependency by giving Indians real power in its administrative hierarchy, including the top positions in Washington, Indians will remain isolated and dependent and will not develop the work and administrative skills necessary to improve their political and economic position. It is very likely that if Indians had power in and could run the BIA, their condition could improve to the extent that the BIA could be dismantled—marking the end of federal paternalism and the beginning of Indian independence and self-governance.

BLACK AMERICANS[8]

ECONOMIC DISCRIMINATION AGAINST BLACK AMERICANS

While it is not clear just when slavery became institutionalized, by 1670 most blacks in America, and their offspring, were condemned to perpetual servitude. Whether the expansion of slavery was encouraged by the emerging plantation system in the South or the existence of slaves allowed for the development of the plan-

[8] For basic references on the history of white racism against blacks, see Turner and Singleton, 1976; Glasurd and Smith, 1972; and Feldstein, 1971.

tation system can never be known (Genovese, 1965; Fogel and Engerman, 1974). The relationship was probably reciprocal, but the increasing reliance of the Southern economy on labor-intensive agricultural crops, such as cotton, tobacco, hemp, rice, wheat, and sugar, caused the rapid expansion of slavery. And once a large slave population existed, fear of revolts from oppressed slaves probably perpetuated slavery, even if it became a less efficient form of economic organization.

While the importation of slaves was outlawed in the early years of the nineteenth century, the already large size of the black population was sufficient to provide labor for not only agriculture, but also for the growing industrial sectors of the Southern economy. Slavery is, of course, the most oppressive form of economic discrimination, since a slave is "property" that can be used, traded, bought, and sold at the owners discretion. As property, slaves possessed few familial, legal, political, and personal rights (Stampp, 1956).[9] And while various Northern groups opposed slavery as an institution, little was done to change this economic situation, except for a very brief period in the post-Civil War period.

Although the period of Reconstruction after the Civil War saw many blacks participating in political and educational spheres, white conservatives soon regained control of state legislatures and were able to destroy Reconstruction programs. By 1900 blacks had been forced off their land (given to them during Reconstruction) and onto tenant farms owned by whites, or they had become part of the cheap labor pool that provided the muscle and the menial services for white enterprises. With the onset of World War I and the increased opportunities in northern industrial cities, blacks began to leave the South in search of new economic opportunities. They encountered the same white violence and economic discrimination that they had left in the South. Except during the height of wartime production, blacks were excluded from skilled jobs in industry and relegated, once again, to a cheap and menial labor force.

During the depression, black migrations to urban areas stopped, while both those in rural and urban areas suffered enormously from unemployment and hunger. In the mid 1930s great masses of blacks received some form of public assistance; but even so, welfare allocations were differentially bestowed on blacks and whites (Pinkney, 1969:33–34). The New Deal marked a change in attitudes and policies toward blacks; politicians and legislators were now becoming "concerned" about their plight. The Joint Committee on

[9] For more descriptions and analyses of slaves and the slave community, see Blassingame, 1972 and Feldstein, 1971.

National Recovery—a combination of various black rights groups —revealed the differential wages paid to black and white workers in both the private economy and the federally run public works projects. Yet discrimination continued, for it was only under the threat of a massive march on Washington did President Franklin D. Roosevelt issue an executive order banning discrimination against blacks in the growing number of government-financed wartime industries. The large labor unions, particularly the Congress of Industrial Organizations, allowed some blacks into their ranks, although separate locals for blacks and whites were often maintained.

In the post-World War II period, with the persistence of racial discrimination in employment and with white supremacy practices, blacks became increasingly militant and began to press for equality. In response, President Harry S Truman integrated the heretofore segregated armed forces and established the National Committee on Civil Rights. Several states enacted antidiscrimination laws— most notably the New York Fair Employment Practices Law of 1945. Furthermore, the U.S. Supreme Court began to evidence an antidiscriminatory profile, culminating in the 1954 decision prohibiting racial segregation in public education.

Although the economic plight of blacks improved in the postwar period and in the early 1950s, the last decade has seen only slight change in their economic situation. Blacks are still overrepresented in menial, farm, and service occupations; they are underrepresented in professional and managerial positions; black unemployment has remained at twice that of white unemployment; blacks tend to be unemployed longer than whites in equivalent job categories; they earn less in the same job as whites; college-educated blacks earn about the same amount of money as high-school-educated whites; and black income, as a percentage of white income, has actually dropped from 61 percent in 1969 to 58 percent in 1973.[10]

The relatively deprived economic position of black Americans cannot be explained solely in terms of inadequate education, cultural impoverishment, unstable family life, and similar forces. Rather, economic discrimination remains—over 100 years after slavery—a major cause of black unemployment and underemployment. State and private employment agencies still discriminate

[10] For data on black income during the 1960s, see U.S. Department of Labor, Bureau of Labor Statistics, *Recent Trends in Social and Economic Conditions of Negroes in the United States, 1968;* and Current Population Reports, *Consumer Income,* U.S. Department of Commerce, 1970. For somewhat dated, but still accurate portrayals of black economic plight, see Pinkney, 1969: 77–90; Moynihan, 1965; Siegal, 1965; Batchelder, 1964; Seligman, 1970.

against blacks eligible (in terms of education) for white-collar work. Blacks are often assigned occupational classifications not commensurate with their skills; they tend to receive fewer referrals than whites to employers; they are rarely referred to openings in banks, loan firms, and other commercial establishments; and they are less likely than whites to be referred to retail stores and other businesses (Schaffer et al., 1970:44).[11] Blacks have at times been excluded from blue-collar occupations because of the discriminatory policies of trade unions, including those of the plumbers, carpenters, electricians, printers, metal workers, and machinists (Schaffer et al., 1970:44). Typical craft union strategies for discriminating against blacks include: (1) excluding blacks from apprenticeship programs and (2) insisting, in collective bargaining agreements and contracts, that the union—not the contractor or builder—maintain control of the hiring and firing of workers (Seligman, 1970:50–51). Industrial unions, which incorporate diverse workers on an industrywide basis, sometimes still engage in discrimination by forcing blacks into the lower-paying jobs and by segregating blacks into separate locals. The instances of this latter tactic have declined under pressure from the federal government. Yet, the legacy of both these tactics now haunts blacks who are unskilled and hence unable to join unions and, in many cases, unable to "qualify" for apprenticeship programs. The lack of skill among black workers is a result of a historical legacy of discrimination by many unions; this lack of skill has then been used by some unions to justify exclusion of blacks. For example, the U.S. Commission on Civil Rights reported that in the late 1960s, of the 1667 apprenticeships in St. Louis craft unions, only seven were held by blacks; or of the 750 building trade apprenticeships in Baltimore, 20 were black; or in both Atlanta and Baltimore, there are no black apprentices in the plumbers, iron workers, electrical workers, sheet and metal workers, and painters union (Turner and Singleton, 1976). Even among industrial unions that organize workers on an industrywide basis and in which blacks are proportionately represented, discrimination still occurs in the recruiting of apprentices for the better-paying jobs. For example, in one Detroit auto plant, 23 percent of the workers were black, but only one black was involved in the 289 apprenticeships (Knowles and Prewitt, 1969:23).

Employers also engage in discrimination against blacks. For example, in the South, separate white and black pay scales have only recently been outlawed. In many industries in both the North

---

[11] For a more detailed discussion, see the 1968 U.S. Department of Labor report on *Equality of Opportunity in Manpower Programs.*

and South, even those with government contracts, blacks are simply excluded from certain occupations. These practices clearly violate the 1964 Civil Rights Act, but enforcing the laws has proved difficult. The Civil Rights Division of the Department of Justice is simply too small to prosecute all the violations reported by the Employment Opportunity Commission (created by the 1964 Civil Rights Act). More importantly, the government has been hesitant to prosecute companies on whom it depends for "vital" defense contract items, especially those located in the districts of powerful congressional committee chairmen (Schaffer et al., 1970:53). Even within the federal government, there are signs of employment discrimination against blacks. While blacks are overrepresented in government jobs, they are underrepresented in the higher-paying government jobs (Pinkney, 1969:80).

GOVERNMENT BETRAYAL AND NEGLECT

The Civil War was ostensibly fought over the slavery issue;[12] and the fact that it was one of the bloodiest wars in American history might, to an outsider, give an indication of a strong governmental commitment to emancipation. However, the commitment was short-lived and ultimately resulted in the federal government's abandonment of the "black cause" by 1880 in the name of political stability and unification. After this betrayal there followed decades of neglect, resulting in the creation of a black "caste" that only recently shows signs of breaking down.

After the Civil War, President Abraham Lincoln conceived of Reconstruction in the South and the emancipation of blacks as a presidential function.[13] With his assassination and the ascendance of Andrew Johnson to the presidency, Reconstruction efforts began to ignore the situation of blacks in the South. White violence against blacks again became widespread, and a series of oppressive Black Codes were enacted at the state and local levels. To counteract this presidential neglect, Congress took over the responsibility for Reconstruction and proceeded to engage in a comprehensive program for assisting the newly emancipated slaves. During this period of Radical Reconstruction, the South was divided into military districts and ex-slaves became temporary wards of the government. The Black Codes were suspended by the Freedman's Bureau

---

[12] However, as many commentators have noted, the war may actually have been fought over political and economic issues as much as over slavery. Emancipation may have been a convenient justification to suppress the South politically and economically.

[13] For basic references on the Civil War and the period of Reconstruction, see Franklin, 1961; Trowbridge, 1956; Simkins, 1959; and Woodward, 1951.

in 1865, and in 1866, to supplement The Thirteenth Amendment (abolishing slavery), Congress enacted a Civil Rights Act (later to be the Fourteenth Amendment), that gave blacks full citizenship rights. Other federal legislation encouraged blacks to register and vote, with the result that widespread participation of blacks in state and national politics became typical. Although black legislators never controlled any southern state and no black ever became a governor, blacks could be found in high-ranking positions throughout state governments. Coupled with these new political freedoms, blacks began to enter schools and skilled occupations and, hence, initiate movement up the stratification system.

However, this new freedom and social mobility began to decline as federal troops were withdrawn in the 1870s, stimulating a wave of white violence against blacks. By the middle of the decade, blacks had been pushed out of schools, skilled jobs, and many governmental positions. Then, in 1877, the presidential election of 1876 became deadlocked and was thrown into Congress; the Republicans, in order to secure the election of Rutherford B. Hayes, agreed to abandon all Reconstruction efforts and leave the matters of race to the South to decide. Very quickly, blacks were forced once again into almost totally subservient social and economic positions that differed little from those of pre-Civil War days.

After this betrayal, the situation of black Americans was ignored by the federal government. During the depression, some federal assistance was provided for blacks, and President Roosevelt appointed a black committee—known as the Black Cabinet—to advise him on the plight of blacks. But little was really done to assist blacks who remained in the South or who were trapped in the slums of northern cities. Even during the post-World War II period extending into the 1950s, comparatively little federal assistance to blacks occurred, despite the 1954 landmark school desegregation decision of the Supreme Court and the integration of the armed forces. Although public housing and urban renewal somewhat improved the housing conditions of blacks in urban areas, they also confined blacks to the urban cores of large cities, where educational and job opportunities were not as great as in the suburbs. While the federally backed welfare establishment grew during this period and provided many black families with desperately needed assistance, the multitude of abuses and injustices leveled on blacks negated many of its more benevolent features (see Chapter 7).

Probably the most comprehensive effort to assist blacks since Radical Reconstruction has been the War on Poverty initiated at the midpoint of the last decade. Coupled with a more vigorous federal commitment to the Supreme Court school desegregation ruling of 1954, some assistance to blacks occurred. But in less than a decade, the federal commitment to both these goals, especially the War on Poverty, has waned. The conspicuous projects of the mid 1960s—Operation Head Start, the Neighborhood Youth Corps, the Job Corps, Upward Bound, VISTA, and even the Office of Economic Opportunity itself—have become increasingly obscure (see Chapter 7 for details on the War on Poverty). Overall, these programs failed to materially benefit the poor black in any comprehensive way.

EDUCATION

Prior to the Civil War, most black Americans received no formal education, although a few were given training in an effort to extract more skilled labor from them. In the brief period of Radical Reconstruction following the Civil War, however, blacks began to enter the emerging system of public schools, but with the demise of the congressional Reconstruction in the 1870s, virtually all blacks were expelled from southern schools, although a few did manage to secure education in segregated public facilities and church schools.

Since the 1870s, the black population has made significant gains in years of education completed. The percent of illiterates has dropped from 80 percent in 1870 to less than 7 percent in 1970, although this figure is still nearly four times higher than that for whites. The total number of years in school for blacks is higher than that for either Indians or Mexican Americans, although it lags considerably behind that for whites. Most of the educational gains of blacks have occurred at the primary level, where today 99 percent of black youths are enrolled, and at the secondary level, where nearly 90 percent of blacks are still in school. Even though a large proportion of blacks attend college than ever before, the proportion of whites attending college has increased at a faster rate—thus widening the educational gap. Despite the educational gains of blacks, their economic position relative to whites has remained about the same: In 1974 a black high school graduate still earned roughly the same as a white dropout, and a college-educated black earned not much more than a white high school graduate.[14] These data clearly reveal the operation of discriminatory forces in the broader society that cut off opportunities for educated blacks.

Even in this decade of awareness over inequality in the schools,

[14] However, this situation may change since black graduates from white colleges are now in great demand because of pressure from the federal government and from the genuine concern of many corporations. But it will be at least a decade before these improvements are reflected in income data for blacks. In fact, black income as a proportion of white income has declined.

blacks still must endure discriminatory educational practices. While school facilities at the lower education level, even in segregated schools, appear to be becoming more equal, the middle-class environment of the schools tends to alienate many black students. The emphasis by white teachers and administrators on verbal skills and competitive examinations, as well as the use of IQ and achievement tests normed to white populations, apparently suppress the achievement of children who come from somewhat different cultural backgrounds.

Blacks also suffer from educational abuses at the college and university level. In 1968 over 50 percent of the black college students attended all-black colleges, accounting for 80 percent of the degrees earned by blacks. These colleges are grossly underfinanced, as is evidenced by the fact that only 3.5 percent of the $4 billion in federal aid given to higher education in 1969 went to predominately black colleges—whose needs are much greater than that of white schools. Furthermore, black land-grant colleges do not receive their share of federal and state funds. For example, federal and state aid to white colleges averaged $2300 per student, whereas the corresponding figure was $1365 for blacks in 1969. Coupled with the fact that students in black colleges come from poor families with average incomes of $4000 per year, tuition costs must be low and hence cannot finance, to any great degree, black college facilities. The result of these financial squeezes on black colleges is an inferior education. Teachers' salaries are low; physical facilities are barely adequate; and the curricula are narrow and do not allow for training in professional occupations, except teaching (Seligman, 1970:47).

Thus, in terms of quantity and quality of education, blacks still lag behind whites, despite some educational gains—reflected by the fact that blacks are better off than Chicanos and Indians in terms of their educational attainment. But this fact has not yet become translated into significant increases in black income relative to whites, for the incomes of blacks are lower than that of less-educated whites and Chicanos (Miller, 1964).[15]

LEGAL DISCRIMINATION

By 1650, several American colonies had enacted laws distinguishing white and black indentured servants, and blacks were increasingly consigned to servitude for life. By the early eighteenth

---

[15] The somewhat large size of the Mexican-American family may equalize this difference (Moore and Cuéllar, 1970). However, the fact remains that a Chicano family head, with fewer years of school, can get a better job than a better-educated black.

century, the legal framework sanctioning slavery in all southern states was clear:

1. Blacks were to be slaves for life.
2. Slaves were property *and* persons; owners held property rights, while incurring some responsibilities to blacks as persons.
3. Black children were to inherit their mother's position.
4. Marriages between blacks and whites were prohibited.
5. Blacks were not allowed to acquire property.
6. Blacks were not allowed to enter civil contracts, engage in litigation, testify against whites in court, or sit on juries.

In the North, laws were not nearly so severe and varied enormously from state to state. In the early 1800s, the existence of free blacks in the North and total slavery in the South was increasingly debated, and with the entrance of Missouri to the Union in 1821, a vague and platitudinous congressional proclamation allowed northern and southern states to enact entirely contradictory laws, with the North increasingly enacting liberalized laws and the South ever more severe laws. Yet, even with liberal formal laws in the North, informal "Jim Crow" practices—restricting blacks access to jobs, education, recreational facilities, transportation, and housing—often guided actions more than the formal law. Thus, at the dawn of the Civil War, formal law and informal practices in the South were highly correlated, whereas in the North, liberal formal laws were frequently contradicted by informal Jim Crow practices.

With the demise of Radical Reconstruction, Jim Crow practices were extended to all regions of the North and South, especially with respect to black access to public accommodations, public conveyances, and amusement facilities used by whites. Indicative of their broad use and support is the fact that they were sanctioned in a series of landmark decisions by the Supreme Court. For example, the Supreme Court declared unconstitutional the Civil Rights Act of 1875 that had made it a crime to deny people equal access to public places; and in 1896 the Court ruled that segregated facilities for blacks and whites were not a violation of the Thirteenth and Fourteenth Amendments. As it declared: "If one race be inferior to the other socially, the Constitution cannot put them on the same plane" (Pinkney, 1969:28). White supremacy thus became institutionalized by the Supreme Court, with the result that discrimination in virtually all spheres of social life became the tacit "law of the land." It was not until the post-World War II period that Jim Crow began to recede; and only with the 1954 school desegregation decision and with the civil rights acts of the last decade did the American legal system *explicitly forbid* Jim Crow laws and practices. Yet much damage had been done, since nearly a century of legal discrimination had forced blacks into the bottom ranks of the stratification system. And even today, with civil rights laws on the books, the Justice Department has often failed to enforce the legal rights of black Americans.

In criminal cases, police discrimination and abuse, as well as disproportionately strong indictments and long jail sentences for crimes against whites, are typically imposed upon blacks by a legal system staffed predominantly by whites. As a number of studies reveal, blacks in urban ghettos list "police practices" as their most intense grievance—revealing the still uneasy accommodation between black Americans and the legal system. And while police and community groups have made significant efforts to reduce tensions, considerable estrangement between the enforcers of the law and black Americans remains.

In sum, the history of black Americans' treatment under the law is one of inequity. Unlike most minorities, blacks have experienced formally sanctioned discrimination. As a result, blacks have been segregated and excluded from all major social, recreational, and institutional spheres—a situation that forced them to the bottom rungs of the stratification system.[16]

INSTITUTIONALIZED DISCRIMINATION: AN OVERVIEW

This chapter should be read within the context of the forces maintaining inequality and poverty in American society. Running through the general pattern of inequality and poverty are the additional forces of racial and ethnic discrimination. Discrimination at an interpersonal level often reveals the racism and bigotry of people, but it also reflects broader *institutional patterns*. While basic social institutions are, in part, a reflection of people's attitudes and values, the relationship is reciprocal: Attitudes and values are also shaped by basic institutional arrangements. What is more, institutions have a kind of autonomy and capacity to perpetuate themselves, even when values and beliefs change.

These facts should indicate that discrimination transcends "just

---

[16] The only other group to be so *openly* discriminated against by the government has been Japanese Americans, who were placed in relocation camps during World War II. While the abuses of the BIA against Indians, and of the border patrol and Texas Rangers against Mexican Americans should not be ignored, the legal discrimination against blacks remains unparalleled.

plain folk" interacting with one another. People are only actors in a script written by the structure of basic American institutions: the economy, government, education, and the law. To understand why certain racial and ethnic groups are disproportionately represented at the lower end of the American stratification system has required an examination of the historical forces that have shaped current institutional arrangements. These forces have operated somewhat differently on the three minority populations discussed in this chapter, but there are many similarities in the general pattern of institutional discrimination.

In the economic sphere blacks, Chicanos, and Indians have suffered from somewhat similar abuses. Whether as bracero labor, slaves, or a conquered people, these groups have been used as a cheap, unskilled labor pool. Until very recently, attempts to remedy this situation were resisted by those economic interests dependent on such labor. These minority peoples have thus been kept from joining unions in proportionate numbers; and even when they were able to crack the union barrier, they were often forced into the lower job classifications. Coupled with employer discrimination, they have been kept economically deprived and dependent on the welfare programs of government.

Politically blacks, Chicanos, and Indians have traditionally been disfranchised. Members of each group have been treated, at various times, as somewhat less than full citizens—a practice that has delayed their involvement in the political process where they can better press for their interests. As less than full citizens and as economically impoverished groups, they have had to rely on federal programs that are notable for their inadequacy and insensitivity to the needs of these populations. Furthermore, these programs have typically addressed the more superficial conditions of the minority poor and have avoided the hard issues such as housing, integration, and income redistribution.

Educationally, minority populations still must endure discrimination, despite clear recognition of the importance of education for social mobility. Several common patterns of discrimination are encountered by blacks, Chicanos, and Indians. First, these minority groups tend to be residentially segregated as outcast populations from the rest of society. One result of segregation is that minority young are likely to attend segregated schools—in urban enclaves and rural backwaters, or on reservations—that are inferior to schools serving suburban white students. Classroom crowding, lack of teacher credentialing, poor texts, and rigid curricula are still typical of schools serving minority students, even though the gap between facilities serving *poor* whites and minority populations has now closed. Second, when minority students attend integrated schools, they are most likely to suffer teacher and counselor discrimination and to be tracked into separate and inferior lanes on the presumption that they cannot compete with white Anglos. Third, schools rarely accommodate themselves to the diverse cultural backgrounds of minority students; rather, they attempt to assimilate students and force them to abandon their cultural uniqueness and conform to a white, middle-class image of the good student. As a direct outgrowth of these discriminatory practices, minority students are more likely to drop out of school and not go on to college than are white Anglos—thus decreasing their job opportunities and ability to ascend the stratification ladder.

Even in the aftermath of a series of civil rights acts and sympathetic Supreme Court decisions, the institution of law remains a discriminatory force in America. The highly publicized civil rights legislation of the federal government is often not enforced at the local community level, where police and courts oftentimes discriminate against minority groups. More importantly, decades of legal abuse have preceded current attempts to legislate equality. For example, restrictive covenants, discrimination in hiring, separate wage scales for minorities, union discrimination, segregated schooling, poll taxes, and other discriminatory practices were allowed to continue, even though they violated basic constitutional rights. Even today legal action against such policies is sometimes slow and ineffective.

Today in American communities, minority group individuals can still expect to find that (1) they are more likely to be viewed as "suspicious" by police than lower-class whites; (2) they are more likely to be arrested than whites; (3) they should be prepared to be charged with a more severe crime than a white for the same alleged behavior, especially if the crime is against a white; (4) because of their poverty and inability to afford legal defense, they are more likely to be forced to "cop a plea" (even when innocent) and plead guilty to a lesser charge than are whites; and (5) they can expect longer jail sentences than whites when they commit a crime against an Anglo.

The impact of tacit legal sanctioning of economic, political, and educational discrimination is obvious: it blocks access to those institutional spheres necessary for mobility out of poverty. The consequences of more direct discrimination of police and courts against individual members of minority groups are more difficult to assess. At the very least, they deprive individuals of basic constitutional rights, and at the most, they generate fear, distrust, and hatred among large segments of minority populations—not only toward the legal system, but also toward the broader institutions it sanctions. Minority group members thus become less willing to participate in the broader society and more inclined to seek refuge in a racial or ethnic enclave, hence perpetuating their isolation and impoverishment.

PART THREE
AMERICAN COMMUNITY PROBLEMS

Simple definitions of community are difficult, since there are so many different types ranging from rural villages and towns to sprawling suburbs and large commercial and industrial cities. In light of such diversity, a definition of community must be very general and abstract: a community is a self-governing geographical area where people live and meet their basic and acquired needs through interrelated and partially coordinated work activities (Boskoff, 1970:3–37).

Over the last 150 years, under the presures of industrialization, the United States has become an urbanized society. Residence, work, and social life for well over half the population occurs within a few hundred large urban and metropolitan areas. This majority of the population is crowded into less than 2 percent of the land expanse of the United States—a population density rivaling India, Egypt, Japan, and Java. During the transformation from a rural to an urbanized society, four notable trends have been evident:

1. the great rural to urban migrations of indigenous whites into the cities during the middle of the last century
2. the massive immigrations into cities of Europeans and Asians during the latter part of the nineteenth century and the early years of this century
3. the internal migrations of southern blacks from rural areas to cities in the North
4. the rapid exodus over the last 25 years of white middle-class Americans out of the cities into the suburbs

These trends highlight an incredible series of shifts in the way people live in American society. Associated with these transformations is a host of social problems confronting the giant metropolitan areas. A number of such problems are related to the physical ascendance and subsequent deterioration of major American cities, to the burgeoning of white suburbs, and to the creation of vast patterns of residential segregation. It is emphasized in the chapters of this section, then, that *built into the structure* of American communities is a set of problems that can be solved only by transformations in the structure of those communities.

The concept of "community" can be used in a broader sense, however. Humans are only one part of a much larger community: the national and world ecosystem. Ecosystems are composed of functional relationships among species, and between species and their physical environments.[1] While the complexity of these relationships can be enormous, one fact is clear: Each species is dependent on at least some other species and some elements of the physical environment for survival. No matter how ascendant humans believe themselves to be, they too cannot extricate themselves from this dependency on other life forms and minerals in the global ecosystem (Iltis, 1970). It is such a dependency that makes the study of interaction between the ecosystem and society critical.

[1] For more detailed, yet readable discussions of ecosystems, see Ehrlich and Ehrlich, 1970:157–199; Odum, 1969; Duncan and Schnore, 1964; Murphy, 1967: 49–108. For more technical discussions, consult the bibliographies of these works.

Over the last 10,000 years, humans have evolved increasingly complex social systems that have allowed their populations to grow at incredible rates. As a result, humans organized into urban industrial societies like the United States have been able to potentially disrupt, on a scale never before possible, basic relationships within the world ecosystem. The inevitable trend toward complexity and diversity of ecosystems in nature has been reversed with the cultivation of single crops, the use of pesticides, and the stripping of soil and plant life. The basic cycles of materials, involving the circulation of life-sustaining elements such as carbon, nitrogen, and phosphorus, may have been disrupted. Air has been altered chemically in ways harmful to human lives. Crucial life forms, such as the ocean's phytoplankton, that give mammals most of the air they breathe, have been invaded by chlorinated hydrocarbons like DDT. And the life-sustaining capacity of water has been reduced in many parts of the world.[2]

These events are a familiar story and need not be dwelled on. What is crucial in understanding the impact of human societies on the environment is the fact that changes introduced at one point in the world ecological community have consequences for other areas, always extending and magnifying disruption of the environment. The amount of damage that has already been done and the long-range disruptions that will show up in the future cannot be precisely estimated because the chains and cycles of the ecosystem are too complex. But it is evident that considerable ecological damage may have already occurred and that, unless existing patterns of human social organization are altered, the point of no return from an ecocatastrophe could soon be passed. It is, therefore, appropriate that we close this short volume on America's problems with an analysis of how American social structure and culture pose problems for the world ecological community. Patterns of stratification, institutional adaptation, and community organization in America will, in Chapter 11, be seen as posing the ultimate "problem of structure:" the potential destruction of the human species through massive alteration of the ecological community.

[2] For more technical discussion of the impact of pollutants on the ecosystem, see Revelle, 1968; Ehrlich and Ehrlich, 1970:117–198.

Chapter 9

PROBLEMS OF THE CITY IN AMERICA

THE BIRTH OF AMERICAN CITIES

In 1800 only a few cities in the United States had a population over 25,000, and none of these exceeded 100,000 (Strauss, 1961: 91). Compared to London with 800,000 or Paris with 500,000 residents, Philadelphia (70,000) and New York (60,000) were little more than small towns. However, by 1860 New York had a population of more than 800,000 inhabitants (not including Brooklyn) and was the third largest city in the Western world, behind London and Paris. Philadelphia, with over 500,000, had surpassed Berlin in size, while six other American cities had swelled to over 100,000 inhabitants (Schlesinger, 1951). By 1880, with the vast immigrations from southeastern Europe only beginning, 20 American cities had surpassed the 100,000 mark in population (Strauss, 1961:91).

This spectacular emergence of large American cities can be attributed to a matrix of several interrelated forces: (1) industrialization and the creation of urban jobs; (2) the resulting massive internal rural to urban migrations of people in search of these jobs in industry; (3) the immigration of peasants from rural Europe into the cities in search of a prosperous life in the new cities of the New World; and (4) the natural increase of urban residents stemming from the high birthrates of rural migrants and immigrants.

The first large cities in the American colonies, such as New York, Boston, Baltimore, Philadelphia, Charleston, and Newport, were commercial seaports that marketed goods from Europe while distributing indigenous agricultural goods from their own hinterlands. Migrations westward from these initial cities resulted in the emergence of cities beyond the Appalachians, as in Ohio and Indiana.

Unlike those in the East, these cities were populated not so much by rural migrants as by sons of city residents of the eastern seaboard. The westward expansion of urban communities altered the commercial profile of eastern cities to one centered around the manufacture of goods for these new territories. At the same time, industrialists began to establish factory towns along the banks of rivers from which power could be easily derived. From 1815 to 1850, these industrial towns grew and greatly extended urban industrial communities into the interior of the nation along major waterways—a pattern that persists until the present day. As the factories in the seaboard and river cities grew in number and size, farmers from the surrounding rural areas looked to them in search of opportunities not available in the increasingly unprosperous farmland. This rural peasantry was rapidly transformed into an urban proletariat and became crowded into the tenements surrounding the factories. In the 1850s the railroad allowed further urban development to the west, most notably in Chicago and Toledo, and stimulated increased industrial manufacturing in the East—thereby initiating new manufacturing in the Midwest.

THE GOLDEN AGE OF CITIES: A HISTORICAL MYTH?

By the 1850s the urban-industrial profile of American communities was becoming clearly evident. With further industrialization, the demand for unskilled factory labor began to exceed the supply available from rural migrations and natural population increases in the city. Fleeing from impoverished conditions in Europe in search of these job opportunities, waves of immigrants began to pour into the cities, resulting in a new and persistent pattern of urban organization: the ethnic ghetto or enclave. The influx of foreign immigrants was so great that the cities became overrun, creating incredibly crowded and unsanitary living conditions. Because housing was scarce, rents could soar as buildings became increasingly crowded and deteriorated. By 1850 the overcrowded, poor, ethnically segregated and deteriorated American slum, and its absentee slumlord, were permanent fixtures of the American city.

Concomitant to the development of urban slums was the emergence of middle-class residential areas of white-collar workers who managed the factories and provided the services necessary to keep them running. Also, extensive downtown shopping and commercial areas developed to service both the factory and white-collar worker, as well as to distribute and market many of the products of the industrializing economy. Thus, within a comparatively small geographical region, working-class tenements, impoverished ethnic slums, middle-class neighborhoods, factories, and an extensive downtown commercial center typified most urban-industrial cities by the turn of the century.

While the ethnic and cultural diversity, as well as the concentration of so much human activity around a prospering central business district gives—in retrospect—an image of a vibrant polis, today's cities, with all the problems imputed to them, are much safer and more sanitary places to live, in *absolute terms*, than they were at the turn of the century. By 1910, with the development of the automobile, cities became highly congested because the streets and their patterning were not designed for the use of cars and trucks. Furthermore, as industrial production increased, as the sewage facilities of the city were overtaxed by the urban masses, and as the concentration of cars and trucks into the narrow city streets multiplied, pollution of the air and water was initiated— although at that time few considered it a serious social problem.[1]

Partially because cities in America developed so rapidly and spontaneously, they were unplanned and went unregulated by the federal government, which did not deem it appropriate to intervene extensively in the internal affairs of cities. Hence the dangers, unsanitary facilities, grievances of the urban peasants from Europe, and deteriorating conditions of the inner city were viewed as not in the province of the federal government. Furthermore, economically, the vast capital needed to plan cities more rationally was unavailable to the federal government in an era when there was no federal income tax. Cities, from their outset, were politically decentralized and autonomous from the federal government. This tradition of local autonomy—buttressed by a laissez faire ideology—makes federal involvement in city problems difficult and often ineffective even today.

This lack of national policy for cities created a pattern of urban city politics that to this day dominates many large eastern and midwestern cities. The waves of immigrants from rural areas in Europe and the outskirts of urban areas encountered many problems of adjustment that were partially resolved by the local ward heeler of the big-city political machines, such as Tammany Hall in New York, Crump in Memphis, Hague in Jersey City, Curley in Boston, and Pendergast in Kansas City (Dynes et al., 1964:55).

---

[1] Obviously people were aware of what was occurring, and most did not like living in the crowded and congested city, but it was firmly believed that some amenities had to be sacrificed in order to make more money and live at a higher material standard.

Ward heelers provided help, comfort, and vital services to the new city residents, who were poor and insecure in the new urban-industrial complex. They became an intermediary between the slumlord and resident (usually at a price unknown to the resident), and eliminated the bureaucratic entanglements (residency requirements, red tape, and delays) in securing assistance for families requiring aid. The big-city machine was thus established on the principle of a personal relationship between its local representative and the new urbanite, but for a great price: the urbanite agreed to vote for the machine's candidate in elections and, hence, perpetuate the machine and its capacity to render great profits for its leaders. While most of the big political machines in large urban areas have diminished, a *pattern* of political control was established and persists today in many large cities. The persistence of widespread political corruption and patronage, as well as control of a city's resources by a few elites, has persisted to the present day and has often inhibited federal involvement in a city's internal affairs; when such involvement has been allowed, as in urban renewal, local corruption has often been the result.[2] What is important for present purposes is to emphasize that big-city politics had been institutionalized and *built into* American communities by the early decades of this century.

From 1910 to 1930 a new form of internal immigration from rural America became conspicuous: The rural southern black began to migrate to northern cities in search of work. For decades rural conditions in the South had deteriorated, and with the boll weevil's devastation of the cotton-farming industry, along with the industrial expansion and changes in immigration policies accompanying World War I, blacks began to pour into northern cities in search of job opportunities. Because of their poverty and because of racial discrimination, black migrants were forced into the most delapidated and crowded tenements, with the result that the black ghetto was born. Out of these conditions, fanned by white attacks on black residents, emerged the first urban race riots and interracial conflicts. Between 1915 and 1919, Allen and Adair (1969: 31) conclude, 18 major race riots occurred. For example, on May 28 and July 2, 1917, 39 blacks were killed in East St. Louis, Illinois, because they had been used as strikebreakers. Reports indicate

[2] Irving Louis Horowitz (1970) has argued, quite perceptively, that perhaps the old big-city political machines were not so bad after all. They kept people in contact with their leaders—albeit somewhat exploitively—and thereby gave city residents a sense of community. Today big-city political machines have little contact and connection with the people they govern, thus creating the form of city government that is big, heavily bureaucratized, oftentimes corrupt, and detached from its constituency.

that the intense violence, burning, and disruption that followed were subdued only by the use of the National Guard and escalated police activity. Thus, by 1920 urban segregation and exploitation of blacks and the resulting racial tensions were clearly *built into* the structure of major cities in the United States.

Shortly after the turn of the century, the following conditions were endemic to the structure of the American city:

1. overcrowded and impoverished slums with substandard housing and unsafe sanitary facilities
2. ethnic and racial segregation of neighborhoods
3. industrial pollution of the air and water
4. community pollution of waters stemming from inadequate sewage facilities
5. extreme congestion from trucks and automobiles
6. corrupt big-city politics
7. racial tensions and riots

These conditions, which began to appear as soon as large cities emerged in the early 1800s, were well known by scholars and residents of the time. If current city conditions are compared to those at the turn of the century, it is clear that things have gotten better, on an absolute standard. In fact congestion, housing, and sanitation are clearly much better than at the turn of the century. But current urban conditions are not judged and evaluated on a fixed standard. Rather, they are judged on a constantly *escalating* standard—a yardstick that compares city life with the affluence of white, middle-class suburbia. The big city was thought pleasant, or at least endurable, as long as most people were of the working class, but as the ranks of the middle classes began to swell, cities became thought of as abhorrent (Banfield, 1970:66). This sense of relative deprivation may help account for the myth about the "golden age" of cities, for in reality they were never very pleasant places to live by any standards. From the beginning cities have been unplanned, heavily industrial (at least in the East and Midwest), overcrowded, congested, unsanitary, and great polluters of the environment.

Any attempt to improve cities by returning to their golden age would be the pursuit of an illusion, and whether the contemporary large city can be kept from deteriorating in the future is unclear. Cities are presently being abandoned by the affluent taxpayer in favor of alternative life-styles in the suburbs. Left to the poor, the cities are rapidly going bankrupt; and unless new revenues and alternative governmental patterns are found, the cities could potentially become in the future worse places to live in than they were at the turn of the century. Urban trends are perhaps operating against any easy solution to the big city's problems, as is best evidenced by the suburbanization of almost everyone except the poor.

SUBURBANIZATION: THE WHITE EXODUS

The large industrial city that was the hallmark of urban America at the turn of the century was an inevitable by-product of the technology of the times. The technology of early industrial socities did not allow for the flexible movement of energy over long distances by electrical cables. Factories, then, had to be located near sources of energy or at least near railroads or major waterways, where coal and oil could be easily supplied. Since work was concentrated in cities, so was the work force, which, because of limited transportation facilities, had to remain close to the factories. Because the markets for industrial goods were in the central cities, the commercial and trade industries also became tied to cities in the form of central business districts.

Just as the imperatives of early industrial technology stimulated the growth of large cities, changes in that technology and the resulting changes in the economy created a new form of urbanism in the twentieth century: metropolitan areas composed of large decaying cities inhabited by the poor and surrounded by suburbs inhabited by the white and affluent.

TECHNOLOGY AND SUBURBANIZATION

Shortly after the turn of the century a technological revolution occurred. In 1915 there were 2.5 million automobiles, but 20 years later assemblyline production had increased the number of cars dramatically. Cars made it possible to adapt transportation facilities to where people wanted to live. Previously, people had been forced to live near less flexible systems of transport because residential areas had to be located near established routes of trollies and railroads. Now, with the increasing development of roads and highways, more flexible and diffused living patterns outside the city limits could be enjoyed by those who could afford a car and the costs of commuting to work from the suburbs (Dentler, 1967; Greer, 1965).

There were other technological forces contributing to the outward growth of urban areas (Banfield, 1970). Mechanical refrigerators, wide varieties of canned foods, and high-voltage electrical transmission cables allowed people to have the amenities in the suburbs that previously were available only in the central city. Furthermore, the communications revolution involving first the radio and then television enabled suburban residents to remain psychologically tied to cities while being geographically separated from them.

Technological changes also allowed, and in some cases forced, industry to follow residents out of the central city. The development of extensive assemblyline techniques of production required more space than was economically feasible to buy in the central city. The rapid proliferation of a road and highway system and the emergence of a trucking industry allowed producers to disperse their production facilities without losing access to raw materials and markets. These and other technological changes had a profound impact on the way the American economy in the twentieth century became organized. In turn, these changes in the economy facilitated suburbanization.

ECONOMIC ORGANIZATION AND SUBURBANIZATION

As people began to move into the suburbs, marketing and service organizations also relocated to serve the affluent suburbanites. This movement created jobs for white-collar workers, with the result that even more white-collar residents migrated out of the city to take advantage of new jobs and better services. As ever more white-collar, middle-class residents relocated in suburbia, so did more marketing and servicing enterprises in search of a more lucrative market. In this way, a cycle of suburbanization of economically prosperous residents and skilled white-collar industries was initiated and perpetuated.

As the buyers for many industrial goods located in the suburbs, manufacturing corporations also began to relocate near these affluent markets. Since land was cheap and taxes low in the suburbs, many industries could increase their profits by locating beyond the city limits. One result of the movement of servicing, marketing, and manufacturing enterprises to the suburbs was to drain the central city of its skilled and affluent work force, as well as its major enterprises in the central business district.

GOVERNMENT POLICIES AND SUBURBANIZATION

State, local, and federal governments have contributed to the mass exodus of white, affluent, middle-class city residents to the suburbs. During the 1930s, the Federal Housing Administration (FHA), and in the 1940s the Veterans Administration (VA), encouraged the construction of single-family dwellings in the suburbs by insuring mortgages. This policy overcame traditionally conservative banking practices and enabled people who had a little economic surplus to purchase their own homes in the suburbs. The

FHA thus kept the urban exodus alive, even during the depression years. During World War II, housing, building, and rent controls were established, and many industries in the cities were revived, resulting in migrations back into the cities. But after the war, with the help of the VA home loan guarantee and FHA guarantees, movement out of the city became truly massive and led to the dramatic transformation of American cities (Haar, 1960).

State and local governments also contributed to the emergence of suburbia. Initially the central city annexed the new residential areas along its borders. But eventually shortsighted city leaders began to feel that the suburbs were a liability because the taxes they yielded did not pay for the services the city had to supply (police, fire protection, sanitation, streets, etc.). By the time large-city governments began to realize that their tax base had vanished to the suburbs, suburban communities had begun to incorporate in order to determine their own fate, patterns of land use, allocation of tax monies, and just who their neighbors were to be. In state after state legislators from suburban areas, who craved self-government, joined forces with rural legislators, who saw the growth of large cities as a threat to rural power, to enact legislation that made the annexation of the suburbs by central cities very difficult. By the end of the 1920s the delineation between suburb and central city was well established in American metropolitan regions (Greer, 1965).

THE DEMOGRAPHIC IMPERATIVES OF SUBURBANIZATION

As people migrated into the first American cities, city boundaries inevitably had to expand. In 1790 only 5 percent of the population lived in urban areas. Today 75 percent live in urban areas; and by 1980, 90 percent of the population will live in urban regions. Naturally, a demographic transformation of these proportions made suburbia almost inevitable. Since there are limits as to how far city boundaries can be extended, eventually autonomous and yet contiguous suburban communities were necessary to accompany the natural growth and migration of the urban population. The migrations of city residents to the suburbs remained highly selective, however, and usually involved only the white and the affluent, whose place in the central city was taken by blacks, Puerto Ricans, Chicanos, and other impoverished minorities who had migrated from rural regions. Many of the problems inherent in urban America derive from the concentration of the minorities and other categories of poor in the central cities and the affluent whites in the suburbs.

PROBLEMS OF THE CITY IN
METROPOLITAN AREAS

In light of technological changes, federal political policies, patterns of economic organization, and demographic imperatives, the growth of a large metropolitan area with a core city surrounded by white suburbs was inevitable. Whether the consequences of these forces were also inevitable is now a moot question, but the problems of the cities are to a very great extent the result of the white exodus and the growth of metropolitan areas.

POLITICAL FRAGMENTATION
OF METROPOLITAN AREAS

One of the major consequences of the growth of metropolitan areas and the resulting incorporation of separate suburban communities was the political decentralization of decision making in urban America. In the old big cities, political machines represented a highly centralized form of decision making with the result that policies—both good and bad—could be easily implemented across the whole city. In contrast, the multiple communities in a modern metropolitan area now make unified and concerted political action difficult (Greer, 1965). Each separate community has its own local official and city government, which, on the one hand, represents a traditional American ideal of a decentralized and democratic polis, but which, on the other hand, makes planning across an entire metropolitan region difficult. While local governments act autonomously, they are in reality part of a large urban system that, in order to remain viable, must engage in metropolitanwide planning. From this perspective, American metropolitan areas can be visualized as having *built into* their structure the *incapacity* to respond politically and administratively to metropolitanwide problems of housing, crime, traffic, pollution, sanitation, police and fire protection.

In addition to fractionalizing political power, suburban incorporation has resulted in the duplication of many public services. Such duplication often represents an enormous waste of the financial resources of a metropolitan region, since vital services, including police and fire protection, public works, sanitation, and pollution control, can be financed less expensively and administered more efficiently at the metropolitanwide level than at the local level. One consequence of this is that resources that could be used for attacking many problems, such as pollution, congestion, poor housing in the cities, and crime in the streets, are spent in the duplication of services. Thus, in addition to political fractionalization and the resulting decrease in the capacity to act at the metropolitan level, resources necessary for resolving metropolitan problems are sometimes available for either the large core cities or their suburbs.

Political fragmentation is a continual dilemma facing a federalist political system. Decentralization of political power has many advantages, the most notable of which is to minimize the gap between political leaders and the citizenry. Centralization has many disadvantages, the most prominent of which is to create a wasteful bureaucracy that is out of touch with those it is supposed to serve. The dilemma facing America's metropolitan areas, then, is how to restructure government so that the benefits of decentralization can be realized, while, at the same time, maintaining some degree of administrative centralization to deal with metropolitanwide problems. Such a formula calls for a delicate balance that is difficult to effect in the first place and even more difficult to maintain.

THE ECONOMIC PLIGHT OF THE CITIES

The white, middle class exodus to the suburbs has created an economic crisis in the cities. First, the movement of industries, businesses, and commerce to the suburbs has frequently led to the decline of the central business district in many large cities. In turn, the decline of this area has undermined the tax base that the city needs to survive and prosper. Second, the high-income resident, in moving to the suburbs, no longer spends money in or pays taxes to the city, resulting in an even greater erosion of the revenue necessary to maintain a large city. Third, state and federal tax formulas typically create a situation whereby the city pays more in taxes than it receives in services such as education, police protection, highway benefits, transportation funds, and public service revenues. The overall result of these three forces is to make it increasingly difficult for cities to finance and supply necessary services (Grier and Grier, 1966). They can no longer afford "to educate and train their underprivileged, support their unemployed and elderly poor, police their streets, mend their sick, or operate their courts, jails, utilities, and garbage plants" (Abrams, 1969:38).

The city is an integral part of a metropolitan area, yet it has a decreasing base of tax revenue. Coupled with the fact that public services cost more than ever, an economic crisis of severe proportions has emerged. In addition, the residents of contemporary cities—the poor, the minorities, and the aged, not to mention the more affluent city dwellers who exercise greater control over their place of residence—are requiring an increasing number of services in the form of housing, welfare, police protection, and health care.

Under current conditions, the city is decreasingly able to pay the rising costs of these necessary services. In 1932 municipalities were collecting more taxes than the federal and state governments combined. Of all tax monies received, cities received 52 percent (Abrams, 1969:39); but today the intake of cities is less than 10 percent of the total. With rising costs and increasing demands for services in the burdened cities, new fiscal formulas for financing America's large core cities will become increasingly necessary.

SUBURBAN "EXPLOITATION"

Among America's large cities only New York, predicts Mitchell Gordon (1963), will have a majority of its work force residing within the city limits by 1980. Even if this prediction is inaccurrate, it points to a trend of utmost importance for the cities: The large city has increasingly become solely a work place for the suburban-ite. This likelihood means that the commuter will derive a liveli-hood from the city, use many of its facilities (police, transporta-tion, sanitation), and yet pay no personal taxes to it. The city may well become—as it already has in many instances—a service area for the affluent middle-class suburbanites who return home to their suburban community, where they deposit their money, buy their wares, and pay their taxes. Since this trend is likely to continue, new sources of tax revenue and city financing will have to be found.

THE DECAYING URBAN CORE

The movement of much industry and commerce as well as many middle-class residents out of the city has been paralleled by a sub-stantial migration of the poor into the city. While the sons and daughters of many early immigrants have vacated their ethnic enclaves for residence in suburbia, or for more prosperous areas of the large city, the rapid influx of blacks and other impoverished minority groups into the city's tenements has perpetuated the slum and ghetto. To illustrate how rapid the migration of blacks into the cities has been, it can be noted that in 1910, 73 percent of the black population lived in the rural South, whereas by 1960, 73 percent resided in urban areas (Taeuber and Taeuber, 1965). A similar migration of rural Puerto Ricans and Chicanos has occurred.

The massiveness of the influx of the poor into the cities has created extensive demands for low-cost housing, which is available only in the decaying tenements that were constructed around the turn of the century. Since the demand for low-cost housing has been great and the supply low (especially for blacks, who have been openly discriminated against), landlords have maintained the tradi-tion, first initiated in the last century, of charging comparatively high rents and providing little property maintenance and few improvements. While in absolute terms the quality of ghetto housing is now superior to that at the turn of the century, the standards of what constitutes decent housing have risen as the level of affluence in the broader society has escalated. Thus, housing still is a major social problem for the urban minorities who are forced to live in dwellings that are substandard and dilapidated by these escalated standards.

While the persistence of substandard housing at the city's core is often the result of personal greed by landlords and of the inability of the poor to afford better living conditions, the urban housing blight has other sources—many of them *built into* the structure of American institutions and communities. The federal government has never really, until very recently, approached the question of housing on a national level. For example, in a society with a federally conceived and financed highway system and with a national farm policy, there currently is no national urban policy, even though American society has been urbanized for half a century. There has traditionally been no national research—until just the last few years—on how to deal with the construction and distribution of housing. Research financed by the federal government on housing lags billions of dollars behind that financed by the government for agriculture, manufacturing, medicine, and other areas of applied technology. Even massive federal programs such as Urban Renewal, Public Housing, and Model Cities have had little impact on the housing blight. In many cases, as with the FHA and VA housing mortgage insurance programs, the federal government has encouraged urban blight by stimulating the building of new houses in the suburbs rather than in the cities. Probably the best demonstration of how unsystematic and uncomprehensive the federal government's approach to urban problems has been is the fact that the Department of Agriculture has existed for 100 years, while it was only in 1965 that the Department of Housing and Urban Development was initiated (Dentler, 1967:296–319). If one compares the funds available to each of these cabinet offices, and their respective power, the neglect of urban conditions by the federal government becomes even more marked.

The structure of the housing industry also helps to account for the current blight in the cities (Dentler, 1967:302–319; Greer, 1965). The building industry is a private enterprise system that naturally seeks to make a profit. Contractors are therefore likely to build in middle- and high-income areas in the suburbs where profits are greatest. The housing industry is also a *local* industry with few national corporations of the magnitude of Ford and General Motors. Yet the housing industry provides one of the most important commodities, a home, and does an annual business of close to $25 billion, employs over 5 million workers, and creates a vast market for other industries. However, because the housing industry is so decentralized, it goes comparatively unregulated by the federal government, with the result that clear national housing policies—should they come to exist—would be difficult to implement, as has been the case with the Urban Renewal program, Model Cities, and other federal programs.

Other features of the building industry prevent the introduction of money-saving innovations and technologies that could reduce costs to a point where it would be profitable for contractors to build low-income housing. For example, current technology would allow for mass production and assembly of almost all components for a house—from the roof to the plumbing—in factories. Most trade unions in the building industry, however, require (in their contracts) on-the-site assembly (and production) of houses. Production of housing in factories would, of course, displace many workers; and until new jobs can be guaranteed for workers in the building industry, unions are naturally going to resist changes in the present mode of home construction. Also, many local building codes prevent the introduction of new building materials that could reduce the cost of home construction. Like the entire building industry, building codes are locally established. Typically, the requirements of these codes pertain to the use of specific materials rather than the performance of materials. Instead of stipulating that building materials be of a certain strength and durability, local codes usually specify the actual material that must be used by a contractor and architect. Local contractors, subcontractors, and building suppliers, operating as a powerful vested interest, can often assure a material emphasis in building codes by exerting pressure on local officials who establish these codes. At times the FHA reinforces this roadblock to the introduction of new building materials by requiring certain materials in homes before it will insure a mortgage.

RACIAL AND ETHNIC SEGREGATION

As the affluent whites moved out of the city, the poor, especially blacks, migrated into the cities. Because they came from rural areas and had few industrial skills and because of racial discrimination, blacks were confined to the worst jobs in the most dilapidated parts of the city. Currently racial and ethnic minorities are locked into the decaying city core and are surrounded by more affluent whites in the suburbs. Furthermore, within the core cities, segregation of the racial and ethnic minorities into ghettos, like that of their immigrant predecessors, remains extremely high. The explosiveness of such "urban apartheid" is all too apparent—as is explored extensively in Chapter 10. For the present, it can be noted that the residential segregation of blacks continues to be high within cities and between the city and suburbs (Taeuber and Taeuber, 1965; Farley and Taeuber, 1968). Such segregation, as will be discussed, is the result of more than racial bigotry; it has been *built into* the structure of the federal government's policies and the demographic forces accompanying American urbanization.

ATTACKING URBAN PROBLEMS: PROBLEMS AND DILEMMAS

As the affluence of the broader society—especially the suburbs—has increased, those trapped in the cities have inevitably had an escalated sense of deprivation. Although slow to respond and somewhat ineffectual when it did, the federal government began to recognize the deprivations of residents in the core cities, as well as the deteriorating physical conditions of central business districts. Over the last 25 years this recognition has been translated into a series of programs designed to "cure" city problems.

THE PUBLIC HOUSING PROGRAM

One of the first programs for providing housing to the poor was the federal Public Housing Program (created by the Housing Act of 1937). The initiation of this program must be viewed in the context of the FHA and VA mortgage insurance programs, which encouraged whites to move into single-family dwellings in the *suburbs*. At the same time, the federal government was building large public housing complexes in the core *city*, usually in ghetto areas. Such dual programs furthered residential segregation by confining impoverished minorities, especially blacks, to the core city, while subsidizing the migration of whites to single-family dwellings in the suburbs.[3] Furthermore, until the early 1950s the FHA often kept affluent blacks from migrating to suburbs by warning realtors, FHA authorities, and bankers in its manuals that racially integrated neighborhoods were likely to deteriorate rapidly and were poor financial risks. The FHA backed up this warning by refusing to insure housing developments that were racially integrated—resulting in the emergence of racial covenants in early American suburbs (Abrams, 1967:59–64; Grigsby, 1964:223). Since this policy existed during the great postwar exodus of whites

---

[3] A 1971 U.S. Supreme Court ruling makes it possible for suburban residents to block the construction of public housing in their communities. This ruling assures that public housing will remain big-city ghetto housing.

from and the migrations of racial minorities to urban areas, it established a pattern of suburban-city segregation. It is in this context that the public housing project was initiated—usually a large, monolithic, concrete and brick structure erected in the middle of the decaying city core. At a time when American values, tastes, and preferences were shifting to the single-family dwelling, the federal government was forcing the poor to live in "supertenements." As Catherine Bauer Wurster (1966:247) commented: "Life in the usual public housing project just is not the way most American families want to live. Nor does it reflect our accepted values as to the way people should live." Furthermore, public housing in *government-managed* housing—a plight that only the poor must endure. Compounding this situation is the overall architectural design of housing projects: They have a standardized institutional appearance, much like that of a hospital or prison. For example, the Robert Taylor Project in Chicago, where 28,000 people are confined to several huge high-rise buildings can be typified as a $70 million ghetto that residents refer to as the "Congo Hilton" (Schaffer et al., 1970). Even though public housing projects may be initially clean, the lack of maintenance funds coupled with their high population densities, often make older projects dirty, unsanitary, and trash strewn.

In addition to their physical appearance, public housing projects, by imposing income ceilings on their residents, create income homogeneity, which adds to the projects' institutional profile. Furthermore, in a society that values freedom from government constraint, the whole concept of a government-managed home is automatically stigmatizing. The result is that those who can afford to would often rather live in a dilapidated "private enterprise slum" where more diversity is possible.

Recently, recognizing the error of the original Public Housing Program, new legislation has been passed in an attempt to remedy some of its deficiencies. For example, the Turnkey Program allows public housing to be built and managed by private corporations and encourages the building of more dispersed, low-rise buildings. While these new kinds of projects may mitigate the institutional and managed character of traditional public housing, two fundamental problems remain with such programs: (1) The black poor are not allowed to *own* their houses as are whites in the suburbs.[4]

[4] Some might argue that the poor cannot afford houses and hence should be thankful for the public housing subsidy. What this line of argument ignores is that most whites could not afford houses until the FHA and VA were established. To argue now that the government should not subsidize the poor in home ownership is to contend that the best housing subsidies should go only to the affluent. It is a curious reversal of the concept of subsidy to maintain that it should *not* be applied to those most in need.

(2) Projects still encourage the segregation of blacks in the cities and whites in the suburbs. New approaches to public housing will not quickly or effectively undo the inequities that have existed between 1935, when the FHA was created, and the 1950s, when FHA policies were finally changed. The reason is that, for close to 20 years, whites have had their ownership of single-family dwellings in the suburbs subsidized by the federal government (FHA and VA), while blacks and other minorities have been shunted into public housing complexes where only their rent was subsidized. Even as recently as 1967, the FHA continued to discriminate against the poor by affirming that "blighted areas" in the core of cities could not be insured for mortgages—thus preventing blacks and other minorities from owning even dilapidated homes and forcing them into slum rentals or public housing. Only after the Detroit riot of 1968 was this policy modified (Harrington, 1968).

THE URBAN RENEWAL PROGRAM

The Housing Act of 1949 created the Urban Renewal Program, which focused on the overall physical and economic needs of the cities. The goals of the program were stated somewhat vaguely: (1) to provide a decent home for every citizen; (2) to assure well-planned, rationally organized neighborhoods; (3) to beautify American cities and communities (Greer, 1965).

As lofty and laudable as these goals would appear, they were implemented within constraints that made their realization most difficult. First, America's large cities had expanded under pressures of early industrialization when sources of power and transportation were limited—thus forcing a centralized-city pattern of land use. It is unlikely that patterns of land use appropriate to the nineteenth century are always viable in light of the massive technological, economic, and demographic changes over the last 50 years (Greer, 1965; Banfield, 1970). The Urban Renewal Program was therefore committed to basic goals that, at times, went against fundamental patterns of reorganization of American urban life. Second, urban renewal was initiated on what are perhaps questionable premises: (1) The existing private enterprise facilities—banks, construction companies, real estate firms, and trade unions—were to provide the vehicle for each project's implementation. Buildings were therefore built by private corporations for a *private market*. Since these same private enterprise processes were responsible for many of the current urban problems—from racial segregation to exploitation of the poor—the wisdom of the government's policy to preserve the sanctity of, and in many cases to subsidize, private enterprise in this sphere can be questioned. (2) Each urban renewal project was to be initiated at the local level and run by the local city government. Considering the political tradition of American cities for corruption and patronage, this provision of the Housing Act was also of questionable wisdom. For indeed, it soon became apparent that urban renewal was, at times, the political tool of big- and little-city government machines. (3) Urban renewal projects tended to be concerned only with physical restoration of the cities, not with changing the social pattern of community life.

The structure of urban renewal has often subverted the implementation of its goals. Generally, a city must first initiate a program through a local agency, which is to work up an urban renewal plan to be approved by the regional and federal renewal agency. If approved, the federal government will supply most of the money needed to acquire necessary land and subsidize the demolition of buildings. Once the land is acquired, the approved plan is contracted to a *private* developer who implements the plan, while being supervised by the local, regional, and federal urban renewal agencies. One of the main shortcomings of this structure is that political biases and pressures from local political officials, as well as from local real estate and business enterprises, greatly determine what is to be renewed in a city. While the federal government oversees the project, the local redevelopment agency is under heavy pressure from local political and economic interests. One consequence has been that downtown areas where business interests are strongest have been renewed, usually at the expense of the poor. For example, downtown blight has frequently been eliminated by displacing the poor from their slum residences and forcing them into either public housing or into even worse slums. When new housing is finally built in the former slum, it has tended to be in the form of upper- and middle-income complexes, since this kind of housing is most profitable on a *private* real estate market.[5] Even when low-income housing has been built, it typically is more expensive than the old and often suffers from the same drawbacks as public housing.

Because urban renewal has been, since its incipiency, committed to reviving the old urban polis, many cities have "renewed" their downtown area into a kind of cultural-economic center of office and civic buildings as well as cultural attractions such as music

[5] Building low-cost housing and showing even a small profit is probably impossible for a private developer, especially since building codes and labor unions prevent the use of cheaper assemblyline methods of construction. Clearly such low-cost housing must be subsidized by the federal government so that the poor can afford it and the developer can make a reasonable profit. As of yet no effective fiscal formula has been developed to allow aid for the poor.

centers and museums. These projects have been designed to entice middle-income residents to move back into the city, but unfortunately these residents have tended rather to visit the renewed facilities—leaving their tax money in suburbia. Oftentimes, the net impact of urban renewal has been to provide new recreation areas for the suburbanite, while displacing the poor and forcing them into other, already overcrowded ghettos or, even worse, public housing projects (Anderson, 1964). Since the poor have not been as well organized or as powerful as the political and economic elites of cities, restoration of downtown areas has usually taken precedence over low-income housing, with the result that "at a cost of more than three billion dollars the Urban Renewal Agency has succeeded in materially reducing the supply of low-cost housing in American cities" (Greer, 1965:3).

Where attempts at slum elimination and restoration do take precedence over political and economic interests, blacks and other poor, as in public housing, are still forced to stay in the core city. Furthermore, while there can be little doubt that in terms of physical facilities urban renewal has improved the conditions of some ghettos, it has not attempted to touch upon the social problems such as crime and drug use. In their desire to plan neighborhoods rationally, local agencies have often ignored the social and human side of a neighborhood in the name of mere physical restoration. Social isolation in towering, impersonal complexes and victimization in untended elevators and corridors are tragically recurrent themes.

Perhaps many of the problems of urban renewal stem from its failure to focus on the whole metropolitan area, for if one considers the cities to be "sick and decaying," the solution to their problems can probably best come from metropolitanwide programs. In focusing only on the symptoms of decay, urban renewal has often ignored the "disease" that is built into the technological, economic, and demographic underpinnings of the modern metropolis.

THE MODEL CITIES PROGRAM

In 1966 Congress enacted the Demonstrations Cities Act in an effort to overcome some of the deficiencies in the Urban Renewal Program. In general, the Model Cities Program created by the act attempts to revitalize a city's economy by strengthening its tax base while providing for improved low-income housing. Unlike urban renewal, the Model Cities Program requires a more comprehensive plan to improve the housing, employment, business, and social service picture in a city. Furthermore, cities must select for development districts that evidence a large proportion of deteriorating housing (Schaffer et al., 1970). The resulting renewal or development plan must receive the approval of local groups and leaders *in the renewal area;* it must provide adequate relocation procedures for those displaced; it must involve and employ local residents in the program; and it requires attractive building design utilizing the latest technology and the altering of building codes if necessary. City governments that submit a plan that includes these provisions are awarded a cash bonus or subsidy to pay for up to 90 percent of development costs. Additional grants can be obtained from the government to improve various municipal services, such as libraries, schools, sanitation and recreation facilities, in the development area.

While the Model Cities Program eliminates many of the problems of urban renewal, several drawbacks remain (Greer, 1965): (1) The program still is initiated by local officials who are more often interested in development of the business area than the slums. The program also is subject to pressures from local vested interests, such as building and real estate industries. Yet the program, in requiring low-income housing development and local residential involvement, does represent a significant improvement over urban renewal. (2) When the Model Cities Program is initiated in large cities, rarely does it cut down on the degree of residential segregation of racial and ethnic groups. While improvements in the downtown area may help recruit middle-income residents back into the city, it does little to break down walls of discrimination and segregation. (3) The program, like urban renewal, focuses only on the city and not on a whole metropolitan area and therefore goes against the tide of suburbanization. In doing so, it subsidizes the downtown business district in its competition with suburban shopping centers. At the same time it perpetuates the segregated position of ethnic and racial groups within the core city, albeit in somewhat improved housing. One of the basic problems of local programs initiated only in the city is that they do little to help the poor migrate out to the suburbs and thereby eliminate urban-suburban segregation.

THE HOUSING SUBSIDY PROGRAMS

After 33 years of subsidizing middle-income homeowners (under FHA and VA programs), the federal government, with the passage of the Housing and Urban Development Act of 1968, initiated a subsidy program for lower-income residents. The act provides for interest-rate subsidies for home purchase among families with incomes between $3000 and $7000. The subsidy comes in the form of a cash gift ranging from $40 to $50 a month to be used for mortgage payments. One problem with the program is that it does not reach the most impoverished, those with incomes below $3000, trapped in the worst urban slums. Another problem is that it does not provide the poor with sufficient funds to meet the high costs of home maintenance.

Another subsidy program initiated with the Housing Act of 1961, but significantly bolstered by the 1966 and 1968 acts, provides for rent subsidies. The poor inevitably have had to pay a very high proportion of their monthly income into housing at the sacrifice of clothing, food, and medical care (Schorr, 1963). The rent subsidy program attempts to keep the proportion down by paying the difference between the actual rent and 25 percent of the monthly income of low- to moderate-income families.

While subsidies may carry little stigma in slum or ghetto areas in large cities, it is not clear what would happen to minority families who attempted to use the benefits of the program to buy or rent in the suburbs, where a subsidy would perhaps carry a burdensome stigma (Glazer, 1967). Coupled with typically discriminatory practices of developers and real estate agents, the program will have minimal impact on moving ghetto residents into the suburbs.

GRANTS-IN-AID AND REVENUE SHARING

Over the last decades, states and cities have received much grants-in-aid from the federal government. Grant-in-aid is the mechanism by which the federal and local governments—state, county, city—share financing and administering vital programs. There are a wide variety of grant-in-aid programs, but they reveal a number of common features: (1) Federal tax revenues are given to states and local communities for specialized activities, such as education, welfare, health care, city development, and housing. (2) State and local governments are to administer the programs financed by grants-in-aid, but there are usually clear guidelines as to how, for whom, and for what the combined federal and local monies can be used. Moreover, there are usually specified auditing procedures for determining if local governments are conforming to federal conditions and guidelines. (3) Early grant-in-aid programs required the local government receiving federal grant-in-aid money to "match" each federal dollar with locally derived dollars; but, during the 1960s, the great majority of grant-in-aid programs were enacted with more than 50 percent federal participation, and with some totally financed by the federal government.

Grant-in-aid has now become one of the principal ways federal monies are channeled back to state and local governments. There are now close to 600 grant-in-aid programs, and this form of assistance constitutes over 25 percent of federal outlays for domestic assistance, with much of this assistance going to cities.

The grant-in-aid program has established useful relations among federal, state, and local governments, but despite its many accomplishments—public housing, model cities, welfare, education, health care, community development, and the like—a number of problems are built into the system (Reagan, 1972:86–88):

First, much grant-in-aid money is bestowed as a project grant that allows those governments with professional staffs, who are good at "grantmanship," to receive favorable financial treatment. Such cities will tend to be the most affluent, and thus, the least in need of federal monies. Large cities represent an exception; they have extensive needs for revenue and they do have effective professional staffs. But suburban governments—the least likely to have need—are equally effective in securing grant money, thereby depriving cities and poor communities of monies.

A second problem is that grants requiring matching monies can force local governments to channel their limited monies into programs that are less than essential. To some extent, the proliferation of large numbers and varieties of grant-in-aid programs has lessened this problem, but this proliferation has created a third problem with grant-in-aid: the creation of so many overlapping programs has caused severe administrative problems. Local governments are often confused about which of several overlapping programs, each with different requirements and administrative procedures, to select for their particular needs.

Finally, grant-in-aid money can do little for communities whose needs lie outside the aid categories. Many intense needs—especially in the large cities and poor communities—are not covered by a grant-in-aid. Moreover, these cities may have used monies that could address these problems to match less essential programs that do provide grant-in-aid money.

Recognizing these problems, *revenue sharing* has been implemented in the 1970s as a supplement, and in some cases as an alternative, to the grant-in-aid system. In 1972, Congress passed and President Nixon signed the State and Local Assistance Act which provided for the distribution of $30.2 billion from 1972 to 1976 to 40,000 state and local governmental units. The amounts to be distributed are determined by complex formulas that are affected by such variables as the nature of the governmental unit (state, county, township, city), its population, its per capita income, its adjusted taxes, and the number of intergovernmental money transfers it receives. The unique feature of revenue sharing is that the money is given with "no strings," matching requirements, administrative guidelines, or restrictive categories. In passing this legislation a number of outcomes were expected: (1) Local governments could have the freedom to take diverse approaches to their unique problems. (2) The severe financial crisis in many communities, especially the large cities of metropolitan areas, would be mitigated, and thus, many of the present tensions over tax revenues between federal and local government would be lessened. (3) The program would equalize federal expenditures on states and communities by applying the same formula to all local governments. (4) The use of progressive federal income tax revenues to finance local government programs would reduce the reliance of local governments on less progressive property taxes; and (5) decentralization of resources and administrative power would ensue, thereby realizing more completely the original goal of a federalist governmental system.

Despite its promise, and its partial realization in some communities, a number of problems have become evident (Reagan, 1972:123–132):[6] First, the federal government spreads limited monies to all communities, thereby avoiding the difficult decisions about what priorities are to guide federal assistance to the cities. The federal government is, by virtue of its more detached position, better able to see national problems than local political leaders who are much more likely to be influenced by local interests groups, professional administrators (city planners, police, fire, etc.), real estate interests, and the Chamber of Commerce—all of which are likely to ignore the more chronic needs of many impoverished cities. For example, the most recent evaluative study of revenue sharing reveals that a disproportionate amount of money has been used on capital improvements—city halls, police cars, new fire engines—and not on health, education, and welfare of residents, especially the poor.

Second, cuts in grant-in-aid programs have occurred under the presumption that revenue sharing can make up the difference. Such an assumption ignores the needs of the cities for even more revenues, regardless of their source. Third, revenue sharing could help perpetuate an overall urban pattern that may, in the long run, be fiscally and politically unviable. Revenue sharing might help maintain the problematic political and fiscal structure of metropolitan governments, and thus, it could delay the crisis that could prompt reorganiztion of America's large urban areas.

[6] Unfortunately, data on the uses and impact of revenue sharing are only just becoming available. The most recent published study is *General Revenue Sharing: The First Planned Use Reports*, Washington, D.C.: Government Printing Office, 1973. For references on current research, see *Proceedings of the Conference on Revenue Sharing Research*, Washington, D.C.: GPO, 1973.

The principle vehicles—grant-in-aid and revenue sharing—by which the federal government addresses community problems reveal their own problems of structure. Both grant-in-aid and revenue sharing are probably necessary approaches to urban problems, but unless they are used to induce, and perhaps coerce, fiscal and political reorganization of America's metropolitan regions, their full potential may go unrealized.

HOUSING AND URBAN DEVELOPMENT

In 1965 the Department of Housing and Urban Development (HUD) became a full cabinet-level office. However, it currently does not have the status, tradition, power, or financial resources of other cabinet offices, such as the Department of Defense, Agriculture, or Health, Education, and Welfare. Yet, if in the future a national housing policy with adequate financing can be generated within this new department, there is hope that the largely unsuccessful programs of the past will not be duplicated in the future.

The current dilemmas and problems of America's cities will require concerted efforts on three fronts: (1) the development of new housing technologies; (2) a federal commitment to city development that regulates more extensively the housing industry; and (3) the imposition of new political and fiscal organization on metropolitan areas. A good proportion of HUD's funds are channeled to its office of Urban Research and Technology, where new ideas and approaches to home construction and city planning are being developed. For example, mass-produced homes in factories, regional city planning, and experimental cities are on the drawing boards of this agency. Unless these technologies can be implemented by the basic reorganization of the housing industry, however, progress in changing housing and city patterns in American communities will probably be difficult. As long as the building industry remains local and decentralized, with local contractors, local building trade unions, local building codes, local real estate enterprises, and local government regulation of home construction and city development, there is little possibility for significant progress. While this conclusion may appear harsh, the federal government will probably have to cease relying on the "talents" and "good will" of local building industries and governments to generate more payoff in its programs.

THE FUTURE OF CITIES: PROPOSED DIRECTIONS OF CHANGE

The problems of cities that are incorrectly associated with recent decades were clearly evident, as noted earlier, by the turn of the century. These problems are thus well institutionalized, and programs to alter them will probably involve more than accommodation by the federal government to the housing industry and local governments. The reverse will likely have to be the case in the future, for a national program for the cities may well have to be *imposed* on American communities. While such a conclusion may seem regrettable, solutions have been imposed in other areas, such as agriculture, transportation, commerce, national defense, and many other spheres.

In the face of the diversity and extensiveness of its problems, developing concrete proposals for changing and improving the central city in metropolitan areas is difficult. When the conceptual inadequacies of proposals are placed up against the manifold sources of political, economic, and social resistance, such proposals may take on a utopian character. Nevertheless, there is at least a direction toward which change should move if the cities are to become attractive places to live. While certainly an incomplete proposal and clearly not politically practical at the moment, some desirable directions of change are briefly discussed:

1. A new form of panmetropolitan governmental authority will probably need to be established over both the central city and the suburban fringe. County governments may have to be eliminated in metropolitan areas, and their place taken by a metropolitan authority. On the basis of population and other criteria, each city within a metropolitan area could have representation on the decision-making body of the metropolitan authority. The most important function of this authority would be to set the tax rate for the entire metropolitan region, collect and pool the property tax, and redistribute these revenues in accordance with a formula weighted by population size and per capita income of residents. The greater the size and the lower the per capita income of residents, the more revenues a community would receive from the metropolitan authority.

2. In addition to allocating tax revenues, the metropolitan authority could be responsible for financing certain services that can be more efficiently undertaken at a metropolitanwide level. These would include police and fire protection, transportation, health and social services, and pollution control. However, the local governments of the metropolitan region would be responsible for the staffing and administration of these services. Within very broad fiscal and policy guidelines, diversity in the way these services are administered could be encouraged as local governments attempt to meet the unique needs of their population.

3. Aside from administering these metropolitanwide services,

local governments would be free to use the liquid tax resources received from the metropolitan authority in any way considered desirable by their elected officials. Additionally, local communities would have administrative control of their schools, which would not be financed by regressive property taxes, as is currently the case, but by federal revenues. Also, local communities would have the option of applying for federal urban renewal, Model Cities, business development, and mortgage subsidy funds, and federal policies would give priority to areas of the core city.

Such guidelines for future action on the cities are devoid of the details that give a proposal other than a utopian character. Yet, it must be recognized that old patterns of city government, outdated fiscal formulas, chaotic and wasteful ways of providing public services, the growing problems of community pollution, and the exploitation of cities by the affluent suburbs may require a radically different form of urban polis. The new forms of government in metropolitan areas should seek to maximize the economies and equities that can come with centralization, and at the same time provide for responsiveness of city governments to the unique needs of their residents. Such is the dilemma of structure facing America's cities.

Chapter 10

COMMUNITY SEGREGATION IN AMERICA

AMERICAN COMMUNITY SEGREGATION

Where people live in America is to a great extent a reflection of their race. Black Americans are increasingly being confined to the decaying cores of large cities and surrounded by whites in the sprawling suburbs. Of the total metropolitan population in the United States, over 80 percent of its black residents live in the core downtown area of the big cities. Since over 40 percent of the black population of the United States lives in the 20 largest of these metropolitan areas in both the North and South, segregation involves the confinement of blacks to the extreme vicissitudes of the decaying cores of America's larger cities. As Charles Abrams (1969: 38) once remarked: "An urban society in which there is freedom of movement and which sees 35 million people move annually from house to house, city to city, and state to state . . . cannot put up a 'No Entry' sign (for blacks) as many suburbs have done." Thus, in many ways, the wall between the big city and suburbia has become the "new Mason-Dixon line" of American society and represents a form of "urban apartheid." For indeed, black Americans are confined to large housing tracts in ghetto areas where black-owned homes are three times more likely to be substandard than those of whites, and where black-rented units are twice as likely to be substandard as white-rented units (Taeuber and Taeuber, 1965: 140). In order to eliminate such segregation and create racial balance in large cities such as Washington D.C., by the year 2000, George Schermer (1967:120) estimates that every year 1200 black families would have to move out of slums into the suburbs and 4000 white families would have to return to the city. Achieving a balance by the year 2000 in Philadelphia would require that 6000 black families move to the suburbs and 3000 white families move back to the city every year. Similar mass migrations would have to occur in other large cities to significantly break down current suburban-urban apartheid. However, data reveal that large-city residential segregation may have increased during the last decade (Farley and Taeuber, 1968).

Segregation by race is more pervasive than large city-suburban fringe patterns would reveal. In a pioneering study using census data, Karl and Alma Taeuber documented high degrees of residential segregation within 207 American cities (1965). Furthermore, within a city, blacks tend to be segregated not only from whites, but also from other minorities. Even when blacks do manage to maintain suburban homes, they are sometimes forced to do so in segregated developments. For example, the black population in the suburban ring of the Chicago metropolitan area increased from 44,000 in 1950 to 78,000 in 1960, but the apparent improvement occurred in heavily black suburbs or in industrial suburbs with their own black enclaves (Taeuber and Taeuber, 1965).

Racial segregation is thus a fact of American community life. Its persistence will continue to be a major source of strain and conflict. The forces that have created and maintained urban apartheid and all the hardships that go with it are built into the structure of the society—indicating that only major alterations in America's urban profile will eliminate the "dark ghetto" which has become a landmark in virtually every American city.

CREATION OF THE DARK GHETTO IN AMERICA

As late as 1900, three-fourths of all black Americans lived in rural areas of the South (Taeuber and Taeuber, 1958:121–127). Between 1900 and 1970 virtually the entire black population has become transformed from a rural to a predominantly urban aggregate, with well over 70 percent living in urban areas. In 1900 over 90 percent of the black population lived in the South, whereas today only about half do. The extensiveness of the migration into northern urban areas is revealed by the fact that ". . . more Negroes live in the New York metropolitan area than in any single Southern state, about as many Negroes live in metropolitan Chicago as in the entire state of Mississippi, and more Negroes live in metropolitan Philadelphia than in the entire states of Arkansas and Kentucky combined" (Pettigrew, 1969:48). Thus, as blacks have moved from rural to urban locations, and as they have migrated from the South to the North, they have been "ghettoized" and segregated from much of American society.

ECONOMIC AND DEMOGRAPHIC FACTORS

Since their beginnings in the United States as slaves, blacks have been economically impoverished. Such impoverishment was perpetuated after slavery by Jim Crow laws that maintained segregated facilities and by decisions of the U.S. Supreme Court that sanctioned such segregation. There was widespread discrimination and violence against blacks in the South, and their caste position was woven into the American social fabric (Turner and Singleton, 1976). Most blacks had unskilled farming jobs, whether as tenant farmers or as poorly paid labor for large landholders. Around the turn of the century, however, even this marginal economic position of blacks in the rural South worsened (H. Hamilton, 1964): (1) The high birthrates of rural families began to exceed the obtainable food supply. (2) Rapid changes in the form of agriculture were taking place as farms became increasingly mechanized, as new government programs for limiting farm production were enacted, and as the boll weevil devastated the cotton industry. (3) And finally, as a kind of economic coup de grace, cotton cultivation began to shift from the South to the Southwest and West.

Combined with these "push" factors forcing people out of the South were a series of "pull" factors from northern cities. The onset of World War I had stopped the massive immigrations from Europe; as wartime production increased—first from European demand and then from internal demand when the United States entered the war—the need for labor in northern factories increased. Recruiters from northern cities began actively to encourage rural blacks to leave the South, with the result that an estimated 400,000 to 1 million blacks left to work in northern industries between 1914 and 1920 (Franklin, 1948:465; H. Hamilton, 1964). Since industrial jobs were located in the large cities, black migrants began to settle in the cores of densely populated urban areas. In addition to these new economic opportunities, the persistent brutality, lynchings, and intimidation of blacks in the South made almost any new opportunity or hope of a new life seem bright. However, as blacks settled in northern cities, they were again subjected to white violence and to discrimination, which forced them into the worst of housing slums (Pinkney, 1969:31). John Hope Franklin (1948:471–476) recounts that the summer of 1919 became known as the "red summer" because of the violence and bloodshed that took place. From June to the end of September, 25 race riots erupted in cities; 14 blacks were killed in one incident, and 23 blacks and 15 whites died in Chicago in another outbreak. Thus, initial migrations of blacks out of the South and into northern cities resulted in the emergence of patterns of residential segregation and white-black antipathy that persist today.

During the 1930s migration of blacks into the North declined as the depression shut off economic opportunities. With the industrial boom stimulated by World War II, migrations again became extensive and marked a massive shift in the distribution of blacks in communities. As with their predecessors, these wartime and postwar migrants were subjected to job and housing discrimination as well as white violence, resulting in their confinement to slums.

Equally important to the plight and entrapment of blacks in the urban slums was the timing of their migrations—the last of a series of migrations that began around 1820. Since 1910 millions of blacks —6 million since 1950 alone—have come to the ghettos from the South, but they have brought with them few marketable skills. Because of employment practices in the South, blacks had been kept out of skilled jobs that might have given them the work backgrounds useful in northern cities.[1] Furthermore, blacks came to the cities at precisely that point in time when strong backs were decreasingly needed, for new technologies were rendering obsolete, at an escalating rate, unskilled and semiskilled jobs. Thus, unlike their white predecessors, black migrants had difficulty even finding unskilled jobs from which they could work their way up and out of poverty. And during the post-World War II period, when wartime production and jobs declined, large numbers of blacks moved into the cities just as new technologies took away jobs that had previously been an economic springboard to other generations of white migrants. Furthermore, as industry began to move to the suburbs, blacks could not move with it because they lacked necessary skills and, more significantly, whites and the federal government blocked black migrations to the suburbs. Even when suburbanization of blacks occurred, they were at times forced into "mini" ghettos where white discrimination and few job skills kept them trapped in poor housing and economic impoverishment.

Today considerable migration of blacks into large northern cities still occurs, but the stereotype of the rural sharecropper encountering the big city is no longer very accurate. The more typical pattern is for young blacks to come to the North from a southern city or from another northern city. The modern migrants are younger, better educated, more cosmopolitan, far more militant, and less religious than their parents (Pettigrew, 1969:49). These migrants have grown up with promises of change and betterment in eco-

[1] There were many skilled blacks in the South, but they represented only a small proportion of the total black population. However, these skilled blacks were underrepresented in the migrations to the North.

nomic conditions; but as they migrate, it becomes evident that they still must live in ghettos and that economic opportunities are not that readily available.

Currently, the black population increase in the core of American cities stems as much from high birthrates as from migrations. In 1968, 15 million blacks lived in metropolitan communities, with 11.8 million of these living in the central core of large cities. Nearly 90 percent of the nation's black population growth, including both migrations and birthrates, occurred in central cities; if this rate of growth continues, around 17 million blacks will soon live in the cores of large cities (Schaffer et al., 1970:31). And if migrations stopped today, the natural population increase in central cities would swell the black population to nearly 16 million in the urban cores (*Report of the National Advisory Commission on Civil Disorders*, 1968:227). By the end of this decade, New Orleans, Richmond, Baltimore, Jacksonville, Cleveland, St. Louis, Detroit, and perhaps Philadelphia, Oakland, and Chicago will have a majority of black residents. If industrial migration to the suburbs continues and if patterns of segregation and discrimination in housing continue, American cities could potentially become the most volatile in history. Coupled with the fact that black birthrates did not begin to decline until the beginning of the last decade, the 1970s will see a high proportion of young blacks, and the potential for urban riots will probably remain high (Pettigrew, 1969:50), even though it appears that racial violence has declined in the 1970s.

RACIAL DISCRIMINATION

Discrimination against black Americans is very much a part of the American heritage. Probably the most blatant form of discrimination has been violent acts of intimidation by whites. White violence and lynchings were common practices in the rural South in this century. For example a crowd of 3000 whites in Tennessee once turned out to watch the burning of a black in response to a notice in a newspaper advertising the event. Similarly, white violence and threats of violence against blacks occurred during the early migrations of blacks into northern cities.

The *pattern* of discrimination in urban America has helped, in fact, to account for the ghettoization of the black population. When blacks ventured into white residential areas, they were often beaten (Pinkney, 1969). For example, in the East St. Louis riot of 1917, the Chicago riot of 1919, and the Detroit riot of 1943, the whites initiated violence against the blacks (Allen and Adair, 1969:31–37). For fear of intimidation by the white majority, blacks moved into racial enclaves where housing was the most deteriorated.

Housing discrimination has greatly contributed to racial segregation in the United States. Blacks have typically had to pay high rents for deteriorated housing. For example, the Taeubers (1965: 139–140) have documented that, in northern metropolitan areas, the median monthly rents of whites and blacks are not significantly different; however, the difference in the quality of housing is extremely great, with black rentals twice as likely to be substandard. A similar study of housing costs of blacks and whites in the Chicago area disclosed that on the whole nonwhites had to pay around $15 per month more than whites for the same quality of housing. Given the large differences in family income for blacks and whites, blacks must devote a much larger proportion of their total income to secure housing, even substandard housing. The Taeubers (1966: 140) conclude that in 1960 about 33 percent of blacks spent over one-third of their income on housing, whereas around only 20 percent of whites had to do so. Black families, then, must sacrifice such things as quality food, health care, and recreation to secure housing that on the whole is of poorer quality than that for whites who earn comparable incomes.

Housing discrimination has been as intense in the suburbs as in the city. Housing developments in the suburbs initially had restrictive covenants excluding blacks. When these were declared illegal and proved unenforceable, communities used new discriminatory strategies, such as changing zoning regulations in order to prohibit black housing developments. For example, Charles Abrams (1966:516) reports that when a union tried to build houses for its black members in Milpitas, California, the area was rezoned for other than residential use, and when a private developer submitted plans for integrated housing in Deerfield, Illinois, the proposed land site was condemned for use as a park.

Resistance of white suburban governments to the entrance of blacks into better housing is one of the most oppressive forms of racial discrimination in American metropolitan areas. This resistance has been reinforced by presidential policy statements and a 1971 U.S. Supreme Court ruling. In 1971 President Richard Nixon pledged that, while the government would "vigorously enforce laws against racial discrimination in housing," it would not force affluent suburbs to accept housing projects intended for the poor. Since most poor blacks probably cannot get out of the ghetto without such housing projects, this policy statement condemns most blacks to the large ghetto of the central city. A Supreme Court ruling buttressing this policy upheld state laws that give voters in a community the right to block the construction of low-rent housing—thus making it easier for communities to exclude poor blacks.

GOVERNMENT POLICIES AND PRACTICES

In the last chapter, some of the federal programs designed to "rescue" the cities were reviewed. On the whole these programs have been less successful than anticipated and have worked at cross-purposes with other programs. Moreover, many of them have contributed to racial segregation within cities and between large cities and their suburbs.

The Federal Housing Administration (FHA) was established under the New Deal in the depressed 1930s. The philosophy behind the FHA is that the building industry relies on a contant flow of mortgage money that the federal government must guarantee. The outgrowth of this philosophy was for the federal government to insure mortgages lent out by private banks and loan associations. If a borrower forfeited on a mortgage the federal government agreed to buy the mortgage up. Under this program, lenders and builders have been able to make profits with little risk or real investment, for the FHA, and later the Veterans Administration (VA), was to serve as a stimulus to the building industry, while becoming "a sales tool for realtors" (Abrams, 1969:37). While there is little doubt that the FHA and the VA mortgage insurance programs stimulated the building industry and subsidized lending institutions with close to $4 billion in bought-up mortgages, they did little to improve the housing conditions of the poor. In fact, they actively discriminated against blacks in several conspicuous ways:

1. FHA refused to underwrite racially integrated neighborhoods because, as its manual (until 1950) proclaimed: "If a neighborhood is to retain stability it is necessary that properties shall continue to be occupied by the same social and racial classes" (Abrams, 1966:523). From 1950 to 1962 the FHA was officially neutral on racial integration, but in practice it was segregationist (Pettigrew, 1969:58). Not until President John Kennedy's executive antidiscrimination order in early 1962 did even the tone of federal housing policy change. But even then it remained, as Pettigrew summarizes, "ineffectively integrationist."

2. The FHA subsidized the white middle-class exodus to the suburbs while preventing blacks from joining in the suburbanization of communities. Without FHA, and later VA, insurance, lending institutions would not have allowed moderate-income whites to assume home mortgages. By subsidizing the lending institutions in home mortgages, the FHA thus encouraged whites to move to the suburbs, where single-family dwellings could readily be built.

Public housing, also initiated during the New Deal, was designed to alleviate substandard housing for whites in large cities. Only with the extensive migrations of blacks into American cities during the post-World War II period did it come to profoundly effect the pattern of segregation in America. Originally, public housing was run exclusively by the federal government in an effort to keep it out of the hands of the big political machines of the cities. Furthermore, public housing was initially set up, much like the FHA, to stimulate the sagging building industry; not until 1937 did it acquire the social purpose of eliminating substandard housing for the poor. About this same time, public housing was taken out of the exclusive control of the federal government and was turned over to local city governments, which, it was thought, could do the job "quicker, cheaper, and better than [the] federal bureaucracy" (Abrams, 1969:35). The change in policy had two consequences for racial segregation: (1) It probably forestalled indefinitely the possibility of federally initiated and controlled public housing projects in the suburbs. Once turned over to the cities, public housing was built almost exclusively in their cores. (2) Because public housing tended to be built in existing black slums, it perpetuated patterns of racial segregation within the city by providing the only low-cost housing available for blacks; in doing so, it kept blacks from migrating to the suburbs.

So far, urban renewal has largely been a subsidy for the downtown business district and private developers of middle- and upper-class housing in cities. Urban renewal has cleared vast tracts of city land and has managed to displace blacks from their slum homes into the equally degrading and dehumanizing public housing projects. While slum housing is not pleasant, many residents have preferred to live in it rather than in the standardized, high-rise, government-run housing complexes.

Over the last decade, Congress and the Supreme Court have moved to break down housing discrimination. The Civil Rights Act of 1968 prohibits discrimination in either the sale or rental of apartment complexes or housing developments. Real estate brokers are also prohibited from discriminating in the sale of individual, single-family homes. While the law did not prohibit discrimination on the part of owners selling their own property, the Supreme Court, in *Jones* v. *Mayer*, did. Such policies can perhaps lead to the breakdown of discrimination in the suburbs. Coupled with rent and home ownership subsidy programs (see Chapter 11), mobility out of the cities may become increasingly possible, for the first time, for the minority poor.

However, two constraints operate against any immediate changes in residential patterns: (1) Enforcement of open-housing laws is difficult since the Civil Rights Division of the Department of Justice is grossly understaffed and underfinanced. (2) These laws operate at cross-purposes with the Urban Renewal and Model Cities programs of the government that tend to confine the poor to the core city. And to the extent that the government fails to back up the open-housing laws, some have argued that it *actively* discriminates against blacks and other minorities trapped in the core cities.

THE DARK GHETTO

In everyday language, the terms *slum* and *ghetto* are used interchangeably. However, in a more specific sense, the two terms denote different features of communities. *Slum* refers to the physical and economic conditions of a residential area, such at its population density, quality of housing, the poverty level of its residents, sanitation facilities, and other public services. *Ghetto* pertains to the degree of residential isolation of a minority population and the degree of organization and cultural unity among that population, such as Jews in Europe before World War II or blacks in the United States today.[2] A ghetto is thus an isolated and segregated neighborhood in the larger community where distinct patterns of leadership, neighborhood organization, and cultural identity among residents are evident.

In the United States, black residential areas in both urban and rural communities are almost always slums of substandard and overcrowded housing, poor sanitation facilities, and low-income residents. The degree of social organization and cultural unity within these slums appears to vary greatly in different areas within a city and from city to city. In the past the label "black ghetto" has not always been completely accurate because in many cases patterns of social organization and cultural unity in black neighborhoods were weak.[3] But recently, with the blacks growing political awareness of cultural bonds and conditions of economic exploitation, black slums can increasingly be labeled ghettos.

GHETTOIZATION OF RURAL BLACKS

Perhaps the most cohesive black ghettos are those in small, rural, southern towns. In these towns, with their segregated resi-

[2] Many authors use the term *ghetto* to refer to the existing degree of *community* (in a sense not used in this book): primary and diffuse relations, strong in-group feelings of solidarity, social organization along kinship lines, social control by custom and tradition, and norms enforced by the entire community. These denote features of ghettos, but we will refrain from terming them *community*. See Wirth, 1928, for an illustration.

[3] Obviously *some* social organization exists, but the degree of social organization and cultural unity varies enormously.

dential slums, housing for blacks is generally unpainted and poorly constructed, in need of repairs, and often without indoor sanitary facilities. A civil rights volunteer described a typical black ghetto in a rural town in Mississippi as follows: "The Negro neighborhood hasn't got a single paved street in it. It's all dirt and gravel roads. The houses vary from beat-up shacks to fairly good-looking cottages. The beat-up places predominate. There are lots of smelly outhouses, and many of the houses have no inside water" (Pinkney, 1969:56).

The condition of black neighborhoods reflects the incomes of their residents. The majority, often nearly 80 percent, earn less than $3000 per year. To earn even this small sum, rural blacks are usually dependent on the white community, for the best jobs available are usually those of sharecropping for white farmers and menial ones in homes and businesses owned by whites.

Rural southern ghettos pivot around the church. Although things are changing rapidly with rural politicalization of blacks, the church has traditionally provided an approved and tolerated (by whites) place "for social activities, a forum for expression on many issues, an outlet for emotional repressions, and a plan for social living" (Johnson, 1941:135). It is because of such organization around the church that the Reverend Dr. Martin Luther King, Jr. in the 1960s, could mobilize rural blacks for many movements, such as voter registration and boycotts (Pinkney, 1969:57). (Conversely, because of the lack of a single communitywide organization—such as the church—in urban communities, Dr. King was less successful in organizing city blacks.)

It is from the rural slums that the original black urban migrants came in hope of finding new opportunities. However, they were soon to find that dilapidated, unsanitary, and crowded housing conditions, white discriminatory practices, and white control of blacks' economic fate did not change with their movement to urban slums. And at times, they had to endure these conditions without the benefit of a well-organized church. This situation can help explain why much of the political activity in black urban ghettos over the last decade has revolved around finding an alternative to the church in generating ghettowide social organization and cultural unity.

URBAN SLUMS AND GHETTOS

Just how much social organization and cultural unity exists in black urban areas is not clear. Kenneth Clark has described the high degree of social and cultural *dis*organization in Harlem, as well as that area's economic and political dependence on the surrounding white community. He emphasized that, because black males in Harlem cannot secure well-paying jobs, high rates of family instability are evident: "One out of every five men is separated from his wife, and about two out of every seven women are separated from their husbands" (Clark, 1965:47). Family structure in Harlem is thus highly unstable, with only about half of all children under 18 living with both parents. Clark also documented the high degrees of mistrust and suspicion among Harlem residents: For "the residents of the ghettos," he reports, "who have learned from bitter experience, any form of altruism appears to be a ruse, a transparent disguise for the 'hustle'" (Clark, 1965:70). In an environment dominated by such mistrust, leadership and community organizations have proved ineffectual. Clark completed his picture of disorganized Harlem by emphasizing the high rates of delinquency, venereal disease, narcotic addiction, illegitimacy, homicide, and suicide.

Economically, Clark continued, Harlem is a consumption- rather than a production-based community. There are few whole- saling or manufacturing enterprises, virtually no office buildings, and only a few corporations, which are, characteristically, owned by whites. Even the "numbers racket" and other enterprises of crime are run by whites and provide few job opportunities for eco- nomic advancement among blacks. On the other hand, black-owned businesses tend to be small and provide few employment oppor- tunities, for they are primarily consumption, as opposed to pro- duction, enterprises (bars, liquor stores, pawn shops, beauty par- lors, fortune-telling establishments, and storefront churches). Harlem does not manufacture anything of significance, concluded Clark, for the New York urban area or for the nation. Economically the ghetto remains tied to and dominated by white enterprises, while the surrounding white community controls its vital public services, such as schools, police "protection," garbage collection, and welfare. Slum buildings are owned by absentee white landlords.

Clark used the metaphor of a *colony* to describe Harlem's rela- tions to the white community. "The dark ghettos are social, politi- cal, educational, and—above all—economic colonies," he said. "Their inhabitants are subject peoples, victims of greed, cruelty, insensitivity, guilt, and fear of their masters" (Clark, 1965:11).

How accurate is Clark's portrayal? Is it a true description of all black slums? Even if it is assumed that domination of economic opportunities and public services by the white community appears to be a common condition of black slums, are they all also dis- organized, filled with mutual distrust, and leaderless? A study by Hill and Larson (1969) of a Chicago slum, called "Old Annex" by the investigators, revealed a pattern of slum organization in marked contrast to Clark's portrayal. Like Harlem, Old Annex is economically depressed and displays high rates of family instability; but unlike Harlem, there is clear-cut community leadership, extended kinship and friendship patterns, an absence of fear and distrust, and many formal organizations and membership groupings engaged in community action. Hill and Larson (1969:160) concluded that, "Just as we have learned that stereotypes are not valid with respect to individuals, so we must constantly guard against the use of stereotypes in referring to . . . ghettos."

If the nature of community organization in ghettos varies so drastically, it seems logical that different strategies for slum and ghetto aid should also vary for different types of ghetto organization. To "renew" a highly organized ghetto such as Old Annex by leveling buildings and relocating residents would probably be self-defeating, for it would not take advantage of community leadership and organization. And in fact, it could actually undermine these viable community patterns. It would perhaps be more appropriate to allocate a lump sum of money, through revenue sharing, to the community and let it organize its own self-assistance programs in welfare, housing, and education.[4] On the other hand, to the extent that Clark's portrayal is accurate, this strategy would be inappropriate in Harlem, for it has no clear organizational and leadership patterns. In Hill and Larson's words (1969:160):

> Clark's Harlem may need to be rescued. Old Annex does not. Old Annex needs to be allowed to test itself, to use its strengths, and to grow stronger through such use. Old Annex deserves the right to exercise responsibility to debate and select its own programs, to choose its own consultants, and to act like any other viable segment of a city.

One of the main difficulties of federal assistance programs, especially urban renewal, is that they have used the white community's leadership and organizational resources to *impose* solutions on viable black communities. Moreover, programs have been stamped out of the same mold and have thus ignored wide variations in the communities being affected, with the result that black residents have at times become further alienated from federal and local governments.

---

[4] Even if ghetto leadership were not of the high quality evident in Old Annex, welfare bureaucrats and government planners are often of questionable calibre. It is probably better to let leadership conflicts within the ghetto work themselves out rather than impose absentee and inept leadership from the federal government.

RIOTS IN URBAN AMERICA: PAST EVENTS
AND FUTURE PROSPECTS

In the 1960s the militant black leader H. Rap Brown is reported to have said that "violence is as American as cherry pie." In a more tempered tone, historian Richard Hofstadter (1968:112) drew the same conclusion: "The historical catalogue of American violence is a formidable one." The destruction of the American Indians and their culture, the white supremacy practices against slaves and freedmen, the bloody confrontations between early trade unions and police, and the student-police confrontations of the 1960s and early 1970s are sufficient to illustrate the violent traditions of American society.

After the bloody 1917 and 1919 riots, blacks, who had previously been relatively nonviolent, began to retaliate against whites during periods of racial tension; and in fact, one might say they were acculturated into the American tradition of violence. As late as 1943, in the Detroit riot, self-defense and retaliation against whites were the most characteristic features of black civil disturbances. The decades after World War II were comparatively peaceful; but in the 1960s black civil disorders in ghetto areas erupted more frequently. Contrary to previous race riots, these contemporary disorders were not direct retaliations to massive white violence, but rather, spontaneous outbursts against whites stemming from seemingly "minor" incidents between small numbers of white police and blacks. The Kerner Commission's report on civil disorders (1968) emphasized the many unique elements in each of the recent racial disorders, but the race riots of the 1960s nevertheless displayed a similar profile.

SCENARIO OF RECENT RACE RIOTS[5]

It is a summer evening in the ghetto and many people are out on the streets to escape their hot and overcrowded living quarters. The police arrest a black for a relatively minor crime. Prior to this incident, tensions between police and ghetto residents had escalated because of verbal abuse and efforts at social control by the police. A crowd begins to gather around the policemen in reaction to what they perceive as another act of harassment. They shout abuses and then begin to throw rocks and bottles at the patrol officers, perhaps even attempting to rescue the police "victims." As the crowd swells, the disturbance grows noisier, and

[5] For a more detailed analysis of the riot process, see the *Report of the National Advisory Commission on Civil Disorders,* 1968; Rainwater, 1967; Allen and Adair, 1969:51–139; and Blauner, 1967.

attention shifts to surrounding stores. Windows are broken and looting starts. Police reinforcements are called in in an effort to control the disturbance, resulting in escalated crowd activity that goes from window breaking to burning. The riot gathers momentum, with widespread burning, looting, and, in some cases, sniping at police and firemen. If local police agencies cannot control the riot, the National Guard is called in to suppress it. When troops are brought in, promises to ameliorate ghetto conditions are made by local political officials. Eeventually the riot is suppressed, leaving behind burned buildings, a score of dead and injured, and ruined businesses.

The key question in presenting this brief scenario of a 1960s riot is: Could it happen again? And would it take the same form? In many ways, riots are spontaneous outbursts stemming from accumulated frustrations. And they are most likely when there are few organizations and channels for social mobility and expression of grievances (Turner, 1975). The slum of the 1970s is perhaps better organized, and there are more channels for expressing grievances. However, the frustrations that erupt into civil disorders remain, making it clear that the potential for protest—even violent protest—remains high. A slumping economy with high unemployment, especially among teenage young adults, represents an explosive mixture that could, at most any time, erupt into widespread protest activity. Such activity may be more organized, less spontaneous, and perhaps less destructive, but at this time it is difficult to determine if ghetto organizations and newfound political muscle among residents are sufficient to prevent violence, or to channel it in different directions.

Who were the rioters? Was rioting the work of criminal gangs? Of political activists? Or was it the collective outburst of a wide spectrum of ghetto residents? Almost all evidence points to the fact that rioters received wide support from the whole black community and that a large proportion of ghetto residents, from 15 percent to 35 percent, actually engaged in looting. Rioters were not a "lunatic fringe," outside agitators, or a revolutionary cadre, but a mass of relatively young and long-term residents of the ghetto. As the Kerner Commission summarized:

> The typical rioter was a teenager or young adult, a lifelong resident of the city in which he rioted, a high school dropout; he was, nevertheless, somewhat better educated than his nonrioting neighbor, and was usually underemployed or employed in a menial job. He was proud of his race, extremely hostile to both whites and middle-class Negroes and, although informed about politics, highly distrustful of the political system.

Why did these blacks riot and why in the pattern portrayed? The Kerner Commission (1968:81–84) found that many grievances are held by blacks, but at different levels of intensity:

first level of intensity
1. Police practices
2. Unemployment and underemployment
3. Inadequate housing

second level of intensity
4. Inadequate education
5. Poor recreation facilities and programs
6. Ineffectiveness of the political structure and grievance mechanisms

third level of intensity
7. Disrespectful white attitudes
8. Discriminatory administration of justice
9. Inadequacy of federal programs
10. Inadequacy of municipal services
11. Discriminatory consumer and civil practices
12. Inadequate welfare programs

The most intense of these grievances probably still exist, although the police in many communities have altered many of their abusive practices. But the employment, income, and housing picture of black Americans has not improved; and thus many of the intense grievances that moved people to civil disorder remain—indicating once again the potential for future disorder.

Two overlapping and yet clearly distinguishable arguments about the general social *structural conditions* causing riots can be discerned: (1) The first concerns the *caste* position of blacks in American society. Riots seen from the caste perspective are interpreted as a demand for a redistribution of wealth and opportunities for mobility into the middle classes. (2) The second views riots as attempts by blacks to escape "colonial" rule by whites. This argument sees blacks reacting to their dependence on the white community for jobs, education, welfare, housing, and subsistence. The colonialism point of view sees riots as a liberation movement against the occupying army—the police and whites. The caste and colonialism arguments overlap, but the solutions to ghetto and riot problems that each one implies are vastly different, if not contradictory. And depending upon which view is taken, predictions about future ghetto disturbances vary.

RIOTS AS A CASTE REVOLT

There is a large body of literature describing the conditions under which conflicts, revolts, and revolutions by an oppressed population are likely to occur (e.g., Davies, 1962; Erickson, 1966; Brinton, 1965; Williams, 1947; Marx and Engels, 1848). Common to all these perspectives are three important conclusions: (1) Revolts do not come from the totally oppressed and downtrodden. (2) Revolts come rather from those whose lot has been getting better in absolute terms but worse relative to the standards of the broader society. (3) Revolts are directed toward the goal of redistribution of wealth in a society.

From this perspective, it is argued that even under the impact of judicial decisions and legislation to promote racial equality—such as the 1954 Supreme Court decision and the civil rights acts of 1964 and 1968—little progress has been made to close the gap between the position of blacks and whites in American society. Blacks in cities receive fewer years of education than whites; they are twice as likely to be unemployed, and when they are unemployed it is for a longer duration than for whites; blacks in cities are three times as likely to be in unskilled and service jobs as whites; they earn only about 60 percent of the income of whites; they are twice as likely to live in poverty as whites; blacks pay more than whites for poorer housing; they are three times as likely to live in substandard and overcrowded housing than whites; and so on (Kerner Commission, 1968). Although the current condition of blacks, in absolute terms, is better than it was before the Civil War or at the turn of the century, many blacks justifiably feel *relatively* deprived because of the growing white affluence they see all around them. The selective looting in riots of television sets, furniture, and appliances—all symbols of middle-class affluence—is perhaps the most visible sign of a caste demanding access to that affluence (Dynes and Quarantelli, 1968). Judicial decisions, legislation, and various government programs have raised expectations that things would improve, but the lack of dramatic improvement in ghetto conditions creates an intolerable gap between expectations and reality.

Proponents of the caste perspective argue that if riots are exclusively actions directed toward admittance to the broader society, programs designed to break down discrimination and provide educational opportunity are the key to stopping riots. Suppression by police and the military represents only a short-run solution. To guarantee equal opportunity, well-financed federal programs providing educational, housing, and economic opportunities will have to be implemented more efficiently and with more foresight than in the past, and current civil rights legislation will have to be more seriously enforced than is currently the case. In regard to the future, the recent drop in black income as a proportion of white income, as well as the failure to improve housing, educational, and job opportunities would argue that revolt is still a likely occurrence in many ghetto areas.

RIOTS AS A COLONIAL REVOLT

Contradicting the solutions of the caste proponents—and predicting their failure should they ever come into being—is the colonization perspective, in which riots are seen as more of a liberation movement against "white imperialists." From this perspective, much of the traditional philosophy and strategy for helping the poor in ghettos is called into question.

Richard Rubenstein (1970) has developed an extensive colonial perspective for examining violence in America. In general, his thesis is simple: "Groups become conscious of their independence when they lose it, and resort to violence when violence seems the only alternative to total dependence on more powerful groups or individuals." Revolt and violence occur only after a subpopulation, such as blacks in America, becomes an internal colony of the dominant population. This process of internal colonization and revolt occurs in a series of stages: (1) Groups become isolated from the economic and political spheres. These groups usually have a collective identity, but they remain loosely organized, isolated from the mainstream of social, economic, religious, and political life in a society, and economically dependent on that society. (2) This outcast population is drawn into closer contact with government and powerful economic interests. Realizing the abuses of government and economic organizations, the population begins to pursue political activity along nonviolent lines under the leadership of middle-class members who seek to integrate them into the larger society. (3) The outgroup secures a local power base and can enter into coalition politics on a national level, thereby deriving its share of power and privilege. (4) These initial political gains do not eliminate the outcasts' dependence on the broader society, and members feel themselves losing control of their community and slipping into permanent servitude and dependence. It is at this stage that riot and revolt become most likely and community leadership becomes increasingly militant. If the dependence of the groups on the society is not changed, a war of liberation, that can involve paramilitary mobilization and guerrilla activity, is initiated (Rubenstein, 1970:45).

Such processes of internal colonization and revolt can be used to visualize civil disturbances of the 1960s in the urban ghettos of American society. Proponents of the colonial perspective argue that the twentieth century has seen the progressive colonization of blacks into ghettos, resulting in increasing exploitation by and dependence upon white institutions, despite political movements in the nation's ghettos to alleviate this state of affairs. For example, among the high intensity grievances of blacks reported earlier, police practices, underemployment, poor housing, ineffective political structures, and inadequate education were all prominent. These grievances may reflect not so much perceived inequalities as intense dissatisfaction with black dependence on whites for housing, jobs, political favors, police protection, and education.

The grievances of blacks probably reflect not only dissatisfaction with black dependency, but also outrage over white *exploitation* of black colonies—a form of internal imperialism. For example, police policies directed toward restoring law and order in ghetto areas are more like police occupation of a colony than serious and sensitive attempts at law enforcement. Since police forces in most urban areas have only token integration, it is not unlikely that the platoons of patrol cars moving through the ghetto with their white occupants would be perceived as a white occupation force. With respect to housing, real estate agencies and developers are so thoroughly entrenched in federal programs—from public housing and urban renewal to Model Cities—as to make housing programs often little more than slum takeovers (in the minds of residents) by white interests. In addition, the abuses of white absentee landlords aggravate black outrage, as do such white economic institutions as the white-owned store and the white-controlled finance company, with its high interest rates.

To exacerbate matters, political machines in most large cities have only recently been concerned with the welfare of ghetto residents, and when they are, there is little that financially depressed city governments can do about many of the problems of ghetto residents. Even black mayors of large cities are often inhibited by the high degrees of patronage and corruption in the governmental bureaucracy from doing even what little they can do to ameliorate ghetto conditions. In fact, the whole welfare system—predominately staffed by white civil servants—forces blacks to suffer indignities and invasion of privacy by an intruding and questioning federal bureaucracy. And finally, with only a few exceptions, the school systems in ghettos have been controlled and run by white-dominated school boards and school administrations. Thus, as Rubenstein (1970:127) summarizes:

> The same invasion which raised group expectations by offering a vision of middle-class life in an integrated America deepened the dependence of blacks upon the white community, for whether the colonizer was a venal slumlord or a do-good welfare worker, the result—increasing dependence—was the same.

Young blacks who are aware of their colonial status are the most outraged by their lack of control over their lives, by their inability to secure and keep jobs, by their need to send their women out to clean floors, by self-destructive dependence on alcohol and drugs, and by their participation in white exploitation of "their brothers" (Rubenstein, 1970:128).

If riots are a revolt of a colony led by the angry young, the implications for governmental policies are far reaching. Government-created jobs, more government welfare, a government take-over of ghetto schools, and more government housing are going to feed, not quell, anticolonial forces in ghettos. Whether the colonial revolt has or will reach the stage of paramilitary forces and guerrilla warfare in urban areas is not yet clear. What is clear is that a leadership struggle is currently underway in black ghettos, and the way this internal conflict is resolved will greatly influence the course of ghetto and urban violence.

The direction of black leadership in the late 1970s and early 1980s will reflect the sensitivity of the federal government to the anticolonial forces in ghettos. If federal programs increase black dependency while subverting self-determination, leaders advocating more violence could gain a wider following. Government programs at the very least must allow black residents in each ghetto to have control of the ghetto business structure, housing program, law enforcement, and schools. Ghettos must become economically and socially viable communities under black control and regulation. In response to the caste situation of blacks, the federal government must move quickly and rapidly to eliminate economic, social, housing, and educational barriers to blacks. Federal policies will have to strike a delicate balance (something that the monolithic federal bureaucracy has rarely done) between allowing greater self-determination in ghettos and breaking down barriers to economic and social mobility through massive federal intervention *in the white community*. Such is one dilemma of structure in America; and it is a dilemma that must be resolved if riots and other forms of violence in American communities are to become a problem of the past.

Chapter 11

PROBLEMS OF THE
ECOLOGICAL COMMUNITY

The ecological community can be defined as the complex system of interdependencies among species and minerals. These interdependencies can be visualized as chains, flows, and cycles, and as such, they constitute a highly dynamic community in which various life forms seek the niche allowing for their survival. And yet, continuity is necessary for the survival of the life forms comprising the ecosystem, for it is through such continuity that species evolve those traits necessary for survival in their niche. But as will become evident, highly modern societies like the United States now pose a threat to this continuity; and in doing so, could potentially sow the seeds of their own destruction. It is this potential that perhaps presents America with its ultimate problem of structure.[1]

THE NATURE OF ECOSYSTEMS

To understand the operation of the ecological community, and how American culture and social structure pose a problem for its maintenance, it is necessary to outline some of the critical patterns of interdependence in the world ecosystem. One of the most essential flows in ecosystems involves the transference of energy from the sun to all life forms. In this process, the sun's radiant energy is converted to chemical energy by the photosynthesis process in plants; this chemical energy is then passed through the ecosystem in extended "food chains" as varieties of herbivores consume plants, and in turn are eaten by carnivores. In such chains, consuming life forms extract the chemical energy of the plant or animal and utilize it to sustain their life. And in doing so, they store the energy for another organism in the food chain. At each juncture in these

[1] For a more detailed analysis of world ecological problems, see Turner, 1976.

incredibly extended and complex feeding chains, some energy is always lost as heat, because energy transfers are always incomplete. This basic process of energy transfer is schematically represented in Figure 11.1.

A second crucial process in the ecological community involves the cycling of basic substances. Of the many such cycles, the conversion by plants of the carbon dioxide released by respiring organisms into oxygen is one of the most fundamental since it enables all animal life to exist. Another important cycle involves the circulation of such critical minerals as nitrogen, phosphorus, sulfur, magnesium, and some fifteen other essential nutrients. These minerals are cycled through the ecosystem in a fantastically complex process: The billions upon billions of microorganisms, such as bacteria and fungi, living in all corners of the environment, release enzymes from their bodies; these enzymes break down dead plant and animal material and thus make it easier for microorganisms to absorb this material as food. But in addition to supplying the energy needs of their own bodies, these microorganisms, or "decomposers," mineralize organic matter and make it available directly to plants, and in turn, to herbivores and carnivores. For in the process of photosynthesis plants not only require water and the carbon dioxide released by animals, but they also require inorganic compounds, including nitrogen, phosphorus, sulfur, and magnesium. Plants and animals in food chains not only transfer energy, but they also cycle life-sustaining minerals. In contrast to

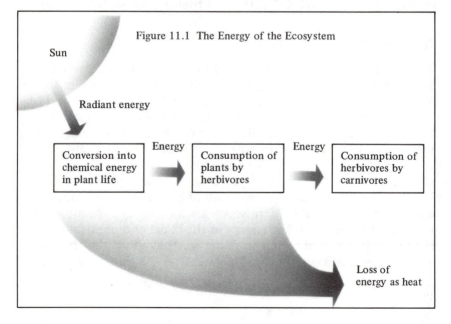

Figure 11.1 The Energy of the Ecosystem

Sun

Radiant energy

| Conversion into chemical energy in plant life | Energy → | Consumption of plants by herbivores | Energy → | Consumption of herbivores by carnivores |

Loss of energy as heat

the energy in these food chains, mineral nutrients are not lost, since the activities of decomposers reinsert them back into the energy chain. In Figure 11.2, the cycling of basic substances is represented.

To the extent that the flows and cycles summarized in Figures 11.1 and 11.2 are disrupted, the capacity for life within the ecological community is reduced (Woodwell, 1967). While the complexity of these interdependencies of the ecosystem presently defies complete understanding, it is evident that life forms are dependent upon each other, since no species can ascend above its dependency on other life forms.

The complexities of these mutual dependencies in the ecological community represents a source of stability, or more accurately, orderly change. Because the web of interconnections among life forms is so vast, and diverse, local changes in some part of the ecosystem will encounter resistance. At the very least, sudden and rapid change will be unlikely, thereby giving plants and organisms time to adjust and adapt to changing environmental conditions. If change is rapid, however, inhabitants of the ecosystem cannot readily adapt to new environmental exigencies, with the result that widespread destruction is likely as the sudden death of some species sets into motion the successive destruction of other dependent species. It is for this reason that "simplified" ecosystems, which have been stripped of their natural diversity, are extremely vulnerable to rapid and highly disruptive changes since the web of interconnections is so simple that it poses less resistance to change than complex webs. However, the interconnections among life forms of ecosystems assure that changes will eventually reverberate far beyond their source. Such amplification of effects will, of course,

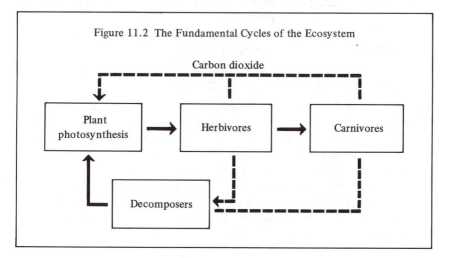

Figure 11.2 The Fundamental Cycles of the Ecosystem

encounter resistance, often allowing species sufficient time to adjust to their new environments. But the fact remains that a change in one element of an ecosystem will ultimately have implications for the flow of energy and cycling of minerals among many more species than those originally subjected to the change. This inevitability should underscore the "lag effects" of changes introduced into ecosystems, because the full implications of a change may take a considerable amount of time to become evident. These change processes may be summarized as the fundamental principles in the ecological community:

1. Simplified ecosystems are subject to more rapid change than highly differentiated systems composed of diverse relations among a wide variety of species. The simplification of ecosystems will thus increase their instability.
2. Alterations of relations in ecosystems will be amplified over time and space, with relatively small changes potentially being amplified into large-scale ecological disruption.
3. The ultimate outcome of changes introduced into ecosystems is difficult to determine due to lag effects. This fact can create a situation in which the point of no return in the destruction of an ecosystem can be passed before it is recognized that a destructive chain of events is irreversible.

These principles of change make it difficult to assess just how severe current ecological problems are. It is not presently known how simplified the world's ecosystem has become with the extensive use of single crop agriculture and chemical pesticides. Nor can the amplified effect of currently observable changes in the quality of water, air, and soil be accurately assessed. And of course, no determination of the lag effects, to say nothing of determining a point of no return, is presently possible. But sufficient change, alteration, and clear disruption of the ecosystem has occurred to warrant its investigation as one of America's problems of structure.

SOCIETY AND THE ECOLOGICAL COMMUNITY

The culture and structure of modern societies clearly have the most disruptive impact on the world ecological community. For it is in societies such as the United States that the appropriateness of high levels of consumption and the utilization of knowledge to manipulate the environment is emphasized. And it is only in such societies that the capacity to extract massive quantities of resources, to create high levels of energy, and to produce large quantities of commodities is evident. The results of these capacities can potentially be destructive, as is outlined in Figure 11.3.

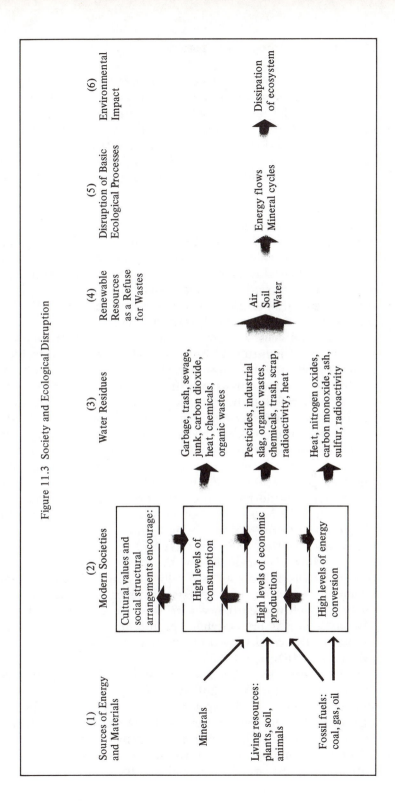

Figure 11.3 Society and Ecological Disruption

The cultural values and structural arrangements of an industrial society are seen as encouraging high levels of consumption, as is indicated in Figure 11.3, column 2. Consumption creates demands for industrial and agricultural goods that, recipocally, stimulate levels of production requiring large quantities of energy. As the arrows in column 2 underscore, these influences are also reciprocal: An extensive productive system encourages consumer demand and sustains the cultural values and structural arrangements in the society that first gave impetus to initial industrialization in modern societies. The consumption, production, and energy-use of modern, industrial economies generates vast quantities of waste residues, as indicated in column 3. In turn, these residues are discharged into the "renewable resources" of air, soil, and water. These resources are renewable because each is capable of rejuvenation through the flows and cycles of energy and minerals. While substitutes for the drain on stock resources (column 1) can be found—albeit at high cost—there are no substitutes for renewable resources; and thus, to use them as a refuse for waste residues (column 4) will disrupt those processes (column 5) that maintain these renewable resources and the vitality of life forms (column 6). For indeed, without air, water, and soil, life is not possible.

The three principles of ecological change enumerated earlier offer a general clue as to the potential dangers of using renewable resources as a refuse. Single crop, large-scale agriculture using chemical fertilizers and pesticides has reduced the complexity of the ecological community. In so doing, its vulnerability to rapid change and the destruction of life forms—including humans—has increased. Moreover, the chemicals of large-scale agriculture run off the soil into the water, mixing with the other residues of urban-industrial societies, and can potentially suffocate wide varieties of life including, it appears, even the phytoplankton from which 80 percent of the world's air is produced. These processes of simplification do not, of course, presently reveal their amplified consequences. And in accordance with the principle of lag effects, some biologists now assert—perhaps prematurely—that the point of no return on the road to ecocatastrophe may be reached within the next decade (Ehrlich, 1969).

Precise and exact information on the disruption of the world ecological community is not available, but it is clear that a considerable amount of disruption has already occurred and that, in light of the culture and structure of modern societies, the potential for further damage is manifestly evident. As the world's greatest polluter, the analysis of the structure of American society becomes critical if the causes of ecological disruption are to be understood.

For with only one-fifteenth of the world's population, American society extracts 35 percent of the world's minerals and energy, while accounting for one-half of the pollutants emitted into the world ecosystem.

THE CULTURE OF POLLUTION IN AMERICA

Many of the dominant values that facilitated the development of America into the world's most affluent society also legitimize those values institutional in the economy, polity, legal system, and community structure that cause the discharge of harmful wastes into the ecosystem. These values can be grouped into four general categories which, for simplicity of exposition, can be lebeled the (1) growth ethic, (2) consumption ethic, (3) technology ethic, and (4) the plentiful nature ethic.

1. THE GROWTH ETHIC. During initial industrialization in America, a growth ethic was perhaps necessary to encourage heavy investment of capital in the productive apparatus. Unfortunately, during this process, the economy became structured around a growth ethic: the more the better. This value was appropriate to an underpopulated, early industrial society where renewable resources such as air, water, and soil were in plentiful supply. Discharging wastes into them saved money, time, and effort and thereby escalated growth in production and consumption. It is now questionable whether these vital resources can continue to renew themselves in the face of the ever-escalating demands being placed on them. To avoid severe ecological problems, many ecologists argue that the growth ethic will need to be replaced by new cultural premises emphasizing stability, recycling, and maintenance of the natural forces of rejuvenation in water, air, and soil (Boulding, 1966, 1970; Ehrlich and Ehrlich, 1970). However, the supports for continued growth emanating from the economy, polity, and consumption habits of the family make any shift in values in American society difficult.

2. THE CONSUMPTION ETHIC. Americans value the consumption of ever-increasing quantities and varieties of economic commodities. Such consumption is considered to cause both progress and prosperity, and it cannot be doubted that such has been one force behind America's economic growth and expansion. Once a large productive apparatus exists, it has a vested interest in manipulating the value of materialism by stimulating needs for consumption. In turn, such stimulation generates greater economic demand lead-

ing to increased production, and so on in a consumption-production cycle. But production and consumption in American society now occur on such a scale that a serious waste residue problem has been created. For as Figure 11.3 underscored, economic production results in the discharge of slag, pesticides, trash, heat, nitrogen oxides, and scores of other harmful residues into the ecosystem. And when high levels of consumption are encouraged by such extensive production of goods and commodities, a disposal crisis is created, as for example, when the phosphates flowing into sewers no longer can be absorbed or when the American landscape becomes scarred with vast quantities of solid wastes.

3. THE TECHNOLOGY ETHIC. Traditionally, the American experience with a wide number of problems has had an easy solution: more technology. There pervades a strong cultural premise that the application of more scientific knowledge can meet any challenge. Such faith in science and technology is now more problematic than in the past, for it delays immediate action on ecological problems while potentially allowing them to intensify to a point where scientific and technological endeavor will be less effective than would be the case if one presumed that no technological solution could be found.

Even today, in the midst of widespread concern over pollution, science is at times seen as a cure-all. For example, the problem of generating enough food to feed the world's population has been turned over to the agricultural experts who, through the selective breeding of grains and intensive use of fertilizers and pesticides, have succeeded in feeding the world—in the short run. But many have argued that this is being done at a long-range cost of simplifying ecosystems and hence creating new problems, while forestalling the imperative of an international program of population control. Even in the area of birth control, the problem has been turned over to medical technologists who continue to seek the "perfect" contraceptive that women and men will readily accept. As these efforts consume attention, considerable time has probably been lost in altering familial, economic, and governmental structures in a direction that will allow for serious control of the population.

The ecological crisis is thus much more than a technological problem; its solution may require some changes in basic values and institutions. Generating the technology is the least of the difficulties in meeting current ecological problems. In fact, to continue to wait on a technological breakthrough is probably unnecessary because, as the President's Council on Environmental Quality noted in

1971, the knowledge to solve many ecological problems is currently available. The technology ethic, then, poses a curious dilemma: It will assist in the solution of ecological problems but, at the same time, blind faith in its powers diverts attention away from the real source of the problem, the basic structure of American society.

4. THE PLENTIFUL NATURE ETHIC. All over the world, and particularly in the United States, nature has been considered a "free good" (Murphy, 1967). As such, using renewable resources such as air and water as a refuse has been allowed to occur, free of charge. The use of nature as a free good represents a pioneer conception of unbounded and inexhaustible resources that can be used for profit and gain, while being necessary for progress (Revelle, 1968). In reality, renewable resources are a "common good"—increasingly in very short supply—that will need to be paid for by polluters.

Even with widespread ecological consciousness, changing this value premise may not be as easy as it appears in the abstract. It will cost the public money to visualize nature as a common good: Industries will have to pay for their pollution, which in turn will mean that they will raise prices; the federal government will have to engage in expensive monitoring and control of pollution emitted by industries, with the result that federal taxes will be raised; and local communities will have to increase taxes to pay for their pollution and to expand their sewage and garbage treatment facilities. Thus, the premise that nature is a free good may persist as an ideology for keeping prices and taxes down. But until there is a strong willingness to pay for a conception of nature as a common good, pollution will continue and the supply of renewable resources in America could diminish even further.

These values, from growth ethic to the plentiful nature ethic, currently dominate American society. They shape social action and at the same time are supported by current structural arrangements in the society. It is this reciprocity between values and structure that makes both highly resistant to change. For as long as values legitimize arrangements that allow Americans to enjoy a "good life," change in either the values or the established modes of conduct that they legitimize will be resisted. And it is in this sense that disruption of the ecological community is a problem of structure in America.

THE STRUCTURE OF POLLUTION IN AMERICA

In analyzing the structure of pollution in America, attention should be drawn to the basic social structures that organize human activities and that have served as a frames of reference in previous chapters: (1) communities, (2) institutions, and (3) stratification. It is the way these structures shape human affairs that problems of pollution ultimately arise.

COMMUNITY STRUCTURE AND POLLUTION

Urbanization involves the increasing concentration of a population into a relatively small geographical area. In the United States, the current population of slightly over 210 million is settled on a little over 1 percent of the land area. Such a high degree of urbanism automatically causes pollution, for the wastes and residues of millions of people and a large industrial complex are being discharged into a very small ecological space. It is therefore likely that the air, water, and land within any large urban area will be polluted and that ecosystem disruption will be high, perhaps setting off chains of events extending considerably beyond the urban area. Were the American population more geographically dispersed, the degree of noticeable air and water pollution would be considerably less. As necessary as geographical dispersion may be for avoiding further ecological damage, however, the current *pattern* of urban organization in America, regardless of population dispersion, will cause ecological problems. For it now appears that ways of treating sewage, disposing of wastes, transportating people, supplying energy, raising revenue, and governing urban areas have evolved in such a way that they pose serious ecological problems.

The pattern of industrialization within urban areas is one source of these ecological problems. During the last century, the first industries tended to settle along major lakes, rivers, and bays. This pattern provided needed power, sources of transportation for materials and goods, and most importantly, a free dump for wastes, since water was seen as a plentiful free good. A pattern of urban, industrial organization which, with the expansion of industry, was most likely to cause ecological problems was thus established 120 years ago. Just as water was considered a free good, so was the air into which wastes could be ejected in the name of progress and productivity.

Because of the long tradition stressing the unbounded right of industry to use the environment as refuse, solving ecological problems will be correspondingly more difficult. However, a number of alternatives are currently available (Revelle, 1968): (1) closed cycle operations, in which water is treated and recycled through industrial plants; (2) export of wastes to an environment more capable of absorbing them; (3) effluent treatment; and (4) plant abatement, by which manufacturing processes are changed so that no dangerous effluents are emitted into the water and air. The technology for all of these solutions exists and could be used, but it is expensive to implement. However, the heavy urban concentrations of industry and their disrupting impact on the national ecosystem will eventually require that these solutions be used by manufacturers in urban areas. The consequences of these solutions will require considerable economic adjustment: Profit margins may be less, and consumers will probably have to adjust to higher prices. Such are the costs of the existing pattern of urban, industrial organization.

The rate of urbanization in America is now creating ecological problems. From around 1800 to 1860, the United States moved from a rural to urban profile. New York, Philadelphia, Boston, Chicago, St. Louis, and other large cities went from literally small towns to massive urban complexes in only half a century. Such a rapid rate of urbanization overwhelmed the sewage facilities of these urban areas, and they simply dumped untreated organic wastes into adjacent waterways. Even with the adoption of sophisticated treatment methods, many large cities continue to be major sources of water pollution because their drainage systems had been, in reality, jury-rigged 100 years ago. For example, in New York, Chicago, Cleveland, and many older cities, treatment of wastes is accomplished by interceptor sewers that were built to catch wastes from the original sewer system and carry it to treatment plants (Revelle, 1968). But during rainy seasons or excessively heavy use, these interceptor sewers are overwhelmed by the water coming from the older system, with the result that untreated sewage overflows into adjacent waterways. Technologically, these problems can be overcome, but the costs to the taxpayer make any change in sewage treatment fiscally and politically difficult. America's waters will thus continue to be burdened as a result of a sewage-treatment legacy inherited from the rapid urbanization of the last century.

Initial urbanization in America was accomplished without the automobile, but suburbanization and the creation of the large metropolitan area was, to a great extent, the product of the car (see Chapter 9). Although the automobile gave people more flexibility as to where they could live, its emissions now seriously pollute the urban air. For example, it has been estimated that three-quarters of all carbon monoxide and one-half the sulfur oxides, hydrocarbons, and nitrogen oxides—the ingredients of smog—are emitted by automobiles (Steif, 1970). As urban areas have become restructured around the car, the implementation of alternative, nonpolluting modes of urban mass transportation is economically infeasible. For example, in Los Angeles the entire metropolitan area is almost completely dependent on automobile transportation, creating a severe smog problem and making alternative forms of transportation economically difficult. Other large cities are not so dependent on cars, but most urban transportation still revolves around their extensive use.

To attack the pollution generated by the urban structure will require some very comprehensive political decisions extending across entire metropolitan areas and into rural areas. Unfortunately, as was noted in Chapter 9, a pattern of community political decision making has been established that presently precludes this possibility (Greer, 1965). American metropolitan areas grew during a period when laissez faire, states' rights, and decentralization of government were valued, with the result that it is most difficult to have unified political decision making over a large urban region. As long as political power in metropolitan areas remains fragmented among suburban communities surrounding the central city, there will be a lessened political capacity to deal with urban pollution. It will be difficult to have planning, waste standards, industrial waste monitoring and enforcement procedures, land-use controls, effluent- and sewage-treatment facilities, and alternatives to automobile transportation systems on a *regional* level.

If the federal government, through additional revenue sharing or grants-in-aids, pours money into this political system in an effort to abate pollution, much of it would be lost on duplication of effort and financial squabbles among competing municipalities. To avoid this eventuality, it may prove necessary to abandon traditional concepts of urban government, for pollution problems do not end at a community's border; rather, they extend throughout an urban region and well into its rural fringe. Governmental boundaries may thus have to be established with respect to ecological regions, rather than political boundaries. The fact that such governmental reorganization seems so unlikely politically and economically should indicate the extent to which pollution problems are built into the structure of community government in America.

In addition to the political decision-making problems, American urban communities have what may now be an antiquated revenue-raising system—a system that makes financing pollution control at the metropolitan level impossible. More than just new sources of revenue will have to be sought; a whole new system of deriving revenue to finance cities will be needed. To use forms of revenue sharing from the federal government to supplement this system will probably be ineffective within the context of the fragmented political structure of urban areas. But to rely on taxes from assessed property evaluations is clearly inadequate. As the present financial problems of cities reveal, the entire tax structure in cities will probably have to be revised: Property taxes may have to be supplemented by commuter taxes on those coming into the central city from the suburbs; pollution taxes may have to be assessed on older cars and on industries that produce wastes; tax incentives and rebates may have to be created to encourage industries to move out of urban areas and cut down their pollutants; sewage treatment costs to the public will probably have to be raised to support research and investment in new sewage systems and treatment facilities; a better formula for sharing state and federal income tax revenues will have to be devised; and most importantly, all these tax reforms will probably have to be metropolitanwide instead of confined to local municipalities. Again, the possibilities of all these reforms would probably seem remote.

In sum, it is clear that ecological problems in the United States are intimately connected to current patterns of urban organization. Urbanism per se creates pollution problems since it concentrates the wastes of large numbers of people and industrial complexes into a small ecological space. But equally significant are the existing forms of urban industrialism, the modes of sewage treatment, the basis of transportation, political organization, and the system for raising revenues. Until these features are changed, it is most likely that pollution and ecological disruption will continue to be built into the American community structure.

POLLUTION AND THE STRATIFICATION SYSTEM

In absolute terms, the lowest income and poverty groupings have a better standard of living than ever. This increase in the standard of living, however, has not been accomplished through a redistribution of the wealth; on the contrary, the poor of today receive no greater share of the total wealth than they did 25 years ago (see Chapter 2). The poor's demand for more affluence has therefore been met by the trickling down the stratification ladder of increased economic output that, in turn, has resulted in increased industrial pollution. Were the wealth to be redistributed, such increased output and the resulting pollution would be substantially reduced and these resources could be directed toward meeting the demands of the poor to share in American affluence. The United States has not made the poor more affluent by making the rich poorer (Boulding, 1970).

The respective amounts of pollution also vary by social class in American society. The greatest polluters are the affluent, who generate the greatest economic demand (and hence stimulate industrial pollution), consume the most polluting goods, and dispose of a majority of nondegradable or nonrecyclable wastes (Wald, 1970). Yet, it is the poor who are most likely to live where land, water, and air have been polluted by the needs of the affluent. Another inequity stems from the fact that programs to eliminate pollution will bear most heavily on the poor, not the affluent. The affluent are in the vanguard of the ecology movement not only because they are sincerely concerned but also because they can afford to be. It is the poor who are likely to have to pay a greater proportion of their limited incomes in the higher prices and taxes that will inevitably result from an attack on America's ecological problems. Furthermore, since it is likely that much of the money to fight pollution will be taken out of the domestic rather than the military budget, the poor will see many of the programs that directly benefit them cut back under future efforts to clean up the environment. As one ghetto resident cynically observed, "friends of the earth are not the friends of the poor." It is therefore not surprising that the poor have been slow to join the ecology band-wagon; they have much to lose (Ehrlich, 1971; Sprout, 1970). The poor also have much to gain from a serious attack on pollution problems, since it is they who tend to live in the most ecologically disrupted areas. But unless the poor are exempted from the costs of such an attack, the fight against pollution could aggravate the present levels of inequality that exists in the United States.

Present ecological problems, and their solutions, are connected to the stratification system. It is the affluent who are the big pol-luters, and it is they who are able to make the sacrifice in income and standard of living that a cleaner environment may require. Until the poor and disfranchised minorities can be assured that monies directed toward the environment are not coming out of the desperately needed domestic programs, they will probably resist federal and state environmental legislation—one more structural roadblock in the way of environmental legislation.

POLLUTION AND THE INSTITUTIONAL STRUCTURE

THE ECONOMY. Economic processes in any industrial society have three principle consequences for the environment: (1) They de-plete *stock resources*, such as oil, coal, gas, and various metals and minerals. (2) They are rapidly consuming *renewable resources*, such as air, water, soil, and plant life. (3) Often as a result of the depletion of renewable resources, they disrupt necessary cycles, flows, and energy chains within the ecosystem (see Figure 11.3). While the depletion of stock resources presents short-run economic problems, it is not as serious as is the exhaustion of renewable resources and the disruption of the ecosystem. In the long run, substitutes can probably be found for various stock resources, but there is no substitute for life-sustaining resources like air and water, as well as those ecological processes upon which human health and food supplies depend.

The exhaustion of renewable resources and ecosystem disruption can be intentional—as when massive doses of pesticides are dumped onto crops or when the by-products of careless industries and consumers are emitted as pollutants into the soil, air, and water. Some of this "economic fallout" directly disrupts the environment and then dissipates; but much of it accumulates in the environment, as is the case with DDT and other chlorinated hydrocarbons, and increases its disrupting impact over time. In either case, it appears that considerable damage is being done to vital resources and ecological processes.

The American economy is structured around growth and continual expansion, as is revealed by the fact that economic health and prosperity are now defined by the annual increase in the gross national product (Boulding, 1970; Murphy, 1967; Hill, 1970; Miles, 1970). More substantively, full employment, monetary stability, and political processes are intimately connected to the continued growth of the economy. Therefore, to assure this "necessary" growth, economic enterprises frequently engage in extensive advertising to stimulate needs and desires in the public for more and more goods. Moreover, many industries continually bring out new models of products to instill a sense of psychological obsolescence in the consumer; products are constantly being packaged in "new," "more convenient," and often nondegradable ways in order to stimulate additional consumer demand; manufacturers sometimes build in obsolescence so that goods will self-destruct at a rate compatible to continued economic growth; consumers have been cajoled into thinking that for each task they must perform, from opening a can to making an ice cube, they need a special gadget; an enormous credit industry has emerged to stimulate purchases beyond the immediate capability of consumers; and if such artificially stimulated demand is insufficient to assure growth, appeals are made to the government to provide a subsidy, impose a protective tariff, or buy surplus goods. All such techniques for assuring growth have generated economic prosperity for most Americans, but they have also caused economic fallout. Economic growth means increased energy conversion and hence greater quantities of carbon dioxide, ash, sulfur dioxide, nitrogen oxides, heat, and carbon monoxide. More production creates greater residues of pesticides, fertilizers, slag, chemicals, scrap, and junk. And more consumption will generate increased levels of trash, sewage, garbage, and carbon monoxide. At the same time, however, economic growth assures close to full employment; and as recent recessions have disclosed, a drop in the rate of growth, or even an actual decrease in growth, produces severe unemployment and other economic dislocations. Thus, the stability of the present structure of the American economy, and the fate of many workers, now depends upon growth, setting into bold relief one of America's most difficult dilemmas: environmental stability vs. economic stability. At present, it appears that, in the absence of visible ecological catastrophies, economic stability is preferred to ecological stability by both the public and political decision makers. Many times, of course, the two issues may not come into conflict, but more often than not, there is a clear conflict between these two desirable goals.

It is between the "horns" of this dilemma, then, that government efforts to control pollution must be viewed. While stricter governmental controls could probably cut down dramatically the amount of this harmful economic fallout, more extreme measures may be necessary to stop agricultural and industrial pollution. Economic growth will probably have to be drastically slowed down since it is likely that, with continued economic expansion, the benefits of increased governmental regulation would be negated by increased energy conversion, production, and consumption. To slow the rate of growth will require some far-reaching adjustments within the economy. For example, in the face of population growth, full employment within the structure of the existing economy may be impossible; therefore new ways—from outright welfare to governmental subsidies and "make work" projects—might have to be devised to get income to people so that they could buy products and hence maintain the economy. A new system of corporate taxation would probably be necessary to derive the revenue required by the nonworking populace. Consumption of Americans' habits would also have to change: People would have to get used to recyclable and degradable packaging, planned resistance to obsolescence, and fewer gadgets. To effect this change in consumption habits would in turn require more government control of the market to regulate the supply and demand of only those goods that would improve the quality of life and the environment. Yet, the very fact that these solutions to economic pollution would probably cause severe short term—perhaps even long term—economic and perhaps political disruption, underscores the built-in roadblocks to easy ecological solutions. Further, such changes would go against deep-seated values of many Americans, once again indicating resistance to solutions for ecological problems.

The existence of such roadblocks would thus require more "practical" but probably less effective solutions to ecological problems. While only a stopgap measure, one short-term approach would be for the government to subsidize, as it has done for many industries such as the railroads and airlines, a waste-recovery industry that could recycle many of the current residues back through the economy (Ehrlich and Ehrlich, 1970). However, recycling should not be viewed as a cure-all for problems of industrial pollution. If only by examining Figure 11.3, it should be clear that the wastes generated in energy conversion and in much of the productive process are not recyclable. While federal standards limiting the emission of these nonrecyclable wastes would certainly improve the pollution picture, it is improbable that all of these wastes can be eliminated; and with rapid economic growth, the impact of federal regulation could prove minimal. Such a possibility reveals that government subsidy of pollution-fighting industries and the strict regulation of emissions by polluting industries may not be the panacea that many experts believe it to be.[2]

Government intervention may thus have to be much more extreme, involving policies that limit economic growth. At the same time, the government would have to cope with the economic and social problems stemming from such a radical alteration of the economy.

To change the economy, however, will require that the public find ways to overcome the power of economic interests and/or to build its own base of power. The largest and most powerful corporations in America emit the most wastes and produce the most polluting products, such as cars and gasoline. Given the current structure of the American government (see Chapter 3), these corporations are able to press their interest more effectively than the public or environmental groups. Despite the impressive pro-ecology advertising campaigns mounted by industrial corporations (another indicator of their power to shape public opinion), they will quite naturally continue to lobby against any pollution legislation that would threaten their profits. Thus, the narrow interests, but enormous political power, of America's corporate structure represent yet another major obstacle to pollution control.

THE LEGAL SYSTEM. Ultimately, the control of pollutants will be done by administrative agencies operating under regulatory

[2] Another interesting consequence of subsidizing companies involved in waste recovery, in plant abatement technologies, and in effluent treatment procedures is that the government would also be subsidizing companies that do the polluting, since some of the big polluters are also manufacturing and selling antipollution equipment to other polluters.

laws. The partially effective laws presently on the books and the problems with formulating future pollution control laws can represent another institutional force that can either forestall or foster ecological problems in America. It is therefore necessary to analyze the difficulties and dilemmas of creating coherent and effective pollution control laws.

One of the difficulties in developing effective laws against pollution is the lack of a legal tradition supporting environmental law; for it was well into the twentieth century before serious conservation laws were enacted in America. At about the turn of the century, the Bureau of Reclamation was established and the National Park Service was expanded, simulating the passage of limited numbers of conservation laws by state and federal governments. It was not until the Dust Bowl of the 1930s, however, that legislators began to realize the potential dangers of unregulated use of renewable resources, and with this realization came the enactment of the Soil Conservation Act (Boulding, 1970). But after this promising beginning, the thousands of conservation laws that have been enacted over the last forty years have proved, by and large, ineffective in abating ecological disruption. Even a cursory review of the federal codes and statutes reveals that most "conservation" laws represent an "administrative handbook" telling corporations how to apply for resource extraction. With some noticeable exceptions, these laws do not prevent harmful extraction.

With this short-lived and largely ineffective legal tradition in "conservation laws," it was perhaps inevitable that recent law enactments suffer from a number of defects:

1. Traditional conservation laws and more recent antipollution laws are often phrased in ambiguous language. Coupled with the court system's traditional favoritism of economic interests, state and federal agencies charged with enforcing these vague laws are naturally reluctant to press charges and take violators to court for fear of having even these weak laws, and perhaps the agency's very function, invalidated (Murphy, 1967).

2. Existing antipollution laws typically mandate weak civil penalties and hardly ever carry criminal sanctions. The frequent result of this situation is for companies faced with relatively minor fines to view pollution penalties as just another "cost" to be absorbed and passed onto the consumer in the form of higher prices. It may be that, until companies are confronted with criminal penalties and heavy civil damages, antipollution laws will not be as effective as they might in preventing ecological disruption. For example, the most comprehensive and unambiguous federal antipollution law ever enacted, the Clean Air Act of 1970, carries no

criminal penalties; and it can be wondered how effective a law without criminal penalties will be. And as recent events have underscored, corporations may be able to weaken even this clearly written law as they exert pressure upon legislators. If the penalties for violation of the Clean Air Act can be circumvented, then weaker pieces of federal legislation will probably prove even less effective, especially when the federal government is subject to pressure by corporations seeking to avoid higher costs and a public reluctant to pay higher prices and taxes.

3. The vast majority of laws do not typically address the sources of pollutants; they more frequently require treatment of pollutants *after* they have been created. For example, because there are few state laws prohibiting the use of phosphates and other chemicals in consumer products, the burden of cleaning the water into which these chemicals are dumped must fall upon sewage treatment facilities. To take another example, the Clean Air Act did not specify that the internal combustion engine must be replaced, only that the ultimate emissions of this engine must be reduced. This creates the possibility that, should it prove technically or economically impossible to meet the standards imposed by the Clean Air Act, considerable time will have been lost in developing an alternative to the internal combustion engine.

4. Finally, many state antipollution laws are enacted with "grandfather clauses" that allow established industries to continue their harmful activities. One result of such a clause is to encourage outmoded and highly polluting industries to stay in a geographical area, while discouraging the new industries—which must utilize expensive antipollution equipment—from becoming established. Thus, in the end, these laws often perpetuate the very industrial processes that the law was designed to discourage.

This ineffectiveness of state and federal antipollution laws is compounded by the *inducements* to pollution found in other types of legal statutes. Present tax codes, for example, sometimes encourage unnecessary pollution; traditional depletion allowances, which allow corporations extracting resources to deduct from their taxes the "depletions" of these resources, encourage rapid and sometimes wasteful resource extraction to obtain the highest depletion allowance. Or, to take another example, property tax laws support depletion allowance laws by allowing lower assessed evaluations for land as resources are extracted, once again providing a potential inducement to careless and rapid extraction (Murphy, 1967). Even when corporations are found liable for their pollutants, they are, under some circumstances, allowed to deduct as a business expense the costs of cleaning up their effluents; and under some state statutes, even legally imposed fines for pollution can be deducted as a business expense. These kinds of laws encourage pollution by offering incentives for wasteful resource extraction and by mitigating the costs incurred by companies that disrupt the environment. Until state and federal tax laws reward careful resource extraction, while more heavily penalizing polluters, profit and cost conscious industries are unlikely to initiate a serious antipollution effort.

In sum, then, it must be reluctantly concluded that the present legal structure in America cannot provide what may be a greater need to control and regulate pollution. The many state and federal conservation codes often facilitate as much as inhibit harmful resource extraction; tax laws sometimes provide incentives for pollution, rather than the reverse; and explicit antipollution codes are sometimes circumvented by political pressures from the polluters and an economically squeezed public. To overcome these problems, a comprehensive national body of laws carrying severe criminal and civil penalties will probably be necessary. This new federal body of law will have to involve not piecemeal legislative acts, but rather, a coordinated writing and rewriting of pollution, conservation, and tax laws. For if present trends continue, there may come a time when the environment can no longer be maintained by the current maze of state and federal codes whose ambiguities, conflicts, and overlaps have made legal solutions to ecological problems problematic.

What may be needed from federal legislators is a set of clear *national* quality standards for the air, soil, and water, with no region in America able to tolerate pollution levels exceeding these standards. Aside from the reluctance of federal legislators to enact such bold legislation, however, there are equally fundamental problems: What are the standards to be? What level of pollution is tolerable? At what point does pollution begin to harm the ecosystem? What are the short-run versus the long-run consequences of various pollutants? These are difficult questions to answer, for despite the heightened scientific concern with ecological problems, a great deal of ignorance exists with respect to the impact of pollutants on the environment. This lack of knowledge places legislators in the position of setting renewable resource quality standards without clear scientific guidelines.

In such a state of ignorance, legislators will tend to avoid enacting expensive laws, or if they do enact laws, they will write ambiguities into them, especially when pressured by well-organized lobbying interests (Graham, 1966). For example, the Water Quality Act of 1965 established rather vague water quality standards that could be voided upon a "due consideration to the practicability and to the physical and economic feasibility of complying with such standards . . . as the public interest and equities of the case may require." Coupled with many courts' sympathetic attitudes toward communities and industries, the Water Quality Act has proven difficult to enforce because arguments as to how polluants serve the public interest by keeping taxes low or by providing jobs for workers in polluting industries are rather easily made.

The only significant piece of legislation that explicitly sought to redress these deficiencies was the Clean Air Act of 1970. In this act, tolerable emissions were stated with deadlines for compliance to these standards being explicit. The auto makers have now been granted several extensions in meeting required standards (excluding California); and currently, with the energy crisis and the specter of more economic dislocations resulting from enforcement of the standards, there is considerable pressure to suspend or weaken the law. If unambiguous standards for clean air cannot be maintained, it is less probable that similar standards can be set for emissions into the soil and water which, in both the short and long run, pose a more serious threat to the ecosystem than air pollution. The "public interest," the threat of an economic recession, or higher taxes can be used to weaken, and even suspend, the enforcement of any future standards for the water and soil. This, eventually, is particularly likely because pollution of the soil and water is not as directly observable as air pollution, and thus, not as disturbing to the public. Equally significant, the interaction of pollutants with the water and soil is more complex than with the air, with the result that legislators will not know just what standards to establish.

Assuming that minimal quality standards for the air, water, and soil may some day be enacted, the next legislative problem revolves around the question of how to induce communities and industries to pay for *all* remaining pollutants that they discharged into the environment. These laws will probably reveal the following basic formula: The more pollutants emitted within minimum standards, the more offenders must pay in penalties; and when offenders are corporations, the more they must pay in fines that cannot be passed on to consumers. Such laws might serve as incentives for industries to clean up the last of their harmful effluents. Enacting this kind of law, however, poses a major dilemma: How are the formulas for assigning these costs to be created? As already noted, there is considerable ignorance as to how pollutants interact with each other in different environments over varying lengths of time to cause varying degrees of harm to different ecosystems. In light of this situation, then, just how are costs for emissions into the air, water, and soil to be assessed? Such is one of the problems of enactment in environmental law; and yet, unless tentative legislative efforts to construct these formulas for assigning costs are made, industries and communities will have few economic incentives to restrict their effluents.

To further remove current inducements for pollution, extensive laws may be necessary. It would seem necessary for effective pollution control that depletion allowances and lowered tax assessments for harmful resource extraction be stricken from federal and state laws. Accompanying the elimination of these incentives to pollute should come laws encouraging research on pollution control and installation of emission-control devices. One approach would involve high tax writeoffs for these antipollution activities, although any such law would have to be monitored carefully by the Internal Revenue Service to prevent industries from simply renaming previous research activities in unrelated areas "antipollution research, development, and implementation." Another strategy might create laws requiring polluting companies to reinvest a certain percentage of their profits into pollution control, while at the same time, preventing these corporations from passing their increased costs onto consumers.

To add legal weight to these kinds of new laws, and to facilitate their enactment where legislative bodies hesitate, some have proposed a constitutional amendment containing an Environmental Bill of Rights (Nader, 1970; Ehrlich, 1971). In the absence of clear legal precedents for controlling emissions, such an amendment would enable the courts to rule against polluters in environmental lawsuits. Bringing industrywide and class action suits against polluters is presently most difficult, because there are few unambiguous legal doctrines that can provide the necessary legal precedent. In this relative legal vacuum, the doctrine of "balance of equities" has evolved and now guides many pollution suits.

This doctrine charges the courts to consider the "good" consequences (a clean environment) against the "bad" effects (higher taxes and unemployment, for example) of rules favoring environmentalists. The result has often been for the courts to rule that the economic benefits of pollution outweigh the alleged costs to personal health and ecological disruption. A constitutional amendment containing a forceful Environmental Bill of Rights could potentially rebalance legal precedents in favor of environmental groups.

Without such a constitutional amendment, there are few legal traditions with which to press environmental lawsuits. Probably the most applicable of existing legal traditions are the doctrines of "nuisance" and "trespass" (Ehrlich and Ehrlich, 1970:267–274; Landau and Rheingold, 1971). It is not completely wrong to consider pollutants as a "nuisance" to public health and as a "trespass" on individuals' air, land, and water. Yet this argument does appear to stretch traditional conceptions of trespass and nuisance, and thus, they are not likely to prove effective. Equally significant as this lack of legal tradition, one of the key legal weapons of environmentalists—the class action lawsuit—was redefined in 1973 by the Supreme Court. In a landmark water pollution case, the Court ruled that in pollution suits involving several states, the citizens of each state bringing the suit in a federal court must demonstrate $10,000 in damages to their property or health. This ruling will severely limit the capacity of environmental groups to bring class action suits in federal courts, since *each* plaintiff must document $10,000 in damages. Such documentation is difficult when hundreds of plaintiffs in several states are involved in a law suit. Further, environmental groups will have enormous difficulty filing class action suits for entire communities, or any large population, when they must document for each of the plaintiffs—perhaps an entire community—that $10,000 in damages has occurred.

The law, then, can be both a tool to deal with pollution problems and a roadblock to the resolution of these problems. The obstacles to effective laws have been emphasized in order to highlight the extent to which pollution is built into the present body of laws in America. Such need not necessarily be the case, of course, but the problems of calculating ecological damage and of writing pollution control formulas present formidable obstacles to those who seek to write effective laws. And coupled with the economic, social, and political dislocations that the enactment and enforcement of such laws would have, the problems of using law as a tool for pollution control become even more acute. These problems may indeed be surmountable, but they will need to be attacked with political resolve to prevent ecological disruption. Such resolve will reflect the priorities, decision-making processes, and administrative capacities of the federal government.

THE GOVERNMENT. To seriously address environmental problems will probably require reordering of national priorities, for the costs of a comprehensive environmental program will be enormously high—perhaps as much as $50 billion per year for a decade to restore present environment disruptions, and close to that amount thereafter just to maintain these restored ecological balances in the face of an expanding economy. The sources of such high costs are many: For example, tax incentives for polluters will be expensive and inevitably raise federal, state, and local taxes; revenue sharing and grants-in-aids to cities attempting to revamp their antiquated sewage systems will cost a great deal; and the large federal bureaucracy needed to implement, monitor, and enforce antipollution codes will also be expensive.

Conflicting with these costs are the ever-increasing revenue demands in the domestic sphere (Sprout and Sprout, 1971a). For example, welfare costs will continue to rise; proposed national health care systems will be expensive; education costs are likely to continue to increase; law enforcement costs will not remain stable; perpetuation of agricultural and industrial subsidies will continue to tax federal revenues; foreign aid will remain high; and the total revenue needs of the executive departments like Interior, Labor, Commerce, and Housing and Urban Development will expand. While considerable revenue can be raised from closing tax loopholes, raising corporate and individual taxes, thereby expanding the economy and hence tax revenues, it would appear that it will still be necessary to reorder national priorities to generate the large sums of money needed to preserve the ecological community.

If the nation is to maintain current standards of living *and* address pollution problems, the only available source of revenue is the Pentagon's budget. Presently, the military and related agencies receive at least 35 percent (probably closer to 50%) of all federal tax revenues, making them the largest single source of nondomestic monies. To maintain the present military budget *and* address pollution problems would require drastic increases in taxes; or to maintain the military budget, keep taxes down, *and still* attack pollution problems would probably involve, for example, poorer schools, expensive private health care, less police protection, widespread poverty, continued urban decay, and inadequate transport systems. As Chapter 3 documents, the political influence of the Pentagon, and the corporations and labor organizations receiving its contract dollars, is great. This situation underscores the dilemma of addressing ecological problems, because unless the military budget can be tapped, Americans will have higher taxes and lessened social services. The public is not likely to accept these, while the military is not likely to have its budget cut drastically, thus revealing the extent to which pollution problems are built into the political problems involved in reordering priorities. When these political problems are compounded by the economic consequences of reordered priorities—short-term unemployment for workers, and declining profits for the owners of corporations doing business with the Pentagon—then the difficulties of changing priorities to maintain the ecological community become even more pronounced.

Even *if* Congress could render priorities and enact comprehensive quality standards for the air, water, and soil, a new set of political obstacles would probably emerge. These revolve around the present *pattern* of governmental administration in America (Revelle, 1968). As was emphasized in Chapter 3, the United States is a federalist political system with considerable power residing in city, county, and state governments. While there are many advantages to such a system, one of the current problems facing all types of national legislation is the coordination of city, county, and state governments with the federal agencies that administer national legislation. It is perhaps inevitable in a federalist system, and perhaps desirable from one viewpoint, that state and local governments will often have conflicting interests, but one less positive result is to make difficult the implementation of legislation. In order to avoid these conflicts among and between various levels of government, it may be necessary for antipollution agencies to have considerable power over local governments. However, existing governmental agencies, state and local governments, well-organized interests, and even the public in the post Watergate-domestic spying era are likely to resist the allocation of such power. There are many sound reasons for resisting the concentration of power in administrative agencies, but one of the dilemmas of a federalist system is that without this power, it is more difficult to cut through the rivalries and antagonisms among diverse governmental bodies and effectively implement a national pollution control program.

Another problem with the current pattern of administration in America is that, even when they have considerable power, agencies frequently fail to implement and enforce regulatory laws. One type of misregulation involves a failure to maintain various quality standards. For example, the U.S. Department of Agriculture has, on numerous occasions, not held the line on the use of certain dangerous pesticides. A second source of misregulation is the cooptation of federal agencies by those very industries they are established to regulate. For instance, the Department of Agriculture is frequently an advocate of the chemical pesticide industry that it is supposed to regulate; for the public record reveals quite clearly that it has consistently pushed the use of pesticides, while underemphasizing research on and use of alternative forms of pest control (Ehrlich, 1971). A third source of administrative incompetence can be seen in the reluctance of agencies to argue for tougher standards where the standards are weak or ambiguous (Nader, 1970). Sometimes the reason for this reticence stems from the fact that, if agencies push for tougher standards, they could potentially expose their previous laxity in enforcement. A final administrative obstacle to effective administration of regulatory law can be seen in the reluctance of existing agencies to use even the limited sanctions at their disposal. Should an agency finally take action against an offending industry or community, it usually secures a "cease-and-desist" order that requires the violator to stop its illegal activities. Most typically, only after such an order has been ignored will minimal (rarely maximum) civil penalties be sought by regulatory agencies.

This pattern of administration now appears to be well institutionalized, with the likely result that its failings will be repeated even if antipollution laws are enacted. To avoid these administrative problems, it is likely that the current Environmental Protection Agency will be less successful than anticipated. For a supra-agency with power over all other agencies in the federal government might well be necessary for effective enforcement of antipollution laws. Establishing an agency with such far-reaching authority, however, will create many problems. One of these will revolve around opening and maintaining lines of authority to other executive departments in the federal government, as well as to state and local governments (Goldman, 1970), for at a minimum, a supra-agency will probably require authority over the other executive departments, such as Health, Education and Welfare, Commerce, Interior, Agriculture, Transportation, and Housing and Urban Development. In light of the history of rivalry, duplication of effort, and jealousy among these agencies, it will be difficult to create a new agency with authority over all of them. Various departments would probably oppose the creation of this supra-agency in the first place, and attempt to undermine its effectiveness should it even be created. In July 1970, President Nixon formed the Environmental Protection Agency to consolidate pollution control policy and activity, but the record of the last five years with respect to enforcement of the unambiguous Clean Air Act reveals that it has had a difficult time asserting authority over other executive departments. If this situation is to prove typical, then the difficulties in the administration of environmental law will be compounded.

The prognosis, then, for an effective administration of antipollution laws, is one revealing many problems—most of which inhere in the current structure of government in America. These problems are exacerbated by the complexities of the task with which an environmental agency would be charged. Laws and their enforcement cannot simply prohibit the emissions of all pollutants, for such a prohibition is not economically, politically, or socially possible. A more reasonable approach is that, within quality standards set by the law, a way must be devised to induce polluters to cut back their own harmful activities. This inducement can come only by requiring polluters to pay for even those emissions within the limits of national quality standards (which will probably need to be somewhat loose). As was emphasized earlier, there are problems with writing legal formulas for determining what the costs should be, since understanding of the short- and long-run consequences of pollutants to the ecosystem is far from complete. The administrative problems involved in just creating the accounting system represents a roadblock to monitoring and controlling pollution in America. Moreover, the governmental agency charged with enforcing what initially—in light of current ignorance—were somewhat arbitrary cost formulas, will quite naturally be resisted by industry and communities. One result of this situation could be endless legal battles as polluters sought to document that their pollutants should not cost as much as dictated by existing formulas. It is not a completely faciful scenario to visualize an inadequately funded environmental agency embroiled in legal battles to such an extent that it has difficulty enforcing minimal national quality standards for air, water, and soil (Sprout and Sprout, 1971b).

In evaluating the political capacity of the United States to regulate its emissions into the ecosystem, then, it is clear that there are a number of structural obstacles. The reordering of national priorities in the direction of environmental protection will be difficult due to the Pentagon's power. And even should these obstacles be surmounted, the pattern of governmental administration in America reveals an additional set of problems that could potentially reduce effective environmental protection. While these same conditions may have "positive" outcomes for other sectors of the society, they represent severe problems of structure in resolving the problems of the ecological community.

POPULATION AND THE ECOSYSTEM

Humans are multiplying at an accelerating rate. For example, from 1850 to 1930, the world population doubled from one to two billion (Appleman, 1965). Currently the world's population is set at 3.5 billion and will soon double again (Ehrlich, 1970; Hardin, 1969; Miles, 1970; and Wald, 1970). A rapidly expanding population poses a problem for ecological balances since it creates ever-increasing demands for industrial and agricultural goods. In the agricultural sector of the economy, the demands for food cause the use of the pesticides and chemical fertilizers that kill many organisms necessary for life-sustaining energy flows and mineral cycles. Moreover, in order to keep abreast of growing demand, single-crop or a limited-rotation agriculture becomes necessary. Such agricultural techniques strip the ecosystem of the natural stability stemming from diversity, while at the same time making crops extremely vulnerable to pests and disease. In turn, this susceptibility intensifies reliance upon pesticides and various chemical killers. Thus, the short-run demands for agricultural products created by an expanding population can force a pattern of agricultural production which potentially could decrease the soil's capacity to feed the human species in the long run.

In the industrial sector of the economy, population growth escalates the demands for consumer goods that increase the discharge of pollutants into renewable resources. This demand is likely to be particularly severe as the "revolution of rising expectations" among populations of Third World nations stimulates the production of increased numbers and varieties of industrial goods.

The rate of population growth in modern industrial societies is much slower than that in Third World nations, and perhaps, once these latter societies become industrialized, their population growth will begin to level off. Yet, the population base of perhaps as many as 15 billion to be served by mass industrial and intensive agricultural production could create economic demands that can only be met by further ecological disruption. Presently, these large populations of the undeveloped world do not pose an ecological problem, but with rapid growth and industrial expansion they could represent a severe ecological problem in the future. In the immediate present, the comparatively "small" populations and "low" rates of growth of industrialized nations represent the most evident threat to ecosystem balances. For as was outlined in Figure 11.3, the demands of these "small" populations are met with the techniques of mass agriculture and industrial production which deposit large quantities of waste residues into the ecological community (Miles, 1970 Stockwell, 1968).

The patterns of population growth now evident in the United States and elsewhere in the industrial world will perhaps become more prevalent in the rest of the world, but the changes which now appear to be associated with a drop in the birth rate—industrialization, urbanization, and mass production—can be potentially harmful, especially as they serve an expanded population base. For example, some statistics can perhaps underscore the dangers of the Third World developing the same consumption habits as Americans: Consumption of goods by polluting industrial and agricultural processes, as well as the disposal of wastes by each American, is

50 times that of a person in the nonindustrial world (Wald, 1970). Or, to phrase the matter differently, the United States causes more pollution with its current population of 210 million than the combined 2.5 billion inhabitants of the underdeveloped world. The prospect, then, of an "Americanized" Third World is disquieting. But for the present, the population patterns of American society are of most direct relevance to current ecological problems. The critical question thus becomes: What are these population patterns?

Considerable publicity has been given to the sudden decrease in the birth rate to a "no growth" level. From an ecological standpoint, it can be hoped that this recent trend will endure. And yet, even if it does, it will not become translated into a stable population, since the current childbearing population will live for another fifty to sixty years, with the result that their children, grandchildren, and great-grandchildren will be added to the population. Hence, even should the birth *rate* stay at the zero level, it is inevitable that the United States will grow to perhaps as much as 300 million before it finally stabilizes.

One difficulty with extrapolating from birth rates is that in the past they have fluctuated considerably. During the 1930s, for example, concern with the low birth rate was pervasive; and then suddenly with the onset of World War II, all projections of a declining population were rendered inaccurate with the baby boom; and now with new values and birth control technologies, a marked drop in the birth rate has occurred. Is this a long-run trend, or simply a low point in a cycle? While no definitive statement in this

SOCIOLOGICAL INSIGHTS

POPULATION DOWN

Young American women expect to have fewer children. As a result, population projections for the U.S. for the year 2000 have been revised downward.

At the end of this century, the population of this country will range from a low of 245 million to a high of 287 million. The current population is 213 million.

Young American females questioned by the Census Bureau indicate that they plan to bear from 1.7 to 2.7 children. Generally, population projections follow the economic indicators.

area is possible, it would appear that the long-range trend is toward a decline in the birth rate with periodic reversals. It is these periodic reversals that are of concern, because they increase the population base and hence the demand for industrial and mass agricultural goods.

In the United States, then, population policy must be directed to preventing a reversal—even one of short duration—of the current rate of zero population growth. With an equally concerted effort at pollution abatement, perhaps the world's ecosystem can support an American population of 300 million. But if the rate jumps suddenly, even if only briefly, world ecological problems would be correspondingly intensified, especially when coupled with the industrialization of the Third World.

THE ECOLOGICAL COMMUNITY: PROSPECTS FOR THE FUTURE

Only by understanding the basic elements and processes in social and ecological systems is it possible to comprehend the ways in which society has interacted with the ecosystem to create what could potentially become the ultimate problem of structure. The ecological community is composed of highly complex flows of energy and cycles of minerals through the millions of life forms inhabiting the planet. Social systems are composed of humans organized into complex webs of interrelationships that are mediated by cultural symbols. As Figure 11.3 outlined, this organization of the human species into sociocultural entities could threaten the flow of energy and cycling of minerals in the ecosystem, creating not just a crisis of human survival, but one for many other life forms as well.

While data on the matter do not exist, it appears that the structure of many ecosystems is now vulnerable to change from the pollutants of human societies, whereas the structure of social systems appear less likely to the changes in ways that might restore more harmonious relations between society and nature. While the details of ecological disruption are ultimately biological questions, even a cursory appreciation of the nature of the ecological community reveals that human society has (1) lessened, to some unknown extent, the diversity and hence stability of the world ecosystem; (2) altered in a way not fully understood the flow of energy and cycling of minerals, perhaps to the degree that the amplified impact of these alterations will be intense; and (3) perhaps already generated unknown amounts of irreversible destruction to plant and animal species.

Because of its enormous productive power and habits of consumption, American society is largely responsible for this disruption which, by itself, is problematic, but equally problematic is the worldwide process involving restructuring many human societies along the American pattern. While there are notable differences over ideology and forms of social organization existing among the societies of the developing world, these societies reveal a similar pattern of community and institutional organization. For indeed, all are guided by values emphasizing economic growth, higher levels of consumption, the extensive application of technology, and the utilization of nature as a refuse dump. And all reveal the beginnings of community structures and institutional arrangements that will generate large quantities of waste residues.

In closing, it can properly be asked: What are the future prospects for resolving this ultimate problem of structure? And, what will corrective action require of Americans? It does appear that there is some awareness of ecological problems in America; and this awareness may well become translated into actions that reduce the discharge of pollutants into the world's renewable resources. But it could take several ecological disasters, or clearly visible crises, for consciousness to shift into concerted social action. At the very least, there is hope in the fact that Americans realize that some action is necessary. Corrective action, however, may well require difficult adjustments for most Americans: Pollution control will cost money in the form of higher taxes and prices; it will probably require distortions in the job market; it could make "luxuries" of many taken-for-granted goods and services; and it will no doubt require a willingness to save, conserve, and recycle. These represent major changes in the "American way of life," and it is an open question as to whether or not Americans are willing, at this time, to begin making the necessary sacrifices. The next two decades will probably reveal America's capacity to deal with this most ultimate problem of structure.

BIBLIOGRAPHY

Abelson, P. H., "Methyl Mercury," *Science* (July 17, 1970).

Abrams, C., "Housing Policy—1937–1967," in B. J. Frieden and W. W. Nash, eds., *Shaping An Urban Future: Essays in Honor of Catherine Bauer Wurster,* Cambridge, Mass.: MIT Press, 1969.

———, *The City Is the Frontier,* New York: Harper & Row Colophon Books, 1967.

———, "The Housing Problem and the Negro," in T. Parsons and K. Clark, eds., *The Negro American,* Boston: Houghton Mifflin, 1966.

Allen, F., *The Borderline of Criminal Justice,* Chicago: University of Chicago Press, 1964.

Allen, R. F. and C. H. Adair, *Violence and Riots in Urban America,* Worthington, Ohio: Charles A. Jones Publishing Co., 1969.

Anderson, M., *The Federal Bulldozer,* New York: McGraw-Hill, 1964.

Appleman, P., *The Silent Explosion,* Boston: Beacon Press, 1965.

Banfield, R. C., *The Unheavenly City: The Nature and Future of Our Urban Crisis,* Boston: Little, Brown, 1970.

Banton, M., *The Policeman in the Community,* New York: Basic Books, 1964.

Batchelder, A. B., "Decline in Relative Income of Negro Men," *Quarterly Journal of Economics* (November, 1964).

Battan, L. J., *The Unclean Sky: A Meteorologist Looks at Air Pollution,* New York: Doubleday, 1966.

Beegle, A., *Rural Social Systems,* Englewood Cliffs: Prentice-Hall, 1950.

Berelson, B., "Beyond Family Planning," *Science* (February 7, 1969).

Bevan, W., R. S. Albert, R. R. Loigeaux, P. N. Mayfield, and G. Wright, "Jury Behavior as a Function of the Prestige of the Foreman and the Nature of His Leadership," *Journal of Public Law* (Fall, 1958).

Biderman, A. D., "Surveys of Population Samples for Estimating Crime," *Annals of the Academy of Political and Social Science* 84 (November, 1967).

Bittner, E., "The Police on Skid Row: A Study of Peace Keeping," *American Sociological Review* (October, 1967).

Blake, N. M., *Water for the Cities,* Syracuse: Syracuse University Press, 1956.

Blassingame, J. W., *The Slave Community,* New York: Oxford University Press, 1972.

Blau, S. D. and J. Rodenbeck, eds., *The House We Live In: An Environmental Reader,* New York: Macmillan, 1971.

Blauner, R., "The Dilemmas of The Black Urban Revolt," *Journal of Housing* (December, 1967).

———, *Racial Oppression in America,* New York: Harper & Row, 1972.

Blumberg, A. S., *Criminal Justice,* Chicago: Quadrangle Books, 1969.

Bordua, D. J., ed., *The Police,* New York: John Wiley & Sons, 1967.

Boskoff, A., *The Sociology of Urban Regions,* 2d ed., New York: Appleton-Century-Crofts, 1970.

Boulding, K. E., "No Second Chance for Man," in *The Crisis of Survival,* edited by the editors of *The Progressive,* Glenview, Ill.: Scott, Foresman, 1970.

———, "The Economics of the Coming Spaceship Earth," in H. Jarret, ed., *Environmental Quality in a Growing Economy,* Baltimore: Johns Hopkins University Press, 1966.

Brinton, C., *The Anatomy of Revolution,* New York: Vintage Books, 1965.

Brophy, W. A., and S. D. Aberle, *Indian: America's Unfinished Business,* Norman: University of Oklahoma Press, 1966.

Bullock, H. A., "Significance of the Racial Factor in the Length of Prison Sentences," *Journal of Criminal Law, Criminology, and Police Science* (November–December, 1961).

Bullock, P., "Employment Problems of the Mexican American," *Industrial Relations* (December, 1964).

Burch, W. R., *Day Dreams and Nightmares—A Sociological Essay on the American Environment,* New York: Harper & Row, 1971.

Burch, W. R., N. H. Cheek, Jr., and L. Taylor, *Social Behavior, Natural Resources, and the Environment,* New York: Harper & Row, 1972.

Burma, J. H., ed., *Mexican Americans in the United States,* San Francisco: Canfield Press, 1970.

Campbell, A., "The Role of Family Planning in the Reduction of Poverty," *Journal of Marriage and the Family* (December, 1968).

Campbell, A. K., *The States and Urban Crisis,* Englewood Cliffs: Prentice-Hall, 1970.

Campbell, R. R. and J. L. Wade, eds., *Society and Environment: The Coming Collision,* Boston: Allyn & Bacon, 1972.

Caplovitz, D., *The Poor Pay More,* New York: The Free Press, 1963.

Carr, D. N., *Death of the Sweet Waters,* New York: W. W. Norton, 1966.

———, *The Breath of Life,* New York: W. W. Norton, 1965.

Carson, R. L., *The Silent Spring,* Boston: Houghton Mifflin, 1962.

———, *The Sea Around Us,* New York: Signet Library, 1954.

Carter, R. M., and L. T. Wilkins, "Some Factors in Sentencing Policy," *Journal of Criminal Law, Criminology, and Police Science* (December, 1967).

Census, Bureau, *Current Population Reports,* Series P-60, Washington, D.C.: GPO, 1973.

Chevigny, P., *Police Power,* New York: Pantheon Books, 1969.

Cicourel, A. V., and J. I. Kitsuse, *The Educational Decision-Makers,* Indianapolis: Bobbs-Merrill, 1963.

Clark, K. B., *Dark Ghetto: Dilemmas of Social Power,* New York: Harper & Row, 1965.

Clinard, M. and R. Quinney, *Criminal Behavior Systems,* New York: Holt, Rinehart & Winston, 1967.

Cloward, R. A. and R. M. Elman, "Poverty, Injustice, and the Welfare State," *The Nation* (February, 1966).

Coffman, R., "Are Fertilizers Polluting Our Water Supply?" *Farm Journal* (May, 1969).

Coleman, J. S. et al., *Equality of Educational Opportunity,* Washington, D.C.: Government Printing Office, 1966.

Commoner, Barry, *Science and Survival,* New York: The Viking Press, 1966.

Coombs, M., R. E. Kron, G. Collister, and K. E. Anderson, *The Indian Child Goes To School,* Lawrence, Kansas: Haskell Press, 1958.

Cressey, D. R., *Theft of the Nation,* New York: Harper & Row, 1969.

Cumming, E., I. Cumming, and L. Edell, "Policeman as Philosopher, Guide, and Friend," *Social Problems* (Winter, 1965).

Daly, H. E., ed., *Toward Steady-State Economy,* San Francisco: W. H. Freeman, 1973.

Daly, R., *The World Beneath the City,* New York: J. D. Lippincott, 1959.

Daniels, R. and H. H. L. Kitano, *American Racism: Exploration of the Nature of Prejudice,* Englewood Cliffs: Prentice-Hall, 1970.

Davies, J. C., "Toward A Theory of Revolution," *American Sociological Review* (November, 1962).

Davis, A., *Social Class Influence Upon Learning,* Cambridge, Mass.: Harvard University Press, 1952.

Davis, J. P., ed., *The American Negro Reference Book,* Englewood Cliffs: Prentice-Hall, 1966.

Davis, K., "Population Policy: Will Current Programs Succeed?" *Science* (November 10, 1967).

Davis, W. H., "Overpopulated America," *The New Republic* (January 10, 1970).

Day, A. T., "Population Control and Personal Freedom: Are They Compatible?" *The Humanist* (November–December, 1968).

Dennison, G., *The Lives of Children,* New York: Random House, 1969.

Dentler, R. A., "For Local Control in the Schools," *Atlantic Monthly* (January, 1968).

————, *Major American Social Problems*, Chicago: Rand McNally, 1967.

Department of Commerce, "Social Indicators," Washington, D.C.: GPO, 1973.

Department of Labor, *Manpower Report to the President*, Washington, D.C.: GPO, 1969.

Detwyler, R., ed., *Man's Impact on Environment*, New York: Alfred A. Knopf, 1962.

deVilleneuve, R., ed., *The Enemy Is Us: A Rational Look at the Environmental Problem*, Minneapolis: Winston Press, 1973.

Dodd, M., *Studies in the Development of Capitalism*, London: Routledge and Sons, 1946.

Duncan, O. D. and A. Schnore, "The Eco-system," in C. A. Faris, ed., *Handbook of Sociology*, Chicago: Rand McNally, 1964.

Dynes, R. and E. L. Quarantelli, "What Looting in Civil Disturbances Really Means," *Trans-action* (May, 1968).

Dynes, R. R., A. C. Clark, S. Dinitz, and I. Ishino, *Social Problems: Dissensus and Deviation in an Industrial Society*, New York: Oxford University Press, 1964.

Ehrlich, P. R., *The Population Bomb*, rev. ed., New York: Ballantine, 1971.

————, "Eco-Catastrophe," *Ramparts* (September, 1969).

Ehrlich, P. R. and A. H. Ehrlich, *Population, Resources, Environment: Issues in Human Ecology*, San Francisco: W. H. Freeman, 1970.

Ehrlich, P. R., J. P. Hodlren, and R. W. Holm, *Man and the Ecosphere*, San Francisco: W. H. Freeman, 1971.

Elman, R., *The Poorhouse State*, New York: Random House, 1966.

Erickson, K., *Wayward Puritans: A Study in the Sociology of Deviance*, New York: John Wiley & Sons, 1966.

Esposito, J. C., *Vanishing Air: The Ralph Nader Study Group Report on Air Pollution*, New York: Grossman, 1970.

Esselstyn, T. C., "The Social Role of a County Sheriff," *Journal of Criminal Law, Criminology, and Police Science* (July–August, 1953).

Falk, R. A., *This Endangered Planet: Prospects and Proposals for Human Survival*, New York: Random House, 1971.

Farley, R. and K. E. Taeuber, "Population Trends and Residential Segregation Since 1960," *Science* (March, 1968).

Feagin, J. R., "We Still Believe That God Helps Those Who Help Themselves," *Psychology Today* 6 (November), 1972.

Feldstein, S., *Once a Slave: The Slaves' View of Slavery*, New York: William Morrow, 1971.

Feldstein, S., The Poisoned Tongue, New York: William Morrow, 1972.

Fernbach, F. L., "Policies Affecting Income Distribution," in M. S. Gordon, ed., *Poverty in America*, San Francisco: Chandler, 1965.

Flacks, R., "Social and Cultural Meanings of Student Revolt: Some Informal Comparative Observations," *Social Problems* (Winter, 1970a).

———, "Who Protests: The Social Bases of the Student Movement," in J. Foster and D. Long, eds., *Protest! Student Activism in America,* New York: William Morrow & Co., 1970b.

———, "The Liberated Generation: An Exploration of the Roots of Student Protest," *Journal of Social Issues* (July, 1967).

Fogel, R. and S. Engerman, *Time on the Cross,* Boston: Little, Brown, 1974.

Franklin, J. H., *Reconstruction After the Civil War,* Chicago: University of Chicago Press, 1961.

———, *From Slavery to Freedom,* New York: Alfred A. Knopf, 1948.

Freeman, A. M., "Cleaning Up Foul Waters. I—Pollution Tax," *The New Republic* (June 20, 1970).

Freeman, H. E. and W. C. Jones, *Social Problems: Causes and Controls,* Chicago: Rand McNally, 1970.

Friedenberg, E. Z., "Status and Role in Education," *The Humanist* (September–October, 1968).

———, *Coming of Age in America: Growth and Acquiescence,* New York: Vintage Books, 1963.

Gans, H. J., "Culture and Class in the Study of Poverty: An Approach to Anti-Poverty Research," in D. P. Moynihan, ed., *Understanding Poverty,* New York: Basic Books, 1969.

———, "Some Proposals for Government Policy in an Automating Society," *The Correspondent* (January–February, 1964).

de la Garza, R. O. et. al., *Chicanos and Native Americans,* Englewood Cliffs: Prentice-Hall, 1973.

General Advisory Council for Education (England), *Children and Their Primary School,* London: Her Majesty's Stationery Office, 1967.

Genovese, E. D., The Political Economy of Slavery, New York: Vintage Books, 1965.

Gerver, I., "The Social Psychology of Witness Behavior with Special Reference to Criminal Courts," *Journal of Social Issues* (November 2, 1957).

Glazer, N., "Housing Problems and Housing Policies," *The Public Interest* (Spring, 1967).

Goldberg, M., "Schools in Depressed Areas," in A. H. Passow, ed., *Education in Depressed Areas,* New York: Teachers College Press, Columbia University, 1963.

Goldfarb, R., *Ransom: A Critique of the American Bail System,* New York: Harper & Row, 1965.

Goldman, M. I., ed., *Controlling Pollution,* Englewood Cliffs: Prentice-Hall, 1967.

Goldman, M. I., *Ecology and Economics: Controlling Pollution in the 70's,* Englewood Cliffs: Prentice-Hall, 1972.

———, "From Lake Erie to Lake Baikal—From Los Angeles to Tbilisi: The Convergence of Environmental Disruption," *Science* (October 2, 1970).

Goldman, P. and D. Holt, "How Justice Works: The People vs. Donald Payne," *Newsweek* (March 8, 1971).

Goldsmith, J. R., "Los Angeles Smog," *Science Journal* (March, 1969).

Goldsmith, S. F., "Changes in the Size Distribution of Income," in E. C. Budd, ed., *Inequality and Poverty*, New York: W. W. Norton, 1967.

Goodlad, J. I., "The Schools vs. Education," *Saturday Review* (April 19, 1969).

Goodman, P., "The Present Moment in Education," *New York Review of Books* (April 10, 1969).

Gordon, M., *Sick Cities*, Baltimore: Penguin Books, 1963.

Graham, F., Jr., "The Infernal Smog Machine," *Audubon* (September–October, 1968).

————, *Disaster by Default: Politics and Water Pollution*, New York: M. Evans and Co., 1966.

Grebler, L., *The Schooling Gap: Signs of Progress, Advanced Report 7*, Los Angeles: University of California Press, Mexican American Study Project, 1967.

————, "The Naturalization of Mexican Immigrants in the United States," *International Migration Review* (Fall, 1966).

Green, C. M., *The Rise of Urban America*, New York: Harper & Row, 1965.

Greer, S., *Urban Renewal and American Cities: The Dilemma of Democratic Intervention*, Indianapolis: Bobbs-Merrill, 1965.

Grier, E. and G. Grier, "Equality and Beyond: Housing and segregation in the great society," *Daedalus* (Winter, 1966).

Griffin, Jr., C. W., "America's Airborne Garbage," *Saturday Review* (May 22, 1965).

Grigsby, W., *Housing Markets and Public Policy*, Philadelphia: University of Pennsylvania Press, 1964.

Halleck, S. L., "A Critique of Current Psychiatric Roles in the Legal Process," *Wisconsin Law Review* (Spring, 1966).

Hamilton, C. V., in C. V. Daley, ed., *Urban Violence*, Chicago: Center for Policy Study, 1969.

Hamilton, H. C., "The Negro Leaves the South," *Demography* (Winter, 1964).

Hardin, G., ed., *Population, Evolution and Birth Control*, San Francisco: W. H. Freeman, 1969.

————, "The Tragedy of the Commons," *Science* (February 16, 1968).

————, "Parenthood: Right or Privilege?" *Science* (July 30, 1970).

Harr, C., *Federal Credit and Private Housing: The Mass Financing Dilemma*, New York: McGraw-Hill, 1960.

Harrington, M., "Eradicating Poverty," *Playboy* (January, 1971).

————, "Introduction," in L. A. Ferman et al., eds., *Poverty in America*, Ann Arbor: University of Michigan Press, 1968.

————, *The Other America in the United States*, New York: Macmillan, 1963.

Havighurst, R. J. and B. L. Neugarten, *Society and Education*, Boston: Allyn & Bacon, 1967.

Helfrich, H. W., ed., *The Environmental Crisis—Man's Struggle to Live with Himself*, New Haven: Yale University Press, 1970.

Heller, C. S., ed., *Structured Social Inequality*, New York: Macmillan, 1969.

———, *Mexican American Youth: Forgotten at the Crossroads*, New York: Random House, 1966.

Hill, G., "A Not So Silent Spring," in *The Crisis of Survival*, edited by the editors of *The Progressive*, Glenview, Ill.: Scott, Foresman, 1970.

Hirsch, W., *Scientists in American Society*, New York: Random House, 1968.

Hodge, R. W., D. J. Treiman, and P. Rossi, "A Comparative Study of Occupational Prestige," in R. Bendix and S. M. Lipset, eds., *Class, Status, and Power*, New York: The Free Press, 1966.

Hodges, H. M., *Social Stratification: Class in America*, Cambridge, Mass.: Schenkman Press, 1964.

Hofstadter, R., "Spontaneous, Sporadic, and Disorganized," *New York Times Magazine* (April 28, 1968).

Horowitz, I. L., "Separate But Equal: Revolution and Counterrevolution in the American City," *Social Problems* (Winter, 1970).

Horowitz, I. L. and W. Friedland, *The Knowledge Factory: Student Power and Academic Politics in America*, Chicago: Aldine Publishing Co., 1970.

Howard, W. E., "Jet Smoke: Conquest by Camouflage," in *The Crisis of Survival*, edited by the editors of *The Progressive*, Glenview, Ill.: Scott, Foresman, 1970.

Hunter, D., *The Slums: Challenge and Response*, New York: The Free Press of Glencoe, 1965.

Iltis, H. H., "The Optimum Human Environment," in *The Crisis of Survival*, edited by the editors of *The Progressive*, Glenview, Ill.: Scott, Foresman, 1970.

Inkeles, A. and P. Rossi, "National Comparisons of Occupational Prestige," *American Journal of Sociology* (January, 1956).

Jacobs, J., *The Death and Life of Great American Cities*, New York: Random House, 1961.

Jacobs, P., "Keeping the Poor Poor," in J. Skolnick and E. Currie, eds., *Crisis in American Institutions*, Boston: Little, Brown, 1970.

Jacobs, W. R., *Dispossessing the American Indian*, New York: Charles Scribner's Sons, 1972.

Jencks, C., "A Reappraisal of the Most Controversial Educational Document of Our Time," *New York Times Magazine* (August 10, 1969).

Johnson, C. S., *Growing Up in the Black Belt*, Washington, D.C.: American Council on Education, 1941.

Kadish, S., "The Crisis of Overcriminalization," *The Annals* (November, 1967).

Karlen, H. M., *The Pattern of American Government*, Beverly Hills, Calif.: Glencoe Press, 1968.

Katz, M., "Legal Dimensions of Population Policy," *Social Science Quarterly* (December, 1969).

Kauffman, R., "The Military Industrial Complex," *The New York Times Magazine* (April 14, 1969).

Keniston, K., "The Fire Outside," *The Journal* (September–October, 1970).

———, "Notes on Young Radicals," *Change* (November–December, 1969a).

———, "You Have to Grow Up in Scarsdale to Know How Bad Things Really Are," *New York Times Magazine* (April 27, 1969b).

———, *Young Radicals*, New York: Harcourt, Brace & World, 1968.

Kerner, O. et al., Kerner Commission Report. See: *Report of the National Advisory Commission on Civil Disorders.*

Kidd, C. U., *Universities and Federal Research*, Cambridge, Mass.: Harvard University Press, 1959.

King, M. L., Jr., "Beyond the Los Angeles Riots: Next Stop: the North," *Saturday Review* (November 13, 1965).

Kitagawa, D., "The American Indian," in A. M. Rose and C. B. Rose, eds., *Minority Problems*, New York: Harper & Row, 1965.

Knowles, L. L. and K. Prewitt, eds., *Institutional Racism in America*, Englewood Cliffs: Prentice-Hall, 1969.

Koat, R., "Some Implications of the Economic Impact of Disarmament on the Structure of American Industry," in Joint Economic Committee, *Economic Effect of Vietnam Spending*, Washington, D.C.: Government Printing Office, 1967.

Kolko, G., *Wealth and Power in America*, New York: Praeger, 1962.

Kormondy, E. J., *Concepts of Ecology*, Englewood Cliffs: Prentice-Hall, 1969.

Kotz, N., *Let Them Eat Promises: The Politics of Hunger in America*, Garden City, New York: Anchor Press, 1971.

Kozol, J., *Death at an Early Age*, New York: Houghton Mifflin, 1967.

Kramer, J. R., *The American Minority Community*, New York: Thomas Y. Crowell, 1970.

Kristol, I., "The Lower Fifth," *New Leader* (February 17, 1964).

Kuntz, R. F., "An Environmental Glossary," *Saturday Review* (January 2, 1971).

La Fave, W. R., *Arrest: The Decision to Take a Suspect into Custody*, Boston: Little, Brown, 1964.

Lampman, R., "Changes in the Share of Wealth Held by Top Wealth Holders," *Review of Economics and Statistics* (November, 1969).

———, "Changes in the Concentration of Wealth," in E. C. Budd, ed., *Inequity and Poverty*, New York: W. W. Norton, 1967.

———, "Income Distribution and Poverty," in M. S. Gordon, ed., *Poverty in America*, San Francisco: Chandler, 1965.

Landau, N. J. and P. D. Rheingold, *The Environmental Law Handbook*, New York: Friends of the Earth/Ballantine, 1971.

Lapp, R. E., *The Weapons Culture*, New York: W. W. Norton, 1968.

———, *Kill and Overkill*, New York: Basic Books, 1962.

Lenski, G., *Power and Privilege: A Theory of Social Stratification*, New York: McGraw-Hill, 1966.

Levitan, S. A., *The Design of Federal Antipoverty Strategy,* Ann Arbor: University of Michigan Press, 1967.

Levitan, S. A. and B. Hetrick, *Big Brother's Indian Programs—With Reservations,* McGraw-Hill, 1971.

Lewis, O., *The Study of Slum Culture—Backgrounds for La Vida,* New York: Random House, 1968.

Liberson, S., "An Empirical Study of Military-Industrial Linkages," *The American Journal of Sociology* (November, 1971).

Linton, R. M., *Terracide: America's Destruction of Her Living Environment,* Boston: Little, Brown, 1970.

Lipset, S. M., "Youth and Politics," in R. K. Merton and R. Nisbet, eds., *Contemporary Social Problems,* 3d ed., New York: Harcourt, Brace, Jovanovich, 1971.

Lipset, S. M., and E. Raab, "The Non-Generation Gap," *Commentary* (August, 1970).

Lohman, J. D. et al., *The Police and the Community,* Berkeley: President's Commission on Law Enforcement and Administration of Justice, Field Survey No. 4, 1966.

Luce, C. F., "Energy: Economics of the Environment," in W. Helfrich, Jr., ed., *Agenda for Survival,* New Haven: Yale University Press, 1970.

Maccoby, M., "Government, Scientists, and the Priorities of Science," *Dissent* (Winter, 1974).

McClane, A. J., "The Ultimate Open Sewer," *Field and Stream* (May, 1968).

McClelland, D. C., *The Achieving Society,* New York: The Free Press, 1961.

MacDonald, D., "Our Invisible Poor," in L. A. Ferman et al., eds. *Poverty in America,* Ann Arbor: University of Michigan Press, 1968.

McGrath, G. G., R. Roessel, B. Meador, G. C. Helmstadter, and J. Barnes, *Higher Education of Southwestern Indians with Reference to Success and Failure,* Tempe, Ariz.: Cooperative Research Project No. 939, University of Arizona Press, 1962.

McKinley, P., "Compulsory Eugenic Sterilization: For Whom Does the Bell Toll?" *Duquesne University Law Review* (February, 1967).

McNamara, J. H., "Uncertainties in Police Work: The Relevance of Police Recruits' Background and Training," in D. J. Bordua, ed., *The Police: Six Sociological Essays,* New York: John Wiley & Sons, 1967.

McWilliams, C., *North From Mexico,* Philadelphia: J. B. Lippincott, 1949.

Madsen, W., *Mexican Americans of South Texas,* New York: Holt, Rinehart & Winston, 1964.

Marquis, R. W., *Environmental Improvement: Air, Water and Soil,* Washington: Graduate School Press, 1966.

Marx, K. and F. Engels, *Manifesto of the Communist Party,* New York: Appleton-Century-Crofts, 1955.

Mayer, K. W. and W. Buckley, *Class and Society,* 3d ed., New York: Random House, 1970.

Mellanby, K., *Pesticides and Pollution,* New York: William Collins and Sons, 1967.

Melman, S., *Pentagon Capitalism: The Political Economy of War,* New York: McGraw-Hill, 1970.

Miles, R. E., "Whose Baby is the Population Bomb?" *Population Bulletin* (February, 1970).

Miller, H. P., "Is the Income Gap Closed? No," in L. A. Ferman et al., eds., *Poverty in America,* Ann Arbor: University of Michigan Press, 1968.

————, "Changes in the Number and Composition of the Poor," in M. S. Gordon, ed., *Poverty in America,* San Francisco: Chandler, 1965.

————, *Rich Man, Poor Man,* New York: Thomas Y. Crowell, 1964.

Miller, S. M. and P. Roby, "Poverty: Changing Social Stratification," in D. P. Moynihan, ed., *On Understanding Poverty,* New York: Basic Books, 1969.

Miller, W., "The Elimination of the American Lower Class as a National Policy: A Critique of the Ideology of the Poverty Movement of the 1960s," in D. P. Moynihan, ed., *On Understanding Poverty,* New York: Basic Books, 1969.

————, "Focal Concerns of Lower Class Culture," in L. A. Ferman et al., eds., *Poverty in America,* Ann Arbor: University of Michigan Press, 1968.

————, "Lower Class Culture as a Generating Milieu of Gang Delinquency," *Journal of Social Issues* 14 (March, 1958).

Mix, S. A., "Solid Wastes: Every Day, Another 800 Million Pounds," *Today's Health* (March, 1966).

Moncrief, L. W., "The Cultural Basis for Our Environmental Crisis," *Science* (October 30, 1970).

Moore, J. W. with A. Cuéllar, *Mexican Americans,* Englewood Cliffs: Prentice-Hall, 1970.

Morris, R. E., "Witness Performance Under Stress: A Sociological Approach," *Journal of Social Issues* (November, 1957).

Moynihan, D. P., ed., *On Understanding Poverty,* New York: Basic Books, 1969.

————, "Employment, Income, and the Ordeal of the Negro Family," *Daedalus* (Fall, 1965).

Murphy, E. F., *Governing Nature,* Chicago: Quadrangle Books, 1967.

Nader, R., "Corporations and Pollution," in *The Crisis of Survival,* edited by the editors of *The Progressive,* Glenview, Ill.: Scott, Foresman, 1970.

Nagel, S. S., "Judicial Backgrounds and Criminal Cases," *Journal of Criminal Law, Criminology, and Police Science* (September, 1962).

National Welfare Rights Organization, *NWRO Proposals for a Guaranteed Adequate Income,* Washington, D.C.: NOW, 1969.

Neill, A. S., *Summerhill,* New York: Hart Publishing Co., 1960.

New Jersey Graduated Work Incentive Experiment, Washington, D.C.: OEO, 1971.

Newman, D. J., *Conviction: The Determination of Guilt or Innocence Without Trial,* Boston: Little, Brown, 1966.

———, "White Collar Crime," *Law and Contemporary Problems* (Autumn, 1958).

———, "Pleading Guilty for Considerations: A Study of Bargain Justice," *Journal of Criminal Law, Criminology, and Police Science* (March–April, 1956).

Newman, W. M., *American Pluralism: A Study of Minority Groups and Social Theory,* New York, Harper & Row, 1973.

Newsweek, "Justice on Trial" (March 8, 1971).

Niederhoffer, A., *Behind the Shield: The Police in Urban Society,* Garden City, N.Y.: Doubleday, 1968.

Nisbet, R. A., *The Quest for Community,* New York: Oxford University Press, 1953.

Odum, E., "The Strategy of Ecosystem Development," *Science* (April 18, 1969).

———, *Fundamentals of Ecology,* 2d ed., Philadelphia: W. B. Saunders, 1959.

Office of Economic Opportunity, *Further Preliminary Results of the New Jersey Graduated Work Incentive Experiment,* Washington, D.C.: OEO, 1971.

Orlans, H., *The Effects of Federal Programs on Higher Education,* Washington, D.C.: Brookings Institute, 1962.

Ornati, O., "Poverty in America," in L. A. Ferman et al., eds., *Poverty in America,* Ann Arbor: University of Michigan Press, 1968.

———, "Affluence and the Risk of Poverty," *Social Research* (Autumn, 1964).

Orshansky, M., "Counting the Poor: Another Look at the Poverty Profile" and "Author's Note: Who Was Poor in 1966," in L. A. Ferman et al., eds., *Poverty in America,* Ann Arbor: University of Michigan Press, 1968.

———, "Who's Who Among the Poor: A Demographic View of Poverty," *Social Security Bulletin* (July, 1965).

Osborn, E., *The Limits of the Earth,* Boston: Little, Brown, 1953.

———, *Our Plundered Planet,* Boston: Little, Brown, 1948.

Parsons, T., "A Revised Analytical Approach to the Theory of Social Stratification," in R. Bendix and S. M. Lipset, eds., *Class, Status, and Power: A Reader in Social Stratification,* New York: The Free Press, 1953.

Peterson, E., "The Atmosphere: A Clouded Horizon," *Environment* (April, 1970).

Peterson, R. E., "The Student Left in American Higher Education," *Daedalus* (Winter, 1968).

Pettigrew, T. F., "Issues in Urban America," in B. J. Frieden and W. W. Nash, Jr., eds., *Shaping an Urban Future: Essays in Honor of Catherine Bauer Wurster,* Cambridge: MIT Press, 1969.

Pinkney, A., *Black Americans,* Englewood Cliffs: Prentice-Hall, 1969.

Piven, F. F. and R. A. Cloward, *Regulating the Poor: The Functions of Public Welfare,* New York: Vintage Books, 1971.

President's Commission on Law Enforcement and Administration of Justice, *The Challenge of Crime in a Free Society,* Washington, D.C.: Government Printing Office, 1967.

————, *Task Force Report: The Courts,* Washington, D.C.: Government Printing Office, 1967.

————, *Task Force Report: Organized Crime,* Washington, D.C.: Government Printing Office, 1967.

————, *Task Force Report: The Police,* Washington, D.C.: Government Printing Office, 1967.

Proice, D. O., ed., *The 99th Hour—The Population Crisis in the United States,* Chapel Hill: The University of North Carolina Press, 1967.

Quinney, R., *The Social Reality of Crime,* Boston: Little, Brown, 1970.

————, *Crime and Justice in Society,* Boston: Little, Brown, 1969.

————, "The Study of White Collar Crime: Toward a Reorientation in Theory and Research," *Journal of Criminal Law, Criminology, and Police Science* (June, 1964).

Rainwater, L., "The Problem of Lower-Class Culture and Poverty—War Strategy," in D. P. Moynihan, ed., *On Understanding Poverty,* New York: Basic Books, 1969.

————, "Open Letter on White Justice and the Riots," *Trans-action* (September, 1967).

Ramirez, S., *The Mexican American: A New Focus on Opportunity,* Washington, D.C.: Inter-Agency Committee on Mexican American Affairs, 1967.

Reagan, M. D., *The New Federalism,* New York: Oxford University Press, 1972.

Reich, C., *The Greening of America,* New York: Random House, 1970.

Report of the National Advisory Commission on Civil Disorders, Washington, D.C.: Government Printing Office, 1968. Paperback edition by Bantam Books, New York, 1968.

Report of the Special Senate Committee to Investigate Organized Crime in Interstate Commerce, 3d Interim Rep., Senate Rep. No. 307, 82d Cong. 1st sess., 1951.

Revelle, R., "Pollution and Cities," in J. Q. Wilson, ed., *The Metropolitan Enigma,* Cambridge, Mass.: Harvard University Press, 1968.

Ridgeway, J., *The Closed Corporation: American Universities in Crisis,* New York: Ballantine Books, 1968.

Rienow, R. and L. Leona, *Moment in the Sun: A Report on the Deteriorating Quality of the American Environment,* New York: Ballantine Books, 1969.

Robinson, W. S., "Bids, Probability, and Trial by Jury," *American Sociological Review* (February, 1950).

Rodman, H., "The Lower-Class Value Stretch," *Social Forces* (December, 1963).

Rogers, D., *110 Livingston Street,* New York: Random House, 1968.

Rosen, B. C., "The Achievement Syndrome," *American Sociological Review* (August, 1956).

Rosenthal, R. and L. Jacobson, *Pygmalion in the Classroom,* New York: Holt, Rinehart & Winston, 1968.

Rossi, P. H. and Z. D. Blum, "Class, Status, and Poverty," in D. P. Moynihan, ed., *On Understanding Poverty,* New York: Basic Books, 1969.

Rubenstein, R. E., *Rebels in Eden: Mass Political Violence in the United States,* Boston: Little, Brown, 1970.

Rudd, R. L., *Pesticides and the Living Landscape,* Madison: University of Wisconsin Press, 1964.

Savitz, L., *Dilemmas in Criminology,* New York: McGraw-Hill, 1967.

Schaffer, A., R. C. Schaffer, G. L. Ahrenholz, and C. S. Prigmore, *Understanding Social Problems,* Columbus, Ohio: Charles E. Merrill, 1970.

Schermer, G., "Desegregating the Metropolitan Area," *The Public Interest* (June, 1967).

Schlesinger, A., "The City in American History," in P. Hatt and A. Reiss, eds., *Reader in Urban Sociology,* New York: The Free Press, 1951.

Schnore, L. F., "Social Class Among Non-whites in Metropolitan Centers," *Demography* (February, 1965).

Schorr, A., "Slums and Social Insecurity," Research Report No. 1, Division of Research and Statistics, Social Security Administration, Department of Health, Education, and Welfare, Washington, D.C.: Government Printing Office, 1963.

Schrag, C. and L. Keuhn, *Crime in America* (tentative title), to be published by Goodyear Publishing Co., 1976.

Scientific American, Energy and Power, San Francisco: W. H. Freeman, 1971.

Scientific American, The Biosphere, San Francisco, W. H. Freeman, 1970.

Seligman, B. B., *Permanent Poverty: An American Syndrome,* Chicago: Quadrangle Books, 1970.

————, ed., *Poverty as a Public Issue,* New York: Free Press of Glencoe, 1965.

Sewell, W. H., "Students and the University," *American Sociologist* (May, 1971).

Sexton, P. C., "City Schools," *The Annals* (March, 1964).

Sherman, H., *Radical Political Economy,* New York: Basic Books, 1972.

Shoup, D. M., "The New American Militarism," *Atlantic Monthly* (August, 1969).

Siegal, P., "On the Cost of Being Negro," *Sociological Inquiry* (Winter, 1965).

Silberman, C., *Crisis in the Classroom,* New York: Random House, 1970.

Simkins, F. B., *A History of the South,* New York: Alfred A. Knopf, 1959.

Simon, R. J., *The Jury and the Defense of Insanity,* Boston: Little, Brown, 1967.

Skolnick, J., *The Politics of Protest,* New York: Simon & Schuster, 1969.

————, *Justice Without Trial,* New York: John Wiley & Sons, 1966.

Skolnick, J. and E. Currie, *Crisis in American Institutions,* Boston: Little, Brown, 1970.

Smelser, N., *The Sociology of Economic Life,* Englewood Cliffs: Prentice-Hall, 1963.

Smith, B., *Police Systems in the United States,* 2d ed., New York: Harper & Row, 1960.

"Social and Economic Conditions of Negroes in the United States," *Current Population Reports,* No. 24, Washington, D.C.: GPO, 1967.

Solow, R. M., "The Measurement of Inequality," in E. C. Budd, ed., *Inequality and Poverty,* New York: W. W. Norton, 1967.

Special Subcommittee on Indian Education, 90th Cong., part 2, 1968.

Spicer, E. H., *Cycles of Conquest,* Tucson: University of Arizona Press, 1962.

Sprout, H., "The Environmental Crisis in the Context of American Politics," in *The Crisis of Survival,* edited by the editors of *The Progressive,* Glenview, Ill.: Scott, Foresman, 1970.

Sprout, H. and M. Sprout, "Ecology and Politics in America: Some Issues and Alternatives," Morristown, N.J.: General Learning Press, 1971a.

————, *Toward Politics of the Planet Earth,* Philadelphia: Van Nostrand Reinhold, 1971b.

Stampp, K., *The Peculiar Institution,* New York: Alfred A. Knopf, 1956.

Steif, W., "Why Birds Cough," in *The Crisis of Survival,* edited by the editors of *The Progressive,* Glenview, Ill.: Scott, Foresman, 1970.

Steiner, S., *The New Indians,* New York: Harper & Row, 1968.

Stern, A. C., ed., *Air Pollution,* New York: Academic Press, 1968.

Stern, P. M., "How 381 Super-Rich Americans Managed Not to Pay a Cent in Taxes Last Year," *The New York Times Magazine* (April 13, 1969).

————, *The Rape of the Taxpayer,* New York: Vintage Books, 1974.

Stockwell, E. G., *Population and People,* Chicago: Quadrangle Books, 1968.

Stoddard, E. R., *Mexican Americans,* New York: Random House, 1973.

Strauss, A. L., *Images of the American City,* New York: The Free Press, 1961.

Strodtbeck, F. L., R. M. James, and C. Hawkins, "Social Status in Jury Deliberations," *American Sociological Review* (December, 1957).

Study Commission on University Governance, "Education and Society: The Need for Reconsideration," in C. Foote et al., eds., *The Cul-*

ture of the University: Governance and Education, San Francisco: Jossey-Bass, 1968.

Surrey, S., *Pathways to Tax Reform,* Cambridge: Harvard University Press, 1973.

Sutherland, E. H., *White Collar Crime,* New York: Holt, Rinehart & Winston, 1967.

————, "White Collar Criminality," *American Sociological Review* (February, 1940).

Szasz, T. S., *Psychiatric Justice,* New York: Macmillan, 1965.

Taeuber, C. and I. Taeuber, *The Changing Population of the United States,* New York: John Wiley & Sons, 1958.

Taeuber, K. E., "Residential Segregation in the U.S." in K. Davis, ed., *The American Negro Reference Book,* Englewood Cliffs: Prentice-Hall, 1966.

Taeuber, K. E. and A. F. Taeuber, *Negroes in Cities: Residential Segregation and Neighborhood Change,* Chicago: Aldin, 1965.

Ten Broek, J., "The Two Nations: Differential Moral Values in Welfare Law and Administration," in M. Levitt and B. Rubenstein, eds., *Orthopsychiatry and the Law,* Detroit: Wayne State University Press, 1968.

Thernstrom, S., *Poverty and Progress,* Cambridge, Mass.: Harvard University Press, 1964.

Tompkins, D. C., ed., *Poverty in the United States During the Sixties: A Bibliography,* Berkeley, Calif.: Institute of Governmental Studies, 1970.

Train, R. E. et al., *Environmental Quality: The First Annual Report of the Council on Environmental Quality,* Washington, D.C.: Government Printing Office, 1970.

Trowbridge, J. T., *The Desolate South: 1865–1866,* New York: Meredith Press, 1956.

Tumin, M. M., *Social Stratification: The Forms of Inequality,* Englewood Cliffs: Prentice-Hall, 1967.

Turner, J. H., "A Strategy for Reformulating the Dialetical and Functional Theories of Conflict," *Social Forces,* 53 (March), 1975.

————, *American Society: Problems of Structure,* New York: Harper & Row, 1972a.

————, *Patterns of Social Organization: A Survey of Social Institutions,* New York: McGraw-Hill, 1972b.

Turner, J. H. and R. Singleton, "White Racism" in D. Zimmerman and L. Weider, eds., *Understanding Social Problems,* New York: Prager, 1976.

Turner, J. H. and C. E. Starnes, *Inequality: Privilege and Poverty in America,* Pacific Palisades, Cal.: Goodyear Publishing Co., 1976.

Vadakin, J. C., *Children, Poverty, and Family Allowances,* New York: Basic Books, 1968.

Valentine, C. A., *Culture of Poverty,* Chicago: University of Chicago Press, 1968.

Wald, G., "A Better World for Fewer Children," in *The Crisis of Survival,* edited by the editors of *The Progressive,* Glenview, Ill.: Scott, Foresman, 1970.

Waters, L. L., "Transient Mexican Agricultural Labor," *Southwest Social and Political Science Quarterly* (June, 1941).

Weidenbaum, M. L., "Problems of Adjustment for Defense Industries," in E. Benoit and K. E. Boulding, eds., *Disarmament and the Economy,* New York: Harper & Row, 1963.

Wesley, C., "Indian Education," *Journal of American Indian Education* (January, 1961).

Wesley, M., *The Tainted Sea,* New York: Coward, McCann and Geoghegan, 1967.

Westley, W., "Violence and the Police," *American Journal of Sociology* (July, 1953).

Westoff, L. A. and C. F. Westoff, *From Now to Zero: Fertility, Contraception and Abortion in America,* Boston: Little, Brown, 1971.

Wheaton, H. et al., eds., *Urban Housing,* New York: The Free Press, 1966.

Wheeler, H., "The Politics of Ecology," *Saturday Review* (March 7, 1970).

White, Jr., L., "The Historical Roots of Our Ecological Crisis," *Science* (March 10, 1967).

Williams, R. M., Jr., *American Society,* 3d ed., New York: Alfred A. Knopf, 1970.

———, *The Reduction of Intergroup Tensions,* Bulletin No. 57, New York: Social Science Research Council, 1947.

Wilson, J. Q., *Varieties of Police Behavior,* Cambridge, Mass.: Harvard University Press, 1968.

Wilson, O. W., *Police Administration,* New York: McGraw-Hill, 1950.

Wirth, L., *The Ghetto,* Chicago: University of Chicago Press, 1928.

Wolozin, H., ed., *The Economics of Air Pollution: A Symposium,* New York: W. W. Norton, 1966.

Woodward, C. V., *The Strange Career of Jim Crow,* New York: Oxford University Press, 1957.

———, *Reunion and Reaction,* Boston: Little, Brown, 1951.

Woodwell, G. M., "Toxic Substances and Ecological Cycles," *Scientific American* (March, 1967).

Wright, Q., *A Study of War,* Chicago: University of Chicago Press, 1942.

Wurster, C. B., "The Dreary Deadlock of Public Housing," in W. C. Wheaton et al., eds., *Urban Housing,* New York: The Free Press, 1966.

Wurster, C. F., "DDT and the Environment," in W. Helfrich, Jr., ed., *Agenda for Survival,* New Haven: Yale University Press, 1971.

Yarmolinsky, A., *The Military Establishment,* New York: Harper & Row, 1971.

Index

77 78 9 8 7 6 5 4 3 2